Prai

"A detailed, comprehensive, fascinating, and accessible book of folkways and magical traditions. Featuring both historical and practical material, this book will be of interest to those seeking information not only about Hungary's ancient Pagan traditions, but also its unique Catholic folk magic. Tóth is a warm, friendly presence, as she guides us into the realms of Magyar magic and spirituality....So much of the material in this book has not been available to English readers until now, making *Mágia* a must-have for all who love folk magic."

—JUDIKA ILLES, author of *Encyclopedia of 5000 Spells* and *Encyclopedia of Spirits*

"I so loved this book! Margit Tóth has given us a wonderful gift, a treasure-trove of folklore from her own Hungary, much of which has not been available in English translation. Her words evoke a pre-modern time when every aspect of life was intrinsically embedded in the seasons of the year, and magic was the way one lived each day."

—HOLLI EMORE, executive director of Cherry Hill Seminary

"An astounding work of both research and personal dedication, Margit Tóth's *Mágia* introduces readers to the robust world of Hungarian folk belief and practice. This book is deeply scholastic but aims for cultural connection and understanding. The author has parsed original Magyar (Hungarian) source materials, but also works to make the notoriously complex language readable for those who haven't grown up speaking it....So much wonderful lore fits within this book's pages, and those wanting to know more about these practices finally have a stunningly rich guidebook in English to help open up the enchanted world of Hungarian folk magic."

—CORY THOMAS HUTCHESON, editor of *Llewellyn's Complete Book of North American Folk Magic*

MÁGIA

About the Author

Margit Tóth was born in Hungary and spent a large portion of her childhood in New England. As an adult, she has lived all around the United States before settling in the Upper Midwest. Margit has studied world religions for over twenty years, focusing in recent years on the folk religion of her native Hungary.

MÁGIA

Hungarian Myth, Magic,
and Folklore

MARGIT TÓTH

LLEWELLYN
WOODBURY, MINNESOTA

FIRST EDITION
First Printing, 2024

Book design by Samantha Peterson
Cover and interior art by Anikó Czinege
Cover design by Kevin R. Brown

A magyar nép hiedelemvilága reprinted by permission granted by the estate of Tekla Dömötör, c/o Peter Csaszar. All rights reserved.

Llewellyn Publications is a registered trademark of Llewellyn Worldwide Ltd.

Library of Congress Cataloging-in-Publication Data (Pending)
ISBN: 978-0-7387-7427-5

Llewellyn Worldwide Ltd. does not participate in, endorse, or have any authority or responsibility concerning private business transactions between our authors and the public.

All mail addressed to the author is forwarded but the publisher cannot, unless specifically instructed by the author, give out an address or phone number.

Any internet references contained in this work are current at publication time, but the publisher cannot guarantee that a specific location will continue to be maintained. Please refer to the publisher's website for links to authors' websites and other sources.

Llewellyn Publications
A Division of Llewellyn Worldwide Ltd.
2143 Wooddale Drive
Woodbury, MN 55125-2989
www.llewellyn.com

Printed in the United States of America

Dedicated to my family, whose patient and
unwavering support made this book possible.

CONTENTS

ACKNOWLEDGMENTS

First and foremost, I would like to acknowledge all the scholars, named and unnamed, past and present, whose dedicated efforts have kept the lore of past generations safe from being lost to the ages. Many of these individuals worked in eras when the authorities frowned upon those who had such knowledge, which makes their hard work all the more impressive. My special gratitude to Dr. Agócs Gergely, who graciously provided me insight into his research!

This same gratitude extends to all those who are studying folk religions, both in and outside of academia, whether that is through books, online sources, or even direct experience. I've had the chance to connect with so many of you in the past couple of years, and it warms my heart to know that there are so many people out there who share my passion for learning about the topics presented in this volume.

This book was my first attempt at working with a traditional publishing company. Although I had worked in an editorial capacity before, it was my first time on this side of the process. What could have been an absolutely terrifying and daunting process was quite the opposite. Llewellyn has been so encouraging and supportive in this whole process. So many people have been integral to seeing this project through, and I could not begin to name them all, but I would like to name a few. Elysia Gallo, especially, has been an integral part of this process from the very start. It was a stroke of fate that a Hungarian-American editor was able to take me under her wing and help me see this project through, graciously answering many a text at odd hours and sharing her own experiences and insight. (And of course, a special thanks to her partner, Tomi, for his input, including helping the team come up with the project title!) Nicole Borneman, too, has lent her expertise and enthusiasm to the editorial process. Thanks, Nicole!

Llewellyn also found the illustrator, Anikó Kutas-Czinege. As soon as I saw her drawings, I fell in love with her style. I emailed the team back right away about how the pictures reminded me of the illustrations in my childhood storybooks—and I meant that in the best way possible! They're magical and nostalgic and wonderful. I feel so fortunate that she lent her talent to this project.

Finally, I would like to express my endless gratitude to my family. They were patient enough to let me research this special interest of mine for hours on end, and then spent even more hours listening graciously to the various factoids I uncovered during said research. Your encouragement means the world to me!

DISCLAIMER

❧

In recent years, various nationalist groups have risen in popularity in Hungary. In their discourse, these groups frequently use symbolism, traditions, legends, etc. that I discuss in this very book. While many of their goals (such as the revival of old traditions, the use of ancient names, popularization of runic scripts, etc.) may be considered noble, several of these groups also tend to focus on racial purity, cultural superiority, and anti-diversity in theory and in practice. I absolutely disavow connection to these groups, and I believe that anyone who is interested in the traditional culture of the Hungarian people—whatever their race or cultural background, and wherever they are located in the world—is not only free to learn about it, but also *welcome* to learn about it.

During the course of my research, I found quite a bit of material that is, quite frankly, disturbing to our modern sensibilities: animal cruelty, misogyny, violence, psychological cruelty, and more. For the sake of historical accuracy, I included many of these tidbits in this book. I hope very much the reader understands that although I am reporting on these facts, I am in no way condoning or promoting them.

I have also included many historical techniques and beliefs about magic, herbalism, folk healing methods, pregnancy and postpartum practices, and so on in this book. I am *not* personally advocating for any of these specific practices. If you learn something new from this book and feel your life would be enhanced by incorporating it into your spiritual practice, please consider carefully if it is worth bringing into the modern day or if it would be better left for the history books. (This is doubly so in the case of ingesting any herbs; please consult an expert before experimenting with any of them!)

And with those disclaimers out of the way, let's begin!

INTRODUCTION

Early one morning, when I was five and a half years old, I boarded a plane that took me, for the first time in my life, to the United States. My earliest memories of the country centered around the enormous maze of highways leading from the La Guardia airport in New York City to the suburbs that were to be my new home. I was suddenly very far from the small towns and villages of northern Hungary, and even the city of Budapest, where I had been born and spent my earliest years. I adjusted to American life quickly and appreciated countless things about the United States, but the only time I truly felt at home was when I returned to my Hungarian grandparents' house each summer, where I spent the school holidays.

At university, I studied comparative global religion and went on to study world religions in various contexts, focusing on Judaism, folk religions, and more modern Pagan spiritualities. At one point, I attended the graduate program at Cherry Hill Seminary, which included coursework on global Paganisms. During my studies, I came across very limited information on the pre-Christian traditions and beliefs of my own Hungarian forebears. Around the turn of the twenty-first century, the main "flavors" of Paganism in common discourse seemed to be Anglo-Saxon, Celtic, Norse, and possibly Roman and Greek. This did not seem unusual to me. Growing up, I had internalized the oft-repeated notion that Hungary was, and remains, a Christian nation. Christianity did undoubtedly play a vital role in shaping Hungarian culture and history. This is indisputable, but the religion did not spill forth from Rome onto a blank canvas. Countless traditions date back to the times before Christian missionaries first set foot in the Carpathian Basin. Echoes of pre-Christian movements were passed down through the generations, sometimes showing up in the most unexpected places, and they were so deeply ingrained and normalized that, for the longest time, it did not occur to me that even modern Hungarians have personally received a portion of this legacy firsthand.

As a child, I was taught to bless a fresh loaf of bread before cutting into it by tracing a cross into the flour on its bottom and to thank a wilted bouquet of flowers before tossing it outside—never in the garbage!—and I thought it was completely normal to have a *kert őre* ("guardian of the gardens"), a tree in our front yard tasked with protecting our home while we were away on long trips. I was also taught to mentally categorize both tasks and living spaces by whether they were *tiszta* (literally "clean," but with a further meaning of sacred or pure) or not, and even to keep my voice down around the "clean" parts of the house. A few times, I remember asking the adults around me the reasoning behind the actions, but all too often was met with a nonchalant shrug and the reply, "This is just the way we've always done these things." It wasn't until my own children started asking the same questions that I began thinking even more deeply about these habits in terms of my academic background of religious studies.

Before you get the wrong idea, not every child in Hungary receives these guidances. Even in my not-so-distant childhood, they were considered rather old-fashioned or quaint traditions—if they were even considered at all. Until the first part of the twentieth century, the old traditions were still alive, especially in the more isolated rural areas, but they began to fall out of practice in the time period between the two World Wars. In the interwar period, two-thirds of Hungary's territory was lost, and there was massive social upheaval as masses relocated and left their home villages behind. And after the Second World War, there was a systemic erasure of traditional culture, mostly led by (but not limited to) the occupying Soviet forces. For the most part, the younger generations were forced to move into urban centers instead of living in the village communities their forefathers had spent countless generations in, and many expressions of traditional national identity—including religious practices—were treated as suspect by the authorities.

For a time, the old beliefs and traditions were relegated to a handful of elders living in distant villages, as well as the dusty tomes written by *néphitkutatók* (scholars of folk religion). Even in the last decade of the twentieth century, after the fall of the Soviet Union, many of the newly liberated nations were eager to embrace Western ideals instead of returning to the roots of their own heritages. Researchers still had access to vast swaths of information collected over the centuries, but the average citizen was living in a different world than their ancestors had. Between trying to survive political upheaval and economic insecurity, reviving folk beliefs was, understandably, simply not prioritized in most people's lives.

But after winter comes the spring, when what appeared lifeless proves to have only been slumbering. Increasing numbers of people today, in Hungary and beyond, are seeking out the wisdom of their ancestors. Some are researching purely for academic or historical purposes, while others are trying to revive certain elements of their ancestral practices and incorporate old practices into their lives. Some live in the Carpathian Basin, and others live abroad in the wider diaspora; many have never even set foot on their ancestral lands. Still others might feel called to learn about these beliefs for personal reasons, even if they cannot trace their own ancestry to these lands.

Although the information remains somewhat esoteric due to various accessibility barriers, thanks to the magic of the internet, researchers now have access to the research of countless dedicated scholars, such as Dömötör Tekla, Ipolyi Arnold, Diószegi Vilmos, Szendrey Zsigmond and his son, Szendrey Ákos, and Pócs Éva,[1] all of whom have done invaluable research, many of them cataloguing traditional beliefs and customs before the older generations died out, and others systematically categorizing and analyzing said records. Hands down, the most useful starting point for my research was the *Magyar Néprajzi Lexikon* ("Hungarian Folk Encyclopedia"). Although it is not available in English, it is freely accessible to Hungarian speakers, and it provides a wealth of knowledge.

Whenever possible, I extended my studies to the original sources cited in its articles. Many of these sources were articles in the publication *Ethnographia*, a publication of the *Magyar Néprajzi Társaság* ("Association of Hungarian

---

1. In this text, I follow the Hungarian convention of writing the surname before the given name.

Folklore"). For over a century, this society annually put out a hefty tome of original research by various professional and lay "collectors of folklore." Regrettably, many other sources alluded to in the *Magyar Néprajzi Lexikon* that I wanted to consult ended up being dead ends. Volumes of research have been lost to time, often destroyed during the World Wars and the Soviet occupation of the latter half of the twentieth century. Others were simply so obscure that I was unable to track them down—yet. I continue to do more research and uncover more material, and I hope to share further discoveries as I come across them.

For many, language remains a significant barrier in this field. The bulk of my research was done in Hungarian-language sources (all translations in this book are mine, unless otherwise noted), but this is not a possibility for everyone. The Hungarian language, which is not meaningfully related to other European languages, has a reputation for being quite difficult for a non-native speaker to learn. This is not just a rumor; the US Department of State ranks Hungarian as a "'hard language'—languages with significant linguistic and/or cultural differences from English."[2] I've personally talked to many people who wish to learn more about the Magyar ancestral beliefs, but the lack of accessible English-language source material has been a road-block for them. Even with the advent of computer translation, finding source material remains a challenge. This book is my attempt at beginning to correct this problem. In recent years, several authors have written English-language books about the folk religion of Eastern and Central European nations (including Madame Pamita, whose fascinating *Baba Yaga's Book of Witchcraft* was published by Llewellyn in 2022); I am honored to be adding my voice with this volume!

Notes on Language

At first glance, the Hungarian vocabulary in this book might seem intimidating—but don't worry! Hungarian is a phonetic language; that is, each letter (or letter combination) makes exactly one sound, and most of these sounds are present in the English language as well. If you are unfamiliar with the Hungarian alphabet, you can reference the appendix in the back of the book,

2. Foreign Service Institute, "Foreign Language Training."

where I have included a quick pronunciation guide (or you can consult one of many online tutorials). With a little practice, you will be able to sound out even some of the more complicated words in this book, such as the holiday of *Gyertyaszentelő Boldogasszony*!

Two quick points will help the vocabulary in this book make more sense. First, *a* and *az* both mean "the." *Az* is used before a word starting with a vowel; *a* is used before a word starting with a consonant. Second, Hungarian words are made plural (in most cases) by adding a *k* at the end. "Vowel harmony" is a term that means that the letter before the final *k* has to match the tone of the vowels earlier in the word. For example, *tudós* (wise one) becomes *tudósok*, while *macska* (cat) becomes *macskák*. All you have to remember, though, is that if a word ends in a *k*, it's most likely just the plural form of a noun.

Historical Accuracy

The current borders of Hungary encompass a land mass roughly the size of the state of Indiana, although up until the early 1900s, it encompassed much more land—roughly three times as much, in fact. The geography of present-day Hungary is diverse, and it was even more varied before the border changes. Some regions are mountainous and wooded, with caves and valleys, while others, like the central *puszta* ("plains") region known as the *Alföld*, are flat with sparse vegetation. The vast, swampy region of the *Hanság* spawned countless legends of the spirits dwelling in its rivers, lakes, and bogs, and there are temperate, hilly regions ideal for growing grapes. The people in each region were also influenced by different ethnic groups as they lived in close proximity to, and interacted with, one another.

During the course of their wanderings, the Hungarian ancestral nomadic tribes picked up beliefs, practices, and even deities from the various people they interacted with. Even when they settled down on the land, their culture was not frozen in time, but continued to evolve. To further complicate things, there were many sub-groups within the Hungarian nation, such as the *Jászok*, *Csángók*, and *Székelyek*, each of whom had their own variations of the legends, as well as members of other national and ethnic groups living in and around the nation (Saxons, Roma, and Slavic groups, for example), and they all contributed portions of their own lore.[3]

Besides regional differences and variations between ethnic groups, there is also the matter of the passage of time. The modern state of Hungary was formed over a thousand years ago, and the nation's roots stretch back much further than that. A lot can change in a thousand (or more!) years. Customs and beliefs evolve from generation to generation, never mind through the centuries. Whereas one community might have ceremonially washed themselves in the river on May Day, others did so on the summer solstice—and still others on the morning of New Year's! The scholars I quote have dutifully noted all of these differences, which can be endlessly fascinating (if you're into that sort of thing). However, it is not within the scope of this book to try to replicate the breadth or depth of their work. Instead, I have sought to find the underlying patterns beneath the differences, and I present these patterns to the reader.

I want to be very clear: you would not be able to travel to any one particular Hungarian village in any one particular point in time and find all these customs celebrated in exactly the same manner as they are presented in this book. However, despite these variations from one region of Hungary to the next, and from one time period to the next, I can assure you that everything presented in this text was practiced by at least *some* portion of the populace at *some* point in history. Make of that what you will.

Finally, I'd like to point out that although I have consulted numerous sources while writing this book, the research was not focused in a way that it might have been had I been writing, for example, an academic dissertation. Many early researchers were traveling around the villages of Hungary and recording folklore as they saw it, then bringing back the material to share with their fellow folklore enthusiasts. Some of these researchers were academics, while others were simply hobbyists who were passionate about their interest. To me, even the latter group's source material was valuable, but it is important to keep in mind that I did not vet the sources in the same manner I would be evaluating them had this book been written for an academic audience.

3. In this text, I typically do not distinguish between the particular customs of various ethnic groups living within the historical borders of the Hungarian nation. The complex nuances of these group dynamics extend far beyond the scope of this book.

How This Book Is Organized

I have divided this book into five parts. The first is an examination of the worldview and cosmology of the Magyar people—their beliefs in the Creator, the world of spirits, and the afterlife. Next is a look at how magic infused daily life for a person living in a traditional village. The third portion deals with groups of individuals who played magical roles in society—those who were believed to possess just a little more magical know-how than everyone else. Part 4 focuses on the different days of celebration held throughout the calendar year, from the major holidays to many smaller festivals. Finally, some major life milestones and traditional rites of passage are examined in greater detail.

While this volume is not comprehensive, I hope it is extensive enough to serve as a satisfying launching point for those interested in the topic. Whatever reasons you might have for picking up this book, I hope you find what you are looking for. I am so happy you have decided to be part of this exploration into Hungarian myth and magic!

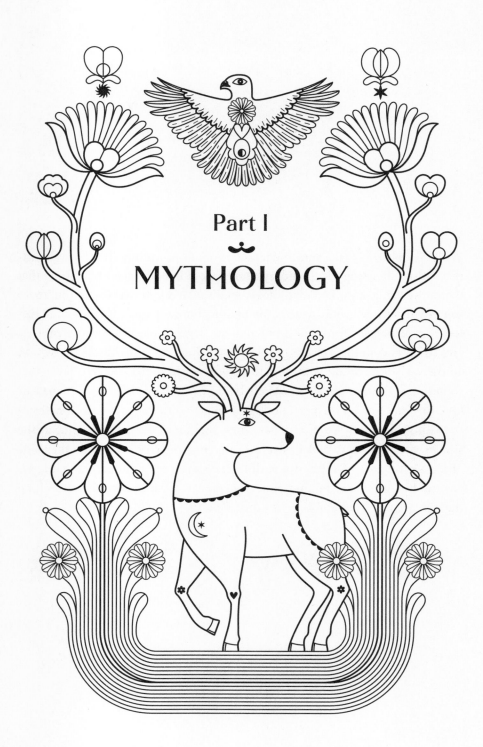

Part I

MYTHOLOGY

While people can make some generalities about prevailing themes and entities within the Hungarian belief system, it would be incorrect to assume that there was a single, unified mythology. As discussed in the introduction, there were many ethnic groups within the nation's borders, each of whom had different explanations for natural phenomena, legends, supernatural creatures, and so on and so forth. Even in this book, which certainly doesn't touch on all the variations found within mythological sources, the reader will see that sometimes, the moon is considered feminine, and sometimes it is masculine. In some stories, the great goddess is married to the god, and sometimes she is his daughter. When a person dies, their soul is said to ascend to the sky, except when it is said to live on in a "mirror world" on the other side of a mystical river. Despite these differences, when I write about "Hungarian mythology," I am talking about oft-repeated patterns and overarching themes. So, with that in mind, let's dive right in.

Chapter 1
THE WORLD OF SPIRITS

The origins of the Hungarian people—who call themselves *magyarok*—are shrouded in mystery. It has long been believed that the Hungarian people's ancestors lived in an idyllic land known as *Etelköz* ("between two rivers") far to the east. Legends known as *mondák* describe how the ancestors wandered around the plains of central Asia; they were a warring people who did not shy away from conflict. Wass Albert, an influential writer, described them in the following way:

> Long ago, far in the east, past where the sun rises, there was a beautiful kingdom of rolling grass and flowering meadows. Its citizens were brave warriors, hunters, and artisans, known for their knowledge and skill. They were famous for their ability to talk to the spirits, and for their wisdom and good humor. They lived in peace unless they were attacked, at which point they defended themselves valiantly.[4]

While these myths live strongly in the Hungarian national identity, they may not be based in truth—at least not entirely. Researchers recently calculated that only 2 to 4 percent of the DNA of modern-day Hungarians can

---

4. Wass, *Selected Hungarian Legends*, 12.

be traced back to central Asia.[5] The other 96 to 98 percent is composed of various European populations, which makes sense considering that at different times, the fertile land of the Carpathian Basin was colonized by several long-standing civilizations, including the Celts and Romans.

Regardless of genetics, some aspects of Hungarian culture are clearly linked to the people of the steppes. The languages most closely related to the famously complicated Hungarian are Khanty and Mansi, the speakers of whom live in present-day Russia. The oldest Hungarian legends also share similarities with those found in Asia, as do many of their notions about the afterlife, the spirit world, and shamanic practices. So, this is where we start our story: in the lands the ancient nomads once inhabited.

Following the Magic Stag

A king who lived far to the east, in the land "beyond where the sun rises," had two adventurous sons, Hunor and Magor. One day, the brothers organized a hunting party. Each chose a hundred companions and started west on horseback. Before long, the hunting party spotted a beautiful stag whose coat glistened like the silvery moon. Its antlers were golden and shone like the sun and stars. This was the Csodaszarvas, the Magical Stag. The animal stood still until the hunting party had almost reached it, then bounded away. Hunor, Magor, and their companions pursued the Csodaszarvas through plains and valleys, rivers and marshes. The animal ran for seven days, never tiring, and the men chased it. They traveled so far that the princes forgot about their father's kingdom entirely, and so did their companions.

On the seventh night, when Hunor and Magor nearly overtook the stag, the Csodaszarvas jumped into a pond and disappeared into its depths, never to be seen again. Hunor and Magor awoke from their trance and looked around. They were in a beautiful land, even more beautiful than the one they had come from. It was a land of forests and meadows, lakes and streams, filled with birds and game

5. Béni, "Genetic Study Proves that Hungarians Are the Descendants of the Huns."

and fish. The men were tired from their hunt and made camp for the night in the beautiful land.

When the moon was directly overhead, the men woke to the sound of singing. Their camp was surrounded by beautiful maidens who were holding one another's hands, dancing in a circle around the men. Each was as lovely as a fairy. The two most beautiful ones approached Hunor and Magor, smiling. "Welcome. We have been waiting for you," they said. Before the night was over, the brothers had fallen in love and vowed marriage to the maidens, who joyfully accepted the proposals. In short order, the rest of their companions also found brides. After a wedding celebration lasting seven days and seven nights, the two brothers decided to go their separate ways to start their new lives. Hunor's descendants would be known as the Huns, and Magor's descendants would be called the Magyars.[6]

According to the *mondák*, the ancestors of the Hungarians were predestined to live in Europe. The myth of *Emese Álma* ("The Dream of Emese") describes how on her wedding night, Emese, the leader's new bride, had a mystical dream. In this dream, the sacred bird of the Hungarians known as the *turul* descended upon the young woman and covered her with its wings. A river sprung from her body and flowed across the land, heading west, until it settled in a beautiful valley. There, a tree grew. It had golden leaves, and golden apples hung from its branches. Emese sat down under the tree and fell asleep. When she awoke, she found herself in the bridal tent once more and knew that she was with child. The *turul* remains an important national symbol of Hungary. Statues of the bird can be found throughout Hungary, and one particularly impressive statue overlooks the city of Budapest from the hillsides above the Danube River.

The Cosmos

The ancient Magyar cosmos is divided into layered realms. Folklorists such as Diószegi Vilmos and Berze Nagy János have explored these themes at length in their writings and compare them to the cosmos of other related nations,

---

6. Adapted from Wass, *Selected Hungarian Legends*, 12–14.

which frequently describe an Upper World, Middle World, and Lower World. In many Hungarian stories and folktales, the hero or heroine travels or was carried vertically into these layered worlds, which have various characteristics. The Middle World is our own realm, the physical world in which we reside throughout our lives. The world above ours is home to various spirits, including the Creator God, *Isten*, who lives alongside the moon, the stars, and the ancestors. Many tales describe this realm as filled with dragons, shining castles of gold and silver, and lush courtyards: "In the highest celestial layer, in the kingdom of the Sun, everything is golden. The grass, the trees, the flowers—and on the trees, there are apples of gold."[7] These golden apples are magical and impart health, strength, and wisdom.

Below the physical realm is the *Alvilág*, the Lower World, a shadowy, mysterious realm where things are not always as they seem. It is filled with magical treasures and lessons to be learned, but it is also bursting with danger. Only those gifted with special powers can enter this realm—and many never return. In many stories, it is said to be filled with snakes, frogs, and lizards. The word *pokol* refers to the Christian notion of hell, and there are many parallels between the two realms. In modern colloquial language, *alvilág* is a word mainly used to refer to the world of criminal activities.

The following story—which features the ideas of the Creator God, a cosmos with a triple realm, and the World Tree—was inspired by Wass Albert's account.[8]

The Creation of the World

Above our own world, past the blue of the skies, is the Upper World. It is a radiant land where even the plants are made of gold and silver. In its center is a palace that shines like diamonds. No human eye could ever look upon it and retain its sight. This is the home of Isten, the God of Creation. Even the sun dims in comparison to him. The courtyards of his palace are filled with trees of jeweled fruit, including the golden apples that are able to heal and contain the collective

7. Bosnyák, "Napkorona, aranyalma, pásztorbot, suba," 7.

8. Adapted from Wass, *Selected Hungarian Legends*, 9–11.

knowledge and wisdom of the world. Isten had two daughters, whom he named Light Sister and Dark Sister. When they were grown, they grew restless, so their father made them a land of their own. This land was the world, but back then, it was empty and barren. Isten told his daughters to go down to it and create upon it. If they needed him, they were to send him a message with the turul, his sacred bird, who was able to carry their words to the Upper World.

The sisters were happy to oblige. Light Sister unbraided her hair, which became seven rivers flowing through the land. When Dark Sister tried to copy her, her work became fetid swamps instead. Light Sister made fruit-bearing trees, berry bushes, and healing herbs, but Dark Sister made poisonous mushrooms, nettles, and weeds. When Light Sister created helpful honeybees and ladybugs, Dark Sister made spiders, snakes, mosquitos, and wasps. Each helpful thing that Light Sister made, her twin sister made a harmful counterpart for. Light Sister was frustrated, and she cried and cried until her salty tears became an ocean, surrounding the land.

Finally, Light Sister went to her father and complained about her sister. Isten grew angry and forbade Dark Sister from shaping the land further. Dark Sister grew angry at this. "My father might have forbidden me from shaping the land, but he said nothing about creating from the mud of the seafloor." So she descended to the bottom of the ocean and carried as much of the mud as she could hold. She even held some of it in her mouth. But Isten saw what his daughter was doing. He ordered everything to grow. The mud, too, expanded, including what had been in Dark Sister's mouth. It contorted her face and turned her ugly. When she got to the surface, she spat it out, and it became a rocky mountain range, perilous to travel upon. Dark Sister was so ashamed of how her face looked that she escaped into a cavity under the land. This became the Lower World, and Dark Sister vowed to stay in its shadowy realm for the rest of time. In this cavity, a tree grew. This was the World Tree, and it became the only way to travel between the Upper World, the Lower World, and the Middle World between them.

Light Sister was happy that Dark Sister was no longer creating destructive things in the land, but she was lonely. So Isten broke off a piece of the sun, from which he created First Man and First Woman. When he was done, he still had enough left over to make First Horse and First Dog. These creatures he sent down into the Middle World, and he told Light Sister to care for them. One morning, First Woman was walking in a meadow and came upon a beautiful golden flower. She picked it up and wrapped it in her shawl, taking it home with her. When she arrived home, she unwrapped the bundle to show her husband. Instead of a blossom, there was a small child, whom they named Golden Child. First Man became First Father, and First Woman became First Mother. To amuse Golden Child, Light Sister created fairies and gnomes and various toys such as birds, butterflies, dragonflies, and snails.

When Dark Sister heard about Golden Child, she too wanted one of her own. She formed a child and named her Treasure. Dark Sister became Dark Mother, and she made Treasure all sorts of toys of her own—gems and precious metal ores. Treasure had a spirit much like Dark Mother's own, and she used her toys to lure humans into traps. She dangled jewels and riches in front of mankind, and when they tried to get them, Treasure played tricks on the people. Over time, she lured them deeper and deeper into the earth, and as they dug they let loose the Dark Mother's creations, the evil spirits known as the rosszak. These brought illness, jealousy, hatred, lies, and nightmares into the world. The worst spirit of all was that of warfare.

Light Sister was so distressed about what was happening to her world that she withdrew from civilization to the wilds. She vowed to live in solitude, but she allowed people to approach her. Because she was worried that humans, who had grown so untrustworthy, would use her gifts for ill gain, she vowed to test those who came to her. If she found them worthy, she aided them, gave them good dreams, comforted them, and showed them how to heal with herbs. But over time, fewer and fewer people turned to her. Eventually, only a few people even remembered her at all, and the rest of humanity had to navigate the world on their own.

Many of the Hungarian fairy tales, legends, and folktales reach back through the centuries. The heroes of Hungarian stories frequently venture to the upper or lower realms in order to find magical items and weapons, fight various foes, and meet spirit helpers. Sometimes they find the way to the Lower World through a hole in the ground or get dragged down against their will by a dragon or other mystical beast. Many heroes who venture into this realm can only return to the surface with the aid of a spirit helper. One legend that is still popular today is *Fehérlófia* ("The Son of the White Mare"). In this tale, the hero—himself the demigod son of a magical white horse—finds himself in the Lower World and has to pay a heavy price to return to the human world on the back of a griffin: he must feed the fearsome creature his own limbs as sustenance. In the end, the griffin not only returns the hero to the land of the living, but offers its own tears to regrow the sacrificed limbs even stronger than before.

The World Tree

The three realms are connected by the *Világfa*, the World Tree, which is also referred to as the *Életfa* ("Tree of Life"), the *Tetejetlen fa* ("Tree Without a Top"), or—like in the title of Berze Nagy János's book—the *Égigérő fa* ("Tree That Reaches the Sky"). The roots of the *Világfa* reach into the Lower World and its branches lead to the heavens, a motif that finds counterparts in several world mythologies, including Norse and Mongolian. The symbol of the World Tree is common in religious art; it is inscribed especially frequently on skin drums used to provide rhythm to spiritual songs and meditations.

Like the characters in stories, shamanic figures known as *táltosok* attempt to utilize drumming, chanting, psychedelic potions, and meditation to fall into a trance and send their higher souls forth to climb up and down the *Világfa*. While the physical body remains behind, the soul of the shamanic figure known as a *táltos* is able to travel between the realms in order to obtain healing, talk to the spirits, prophesy, and gain sacred knowledge. I will discuss these topics in further detail in chapter 11.

The *Világfa*

Tengrism

Academics differ in their view of whether the *ősmagyarok*, the ancient Hungarian ancestors, were monotheistic or polytheistic—or if it is even meaningful to make this type of distinction. Around the year 900, the scholar Ahmad ibn Fadlan described a group known as the *bāšģird*, a people linked closely to the Hungarian ancestors. This tribe had several deities; the deity of the sky was the greatest of them all. Other deities were those of winter, summer, rain, wind, tree, man, horse, water, sun, night, death, and earth. Various tribes also honored specific animal spirits, such as the snake, fish, or crane. Fadlan's text described how these people practiced a form of idol worship, carving phallic amulets and wearing them around their necks, kissing them before battles. When one was asked why they did so, the man responded that he too was created from such a thing, and he recognized no other creator.[9]

Today, several hundred thousand people in Mongolia and Siberia practice a religion called Tengrism, which is an attempt at reconstructing the ancient indigenous religion of the region. Although the theory is not without controversy, some scholars believe that the ancestors of today's Hungarians practiced a form of this faith as well. In Tengrism, the Creator God, also known as the Blue Sky God, lives up in the heavens and is symbolized by the sun. Tengrism also involves honoring one's ancestors and nature spirits—chief of which is the fertile earth spirit—but also includes those of the celestial bodies, landforms, plants, animals, and weather spirits. Though none of these are considered deities in their own right, all of them serve the Blue Sky God. Even today, Hungarians are familiar with sayings such as:

- *Az ég tudja* ("[Only] the sky knows"), used when someone doesn't know the answer to a question
- *Az ég áldjon meg* ("May the sky bless you"), used when someone is very grateful to a person
- *Hála a jó égnek* ("Thanks be to the good sky"), used when good fortune has materialized
- *Az ég szerelmére!* ("For the love of the sky!"), used when someone is very emphatic or emotional about a topic

9. Zimonyi, *A magyarság korai történetének sarokpontjai*, 55.

In Hungarian Catholicism, the most serious categories of sins, such as murder, are known as *égbekiáltó bűnök*; this can be translated as "sins which shout into the skies." Various colorful and offensive expressions about the sky are also used as profanity to this day.

Isten, the One God

In contrast to accounts that ancient Hungarians treated nature spirits as deities, other sources indicate that the Hungarians were monotheistic, worshipping only the Sky God and considering the other spirits to be in a different category of lesser spirits. In the modern day, the word for a god is *isten*; *Isten* is the name by which the one Christian god is referred to as well. (Sometimes, God is referred to as the *Jóisten*, meaning "The God Who Is Good," although this title can have a somewhat childish or old-fashioned connotation.)

Several books about the native faith of the Hungarians include in their introductory chapters points of discourse about the relative ease with which the Hungarian people accepted Christianity relatively easily compared to some other European nations. The authors theorized that this was because the pre-Christian Hungarians were already largely a monotheistic people.[10] The jury still seems to be out on that point, but the fact remains that the word *Isten* came to refer to the Abrahamic God, and it remains so to this day.

A popular blessing called the *házi áldás* ("blessing of the home") is displayed in many homes even today—I myself have an embroidered version hanging in my home that has been passed down through several generations. In its translated form, the blessing states:

> *Where there is faith, there is love.*
> *Where there is love, there is peace.*
> *Where there is peace, there is a blessing.*
> *Where there is a blessing, there is Isten.*
> *Where there is Isten, all needs are satisfied.*

Out of respect for *Isten*, it was strictly forbidden to point at the sun, and if someone were to shoot an arrow at the sun, the worst of punishments would

---

10. Two of these books are Diószegi's *Az ősi magyar hitvilág* (20–28) and Dömötör's *A magyar nép hiedelmvilága* (22–24); many other texts touch on this topic as well.

befall them. I remember hearing people muttering "*Isten nem ver bottal*" often while I was growing up, which can be translated literally as "God does not beat one with a stick." The greater meaning is the spiritual principle that if you do something destructive or harm another person, you will receive this negative energy back through divine retribution (i.e., you will be unlucky in some way).

The Goddess

After missionaries reinterpreted *Isten* as the Abrahamic God, they then rebranded the rest of the spirits known to the Magyars as the *szentek*, the various saints Hungarians faithfully venerated for centuries (and some continue to venerate to this day). Many spirits became patrons of various things they had been associated with—fishing, lightning, wine, mosquitos, and so on. (Some of the *szentek*, such as Luca, retained too many non-Christian elements in folk memory, and the Catholic Church eventually had to make efforts to disassociate the saintly figures with some of the old legends or powers.)

Chief among these spirits was the female demigod, the powerful *Boldogasszony*. One way that *Boldogasszony* may be translated is "Spirit Woman." *Boldog* means joyous or happy, but it also has a secondary connotation of "spirit"; for example, *megboldogult* can literally be translated as "someone who has become happy," but it means someone who has died or gone to the world of the spirits, while *asszony* denotes a mature woman, a wife or a mother. In the words of two folklorists, the *Boldogasszony* "is God's blessed Earth, from which salvation's flower and fruit burst forth." [11] Some described the goddess as the "fairy of Nature." [12] Other healing spells refer to variations of *földanya*—Mother Earth.

Christian missionaries could not eradicate the veneration of the *Boldogasszony*, so the image became conflated with that of the Virgin Mary. To this day, Mary is known as the *Boldogságos Szűz*—the Joyous Virgin. In the words of a modern-day Franciscan monk, Father Daczó Árpád, "The veneration of the Boldogasszony, the Babba, was so beautiful and elevated, that when our ancestors were presented with Mary, the mother of Jesus,

11. Benedek and Kürtössy, "Szeptember 8. Kisasszony napja."
12. Kálmány, *Boldogasszony*, 7.

they were shocked to realize that from time immemorial they had loved and honored her." [13] Depictions of the Queen of Heaven in art, poetry, song, and prayer retained many traces of the pre-Christian goddess. She is often depicted dressed in radiant robes; at times she is even described as "the woman clad in the dress of the sun." [14] Many movements of the Hungarian folk religion allude to this connection, such as village women gathering on certain festivals to go sing to the mountaintops in order to see the face of the Virgin Mary in the rising sun, who was then described as "throwing roses down upon her beloved." [15] On these occasions, the sun was said to be surrounded by colorful tulips (another symbol of the goddess).

Many versions of the *Boldogasszony* describe her having a perpetually virginal daughter known as the *Kisasszony* (a term used for young ladies or maidens). In other versions of her story, there are seven *Boldogasszony* spirits, or else she has seven daughters, although not everyone could agree on who those daughters were. Various potential daughters (or aspects) included:

- *Szülő* ("One Who Gives Birth")
- *Fájdalmas* ("One Who Feels Pain")
- *Gyertyaszentelő* ("One Who Blesses Candles")
- *Gyümölcsoltó* ("Fruit-Grafting")
- *Sarlós* ("One Who Cuts Down with the Sickle")
- *Segítő* ("One Who Helps")
- *Gyógyitó* ("One Who Heals")
- *Havas* ("Snowy")
- *Fogolykiváltó* ("One Who Releases Captives")
- *Csomóoldó* ("Undoer of Knots")

Many of these aspects are celebrated throughout the Hungarian year as liturgical festivals. Some of these are *Gyertyaszentelő Boldogasszony* (held on

13. Szakács, "Boldogasszony, Anyánk!"
14. Domokos, "Hajnal, hajnalnóta, hajnalozás," 249.
15. Benedek and Kürtössy, "Szeptember 8. Kisasszony napja."

February 2), *Gyümölcsoltó Boldogasszony* (March 25), *Sarlós Boldogasszony* (July 2), and *Fájdalmas Boldogasszony* (September 15).

Numerous locations in Hungary are named after the *Boldogasszony*, including lakes, springs, roads, and at least one town. Other places have legends in which she plays a role. One of these regards the forest around the village of Bükkszentkereszt, which is said to be especially favored by the goddess. According to legend, one day the *Boldogasszony* was walking in the forest when she grew tired and sat down to rest on a rock. The rock instantly molded itself to her shape for her comfort. After she had rested and continued on her journey, the impression stayed in the hardened stone. When travelers rested on the same rock, they would find healing from their ailments. Even today, tourists and pilgrims alike continue to seek out this rock, and many report feeling a tingling in their hands and feet when they touch or sit on the stone.

Besides physical locations, there are still many traces of the *Boldogasszony* that can be found throughout Hungary, although few people today associate them with the old goddess. In the folk calendar, people referred to the first month of the year as *Boldogasszony Hava*: "Month of the *Boldogasszony*." Numerous plants are named after her, such as the *Boldogasszony*'s branch, grass, lace, hair, cabbage, leaf, mint, cloak, plum, rose, and thorn. Several of the herbs named after her, such as the *Boldogasszony tövise* ("thorn of the Boldogasszony," i.e., *Silybum marianum*) or the *Boldogasszony tenyere* ("palm of the Boldogasszony," i.e., *Tanacetum balsamita*) were linked to women's reproductive and childbearing health, once again connecting the plants to the goddess of fertility.

Countless organizations in Hungary reference the *Boldogasszony* in their names, including several schools and folk dance troupes. The name of the goddess even materializes in pop culture from time to time. In 2019, for example, the *Magyar Cukrász Ipartestület* ("Hungarian Confectionary Industry Association") declared the *Boldogasszony Csipkéje* ("*Boldogasszony*'s Lace")—a cake creation featuring the flavors of raspberry, white chocolate, lemon, and basil—the winning entry of their annual cake-baking contest. The *Boldogasszony*, it seems, refuses to be forgotten.

Some ethnic groups within Hungary refer to the Virgin Mary as *Babba Mária*. The historian Takács György argues that this title comes from an ancient Middle Eastern goddess known as Kubaba. According to his research, *ku* is a prefix meaning gracious and benevolent; *baba*, or *bába*, is a versatile word that has been used to denote mirages, female spirits, witches, midwives, infants, or humanlike figures such as dolls. Like the *Boldogasszony*, Kubaba was a sun goddess with seven identical daughters.

In the 1970s, a Catholic monk who was researching folk beliefs named Daczó Árpád conversed with villagers in present-day Romania about their beliefs in the *Babba Mária*. They told him that it was she who controlled the weather and chose whether or not a person got injured or stayed protected from harm. She was said to be angry when children ate without washing their hands properly, and to cry if a female whistled a tune, no matter how young or old she was. Children were reassured that she would watch over them as they slept. From cradle to grave, in every aspect of life, everywhere and throughout all of time, it was *Babba Mária* who was the highest power, refuge, and help, "is all-knowing, and is like God...she walks in the sky and sees all, knows all, and cares for everything. From the cradle to the grave, she is in every worldly endeavor the chief protector, refuge, and aid." [16]

When an old woman reported praying to the *Babba Mária*, Daczó asked, "So you prayed to the Virgin Mary?" The old woman replied, "I prayed to the Virgin Mary too, and the Babba Mária, and to the *Jóisten* [Good God] as well." If someone was harmed or insulted, the proper response was to tell the aggressor, "The Babba Mária does not sleep, she knows and she has seen this." [17]

16. Takács, *Babba Mária*.
17. Daczó, "A Gyimesi Babba Mária."

Chapter 2
RELIGIOUS PRACTICE

Whether or not a magical stag or bird led them to the land that is now known as Hungary, the historical record does indeed show that the Magyars settled in Europe around 800 CE. Surrounded and protected by the Carpathian Mountains, the nomads had found their home at last, in the country that came to be known as *Magyarország* ("the land of the Magyars"). Not that the newcomers stayed put altogether. Hungarians whimsically refer to this period in their history as the *kalandozások*, "the adventures," but the reality is that the warring tribes spent many years raiding, conquering, and killing their way through Europe, making enemies with any nations that resisted their arrival.

Unsurprisingly, the leadership of Europe was wary of the Hungarian presence, and alliances came at a high price. The leader Christianized his name from the Pagan name of *Vajk* to that of *István király* (King Stephen) and declared Hungary a formal European state in the year 1000 CE. In a bid to secure the pope's support for the new nation, the monarch officially adopted Christianity as the national religion. His personal convictions aside, this move was politically shrewd; in return for the declaration of fealty, the Pope orchestrated several peace treaties on the unpopular nation's behalf. István and his successors welcomed Christian missionaries into the country. Vying political factions led by old tribal leaders clung to the old traditions, and they tried to use the citizens' reluctance to embrace a new religion to their political advantage. For decades, bloody battles were fought to decide the fate of the nation.

Eventually, the Christians won out, and the native faith slowly began to be lose ground. For his efforts, *István király* and several of his descendants were canonized as saints, and Hungary has been calling itself a Christian nation ever since.

Several important factors might have mitigated how difficult this religious shift truly was for the average individual. According to this line of thinking, the Magyars had historically been exposed to many other religions (including Islam, and to a lesser extent, Judaism) during the course of their nomadic travels. By the time Hungary officially adopted Christianity as its formal religion, religious vocabulary already reflected the varied religious influences. Religious practice was frequently deemed to be a personal matter, and other factors—such as political affiliations—factored much more deeply into many people's identities.

The followers of the traditional religions were—broadly speaking—more generous and accepting of various spiritual paths, and did not, as a general rule, make exclusivist claims that theirs was the only right path. Christianity was viewed as an addition to, rather than a replacement of, the older customs. A number of different religious persuasions existed within the Carpathian Basin when the Magyar tribes were making their claim on the land. According to various international sources, the Pagan leadership was relatively tolerant of different faiths; King Géza was said to have announced that "he was wealthy enough to satisfy two gods."[18] A few notable diehards did strongly oppose the Christian rule, but quite likely for more political reasons than spiritual convictions.

Politics aside, the missionaries were unable to completely eradicate pre-Christian beliefs and customs from the land; these were passed down from generation to generation, coexisting with official church doctrines. Although many, if not most, Hungarians did eventually come to think of themselves as loyal Christians who had little to do with the "primitive" practices of their ancestors, their customs spoke otherwise. The folk religion of the people was not formally written down in the same way that the Christian religion was, but it played just as important a role. People passed down knowledge about which foods to eat on which holiday, when it was forbidden to work, what

18. Dömötör, *A magyar nép hiedelemvilága*, 40.

the symbolism woven into artwork meant, how to deal with souls who had passed into the afterlife, which verses were to be said on special days, and which songs could be utilized to heal or curse. Some people believed in the old superstitions wholeheartedly, while others participated for amusement or simply because that was the way things were done in generations past.

Christian missionaries also emphasized new value systems that not everyone was eager to embrace, such as a focus on punishment or reward in the afterlife. Although facing *Isten*'s wrath was not unheard of in great injustices, the faith of the nomadic tribes placed less emphasis on divine judgment. Rather, a multitude of unseen spirits were constantly about, intimately involved in the world's affairs. Keeping them happy and satisfied meant that they would, in turn, impart their blessings on humankind. Fehér Jenő explains:

> The ancient Hungarian religion…was, in actuality, no religion. It was a moral order in which the supernatural powers were drawn into the living world as real elements. Aside from winning the goodwill of the spirits and avoiding their desire to harm, the Pagan worldview did not require much else from [its adherents]. Keeping the outward formalities, rituals, and traditions is what gave [the people] their peace of mind.[19]

Priests disapproved of these traditions as *babona*, or superstition. Many pled for the political leadership to issue edicts against these traditions, sometimes writing lengthy commentary of the primitive customs the people insisted on following. (Ironically, these religious rants and resulting edicts are a way in which modern scholars can actually study the rites of the early Hungarians!) Eventually, the priests realized that they were better off choosing their battles, and they quietly agreed to tolerate many elements of the folk religion, at times reinterpreting existing traditions to fit into the Christian worldview. In return, the locals learned new prayers and rites—and often ended up using them as magical talismans or spells. The two faiths dovetailed so neatly at times that, in the present day, it is not always straightforward which *babona* were holdovers from pre-Christian days and which arose more recently despite the presence of Christianity in the region. While

19. Fehér, *Középkori magyar inkvizíció*, 206.

priests and scholars argued about theological details, the majority of the citizenry were content to just live their lives, honoring both the old and new religions.

Sacrifices

While there are limited details about the religious practices of the ancient Hungarians, there are records of an old ceremonial form known as the *áldomás*. This rite was practiced during important functions and events, such as the change of leadership or at the start or end of a battle. Through the ritual, the people asked for God's blessing. (Indeed, the word for sacrifice, *áldozat*, has the same root word, as does *áldás*, "blessing.") Magyar leaders were recorded as performing blood oaths; in one famous account, seven tribal leaders poured their blood into a dish, then passed it around for the others to drink. A full *áldomás* ceremony typically included some sort of sacrifice to God (in many accounts, this was a white horse), then a feast which might include wolf meat and milk from mares. The word *áldomás* is still known to Hungarians and used for various important toasts, especially those marking agreements; in the 1845 epic poem *János vitéz*, the leader of the thieves raises a toast by calling for an *áldomás* when a new recruit joins their ranks.

The Magyars made sacrifices to nature spirits and their ancestors under the open skies of the windswept plains and on the peaks of mountains; a royal declaration in the eleventh century denounced those "who, according to Pagan custom made sacrifices by wells, or springs, or trees, or boulders."[20] People expressed gratitude and remorse, and they supplicated for healing, divine guidance, or victory in battle. Some sacrifices were personal, while others were performed on behalf of a household or the entire community. Treasured objects, blessed plants, and animals (frequently dogs or white horses)—and even, some think, humans[21]—were sacrificed.

After the adoption of Christianity, the sacrifices the Magyars offered to the spirits did not disappear completely, but they became tamer. Although small animals such as dogs, cats, and chickens were still fair game in the first

20. Diószegi, *A sámánhit emlékei a magyar népi műveltségben*, 276.
21. Vikár, "A szentiváni ének," 403.

half of the millennium, people (and, generally speaking, horses) were no longer sacrificed. Over time, more and more symbolic objects such as rags and
hairpins were attached to sacred trees, and coins were tossed into springs,
wells, and fountains. Food was thrown into fire, and wine was allowed to soak
into the ground. Loaves of bread and figures of wax or wood could be shaped
to symbolize people or animals. Sometimes, a simple candle was inscribed
with a word describing the intended offering. Even flowers or incense could
be offered as a sacrifice.

Christianity encouraged its followers to make personal sacrifices by cutting their hair, tearing their clothing, becoming celibate, fasting, or giving
up certain earthly comforts. The famed *Szent Margit* (Saint Margaret) was a
princess who had embraced asceticism entirely, wearing belts made of iron
and whipping herself. She slept on the floor and did not wash either her
body or her clothes; she even welcomed the fleas that settled on her. For her
efforts, the leadership named an island in the midst of the stretch of the Danube running between Buda and Pest after her. Today, *Margitsziget* ("Margaret
Island") is a popular destination for both tourists and locals alike; besides
flower gardens, sporting venues, and musical fountains, visitors can even
visit the ruins of the convent where Margit resided during her time amongst
the living. (Growing up, visiting *Margitsziget* was my absolute favorite summer activity, and it holds a special place in my heart even now!)

Taboos

Though sacrifices were a way to please the spirits, it was arguably more
important to avoid angering them. A *tilalom*, or taboo, was an action that
resulted in a punishment of some sort to the transgressor. Countless taboos
were passed down through the generations, but their contexts were frequently
lost, so they can seem quite nonsensical (at best). In their earliest forms,
taboos were likely taken quite seriously and people feared the associated punishments; as they were passed down from generation to generation, people
tended to forget the consequences, viewed the consequences as symbolic, or
simply became altogether unafraid of breaking the taboos. By 1910, the old
taboos had degraded in importance enough that in his book about hunting

magic, Lakatos Károly wrote, "I am convinced that for us Hungarians, there was truly more jest in the whole matter [of *babona*] than serious belief."[22]

Sometime breaking a taboo resulted in direct punishment: a person might be swallowed by the ground; bread baked on Sundays was said to turn to stone; household animals would sicken and die if a person did their washing on Christmas; and prey would hide from hunters who shared a bed with their wife the night before the hunt. Other times, the consequences were not as immediate and might simply serve to put the transgressor in a state of impurity. In everyday language, *tiszta* and *tisztátlan* can mean "clean" and "unclean," but in a spiritual context, they mean something closer to "pure" and "impure." Important tasks such as sowing, harvesting, slaughtering, milking a cow, working in the gardens, or drawing water from a well had to be accomplished in a state of purity. Wearing dirty clothes, having dirty feet, swearing, sexual intercourse (or even simply fondling a sweetheart), or having menstrual or postpartum bleeding could all put one in a state of lacking purity.

A very common type of *tilalom* had to do with performing work (or categories of work) on some days, such as working with fabric on a Tuesday or weaving on a Saturday. All unnecessary work was prohibited on Sundays and major holidays in favor of going to church services; if someone adhered to these prohibitions carefully, they were said to be "keeping Sunday." A *tilalom* could be limited to a certain time of year, moon phase, or time of day. Performing certain chores after sunset was forbidden, such as sweeping, taking out the trash, or lending milk after dark—in the latter case, the household's cows could be cursed. Sometimes one task had to be finished before another; baking bread before the wheat was completely harvested would make the wheat rot. There were even taboos about which chores had to be done within the privacy of the household: if a non-family member witnessed someone churning butter, the milk would not solidify; bread would not rise if an outsider witnessed its dough being kneaded; and so on.

Some taboos were based around gender; if a man milked a cow, the milk would turn sour. Girls and women could not whistle a song, or else they would make the Virgin Mary (i.e., the *Boldogasszony*) cry. Other taboos were

22. Lakatos, *Vadászhit*, 20.

based around a life status or health condition. Pregnant women had a whole slew of taboos specific to them, such as not eating stone fruits or looking at ugly people. (These are discussed in greater detail in chapter 26.) Likewise, postpartum and menstruating women had their own prohibitions, such as drawing water from wells or preserving produce for the winter. There were also, understandably, many taboos about dealing with the dead, such as not stepping in water used to wash a corpse, or not looking through a window of a house in which a dead person lay.

Food-related taboos were common as well. For instance, I was taught that bread must never touch the ground because it was sacred; leftover bread must not be thrown in the garbage, but fed to the birds instead. (In recent years, scientists have issued warnings about feeding bread to wildlife, including birds; I still feel uncomfortable throwing bread out, so I have found the happy medium of composting it instead!) Other food-related taboos were restricted at certain times, like eating meat on Fridays or avoiding unlucky foods on the first day of the year. A custom with many variations throughout Hungary involved a mourning mother, who could not eat fruit (often specified as apples, strawberries, or cherries) until she sent a share of the fruit to her deceased child's spirit via the sacred summer solstice bonfire.

Blessed objects, such as candles, prayerbooks, rosaries, and any blessed herbs, had to be treated reverentially. In the words of one writer, "It was taboo to use foul language in front of [them], and even gossiping [around them] had to be done in quiet tones."[23] As children, my cousins and I knew our grandmothers' religious items were strictly off-limits. Older taboos alluded to pre-Christian times; many a *tilalom* involved avoiding the wrath of nature spirits. As already mentioned, pointing at the sun was forbidden, as was pointing at the moon, rainbows, or stars; the latter acts would cause a person's finger to shrivel up and fall off or get warts. Spitting on a fire was also prohibited lest the person's tongue swell up with blisters. Still other taboos had to do with manners: slamming doors would cause the gates of Heaven to slam shut for a person, and sticking a tongue out at another would cause a person's spirit to be punished in the afterlife by being made to lick a plate of flames.

23. Tomán, "A kegytárgyak élete," 686.

From today's vantage point, it can be hard to distinguish which taboos were genuinely thought to incur the wrath of the spirits and which were a matter of reason, with the spiritual consequences added on as an afterthought to get children (or even adults) to comply. For example, it was forbidden to stand by an open window during a lightning storm. The most reasonable explanation is that people did not categorize issues by physical and spiritual causes—both were believed to be inexorably intertwined.

The Afterlife

The word for soul, *lélek*, is closely related to the word for breath, *lehelet*. When a person dies, they are said to have *kilehelte a lelkét*, or "breathed the soul out of themselves." The soul is the breath, without which the body will die. A person also has a second type of spirit called the *szabadlélek*, the free soul, which is able to temporarily leave the body for short periods of time, such as during sleep, sickness, bouts of great emotion, or shamanic trances. This was also sometimes referred to as the "shadow soul" or the "mirror-image soul." When out of the body, it might take the form of a white mouse, bee, bird, or shadowy version of the body, which returns to the body as the person wakes up. (While I have never seen a physical manifestation of this kind of spirit, I do try, whenever possible, to wake up slowly, in stages. I have noticed a big difference in how I start my day when I have the luxury of waking up in stages instead of being startled awake!)

The *lélek* was able to travel beyond the physical world. *Túlvilág* means "the World Beyond." Another similar term is *Másvilág*, which means "the Other World." *Túlvilág* is still used at times to refer to the afterlife; nowadays, it usually alludes to the Christian concept of heaven. Accounts described several versions of a possible afterlife; frequently, the afterlife was described as similar to the world of the living, but with everything reversed, as in a mirror. Once in the *Túlvilág*, a spirit continued to perform the activities they did while they were alive: they ate and drank, worked, fought battles, and so on and so forth.

The *Túlvilág* was often described as separated from the world of the living by a river or sea. Once a person died, their soul crossed this body of water and started a new life in the *Túlvilág*, periodically returning to visit their loved ones and descendants; a bridge or ferry might aid the soul to cross the waters, while other times they were expected to simply wade through the water. Hair and nail cuttings were collected throughout a person's life and placed into the coffin at their burial in the belief that the soul could use these cuttings to build a bridge to the *Túlvilág*. To make the journey easier and remind the deceased of where they must go, a body was typically carried or passed over a symbolic bridge before burial. This could be a canvas placed over a well or a ditch or simply the passing of the body across the grave before it was lowered down into it.

If a person had committed a great injustice, their soul would be unable to move on to the next world. Instead, the guilty spirit was forced to wander in this world as a ghost until they repaid the debt they owed or righted the wrong they had done. Only when they were purified and relieved of their guilt were they able to move on to the next world. This has parallels to the Christian explanation of a soul being confined to the fires of purgatory—called the *tisztítótűz*, or "cleansing fire"—until, their sins properly atoned, the deceased are able to move into heaven. Family members could comfort the souls of the dead (and perhaps speed up their time in purgatory) by praying for them or having the priest offer Masses on their behalf.

Chapter 3
SPIRITS OF THE SKIES

Szojka Gyula was a university professor who, a century and a half ago, taught at length about the creatures of Hungarian mythology, "those who lived in our mountains and valleys…the gnomes, the kobolds, the spirits of the mines, the mermaids, the fairies of the woodlands."[24] He eloquently stated:

> Eternally young, the sun, moon, and stars sparkled in the unreachable distance above humankind, who was chained to the earth. Humans could thank them for their good fortune, for the growth of their plants and animals. The people could learn from the celestial bodies how to tell time, and could divine their futures from their movements. From these bodies humankind could ask for and receive advice and could pray to them in his misery and helplessness. And so, humankind respected and worshipped them.[25]

Generally, the steady, life-giving *nap* ("sun") is considered a masculine entity and a symbol of God himself. Some simply addressed it as *Öreg* ("The Old/Ancient One"). Many fairy tales talked about the sun witnessing the goings-on in the world. Although sometimes the sun was seen as a passive

---

24. Szojka, *A természet a néphitben*, 6.
25. Szojka, *A természet a néphitben*, 9.

observer, it could also come to people's aid at times. One spell, for instance, directed the caster to go to a lonely place where no one could see or hear them. Then, without eating or drinking anything, they were to pray all day long while facing the sun before stating the conditions of their curse.[26]

The *hold* ("moon"), ever-changing and weaker than the sun, is seen as feminine. Not only were they celestial counterparts, but they were often matched as lovers in legends as well. In one story, the sun and moon married each another, but on their wedding night, the moon wanted to sleep instead of making love with her new husband. The two parted ways. Although both have tried to approach the other, they are rarely seen at the same time. When they are very upset at each another, they will turn their backs on each another completely, resulting in eclipses. The moon grows frail and thin from sorrow, and she eats and grows fat when she is hopeful that the two will reconcile; the sun cries red tears each sunset as he goes to sleep, alone. Other stories, songs, legends, and verses refer to the moon in masculine terms instead, such as the *Hold király* ("Moon King").

Moon phases had a slew of taboos as well as suggested activities. Most were associated with the new moon, which was addressed as *Újhold, új király*—that is, "New Moon, New King." During the waxing moon, people performed tasks that needed energy to grow: sowing seeds, planting fruit trees, casting love spells, or using beauty magic to make one's hair grow longer. On the day of the new moon itself, it was not advisable to start a new task, but a person could place coins in their pocket so that as the moon increased, their wealth would also increase along with it. Magical verses also invoked the healing power of the new moon. There were many variations on the verse "New moon, new king, you have invited me as your guest. I cannot go, but I will send [my illness] instead!"[27]

Numerous legends center on the shadows of the moon's craters, of which I'll mention a handful:

• A fiddler fell in love with a dancer, and she with him. Their spouses became jealous of all the time the two spent together, and they cursed the couple so that they were unable to find a home on earth or in the

26. Jankó, "Kalotaszegi babonák," 281.
27. Szendrey, "A varázslatok eszközei," 400.

sky. Since they did not mention the moon in their curse, the two moved there to live in peace.

- A person cut wood on a day with a work prohibition and chopped down a tree. For his crime, the moon transported him to the sky.
- A man carried a stolen bundle of straw upon his shoulders. When caught by the authorities, he swore by the moon that he had obtained them legally. For his false oath, he was transported to the moon.
- A shepherd placed the lining of his boot on a bush to dry in the moonlight. When the moon did not dry the lining as the sun would have, he cursed the moon. The moon, in return, sucked both him and the boot up in revenge.

Both solar and lunar eclipses were frightening phenomena, and they were almost always attributed to evil forces. Legends explained how the celestial bodies were being eaten by a werewolf, rooster, dragon, or the restless spirit of an infant who had died without baptism. If one put a white bowl of fresh water in the garden and looked into it during the eclipse, it might even be possible to see the reflection of the evil creature in it.

Stars were linked with the world of spirits. The Milky Way was known to the Magyars as the *Hadak Útja*, "Road of the Warriors," the glorious route by which those who had fallen in battle returned to the spirit world; others referred to it as the *Tündérek Útja*, "Road of the Fairies." Some legends told of how each soul had a corresponding star in the sky upon which their fortune depended. When the star had run its course, the person would die; a falling star indicated that a soul had crossed over into the afterlife. Others believed that a falling star meant that a soul was being incarnated at that time, making their journey to the world of the living.

The Wind

In the Hungarian language, the word for "spirit" is *szellem*, while the word for "wind" is *szél* (or *szellő*). The two terms have significant spiritual overlap: people's spirits, or souls, are often linked with the breath of air, and the wind is also said to have (or be) a spirit. In some stories, the *Szélkirály* ("King of Wind") or *Szélatya* ("Father Wind") was said to live on a mountain at the end of the world; in many versions, he had various sons (sometimes named after the cardinal directions) who each had a different personality. In one of my favorite childhood stories, the winds took turns visiting people, each bearing different gifts, which in turn caused the seasons to change. The brothers were eager to prove once and for all which of them was the most beloved by (and beneficial to) humans.

People did not want to anger the *Szélkirály* by complaining about the weather and have him send out his sons to avenge the insult, so even if the wind was bitterly cold and destructive, people only mentioned it in positive terms. Sometimes the wind was described as being "hungry" if a bitter wind was blowing; one could throw a handful of flour, an apple, or some walnuts into an oven to satiate its hunger. As late as 1851, the *Pesti Napló* magazine reported women threw a mixture of flour and salt into the wind to calm it while saying the following: "Calm down, dear wind, and take this to your sons!"[28]

Among the legends that explain the winds, many variations included a *Szélanyó* ("Old Mother Wind") who lived in a cave "a hundred days' journey away" (presumably, from civilization).[29] She was angry and hideous and threatening to those who visited her. Other beliefs hint that winds could listen to humans who knew how to summon them. For instance, a man could summon a gust of wind by taking off his hat or turning his *szűr* (a cloak-like garment) inside out. One could also hang a snake up in the direction the wind should be summoned from, stick an axe into a wall or tree, or simply whistle. If someone was babbling needlessly, they were warned to stop talking lest the winds be set loose.

Whirlwinds were a rare occurrence and were attributed to supernatural causes. A weather wizard called a *garabonciás* could cause a whirlwind by reading aloud from a magic book or riding a dragon through the air; it was also said that the whirlwind was a witch flying through the air. If a person threw an axe, shovel, dagger, or other sharp object into a whirlwind, it might abate completely. This was a dangerous gamble, however—if the object did not hit the witch, she could become furious and throw it back. After a whirlwind, local women suspected of witchcraft were examined; if they had sustained injuries in the storm, that was considered sufficient proof that they

28. Diószegi, *Az ősi magyar hitvilág*, 202.
29. Kandra Kabos, *Magyar mythologia*, 87.

had become harmed while riding in the whirlwind. Yet another explanation for a whirlwind was that the *Szépasszony* (an evil female entity described in greater depth in chapter 5) was dancing through the air, enjoying the chaos of the storm. Onlookers might have observed a beautiful naked woman with long white hair in the midst of the storm, throwing hail in every direction.

Even ordinary wind could be linked to evil entities. In one legend, a beautiful young woman was in love with a young man. Before they could marry, the young man passed away, and the girl mourned him greatly. Her father bade her to marry another man, but she refused. At this, her father grew angry and cursed her. Soon thereafter, the young woman passed away as well, and she was buried on a mountainside. Because of her father's curse, witches tormented her in her grave, night and day, in the form of wind, and they would not let her spirit rest. On nights when the moon was full, the girl's unhappy spirit would emerge to haunt the mountaintop.

Rain

One of the most popular forms of divination dealt with predicting the weather in the coming year. This was no mere curiosity; the amount of precipitation a community received could be the difference between life and death, influencing the growth of crops, the well-being of livestock, and potential hazards such as floods or disease. Physical signs (such as the itching of one's ear) could forecast rain, as could dreams, such as dreaming of a dead person. Weather on certain days of the year could predict what the rest of the season had in store. The weather on the first day of the year was expected to foretell what the weather would be like all year: the weather in the morning corresponded to spring, the weather at midday would correspond to summer, and so on.

Rain had the power to make many things grow and thrive, not just plants. Girls and women who wanted their hair to grow longer stood outside during summertime showers, and young children were sent outside during warm rains so they would grow big and strong. When rainfall was lacking, the community was understandably concerned. Many methods of conjuring rain had to do with appeasing the spirits of the dead. According to various explanations, a recently deceased person might not be "completely" dead yet; if they still needed moisture in some form, this caused a drought in the land. (This was especially likely if the deceased had been a sinner; their soul might have ended up in the fiery dimension of purgatory, which would make them crave water even more than usual.) During droughts, the graves of the recently deceased might be doused with water. Other times, villagers would water the grave of a drunkard in hopes that their soul would absorb the water into the sky and then send it down again in the form of rain.

Other methods of rain-conjuring magic included sacrificing a rooster, throwing a stone into a lake or well, threatening the clouds with an axe, sprinkling water in the four directions, or throwing the underskirts of the oldest woman in the community into a river. Another ceremony involved people dressed up as plants who were watered by the other villagers. According to sympathetic magic, the real plants would also soon receive rainfall.

Rainbows

The rainbow is a bridge between the heavens and the earth—and, thus, a magical route from one to the other. If a rainbow ended in a lake, the rainbow itself (or an unspecified "mythic creature" in it) was said to be able to drink up the water from the lake and send it down again as rain. Fish, frogs, and even humans could be sucked up along with the water.

It was forbidden to point at a rainbow; the punishment for such insolence was the pointing finger drying up, and if someone passed under a rainbow, they would change genders. The first rainbow of the spring was closely examined to see which band of color was the most prominent, although interpretations varied from community to community. According to one interpretation, a thick red stripe foretold wind, green meant heat, and yellow meant a rainy season to come; if all the stripes showed well, the harvest would be good.

Thunder and Lightning

There were many beliefs about lightning, thunder, and storms in general. Out-of-season storms were usually interpreted as omens of bad news to come. (In contrast, thunder in early springtime meant that the year's harvest would be bountiful.) An old-fashioned word for lightning is *istennyila*, meaning "the arrow of God," and accordingly, lightning was often deemed to be a heavenly punishment for wrongdoing. If it struck a tree or house, *Isten* was sending one of his arrows to vanquish a malevolent spirit who was using the tree as its dwelling place or punishing a sin that had been committed there. Such a location was believed to be at risk for being struck again within the next seven years, so it was wise to abandon the place altogether.

Thunderstorm legends explained that celestial beings in the sky were causing a ruckus. They might be sword-fighting and crashing their weapons together, throwing objects around, rolling barrels across the sky, or bowling. *Isten* might be driving his wagon across the sky, lightning being the sparks created by his horses' hooves. In Transylvania, it was said that a thunderstorm was Jesus riding a donkey across the sky. According to another story, at the beginning of the world, God created humans from the earth and breathed his spirit into their forms. The devil saw God doing this and tried to imitate him. He too created a clay figure, but when he tried to breathe life into it, the clay attacked him. The devil defended himself by shooting sparks out of his fingers and then ran away. The clay figure chased after him and has continued chasing him around the world up to the present day. The devil shoots lightning at it, and the figure lumbers after him with thundering footsteps.

During the first storm of the year, the people of the household were advised to run outside and roll around on the ground so that their back would remain healthy that year. They might also bang their heads against a wall or against rocks so that they would not get headaches. The *gazdasszony* could go outside while naked (or at least with her skirts pulled up to expose her bottom) to show that neither she nor her household was afraid of the storm. During subsequent lightning storms, the residents could protect themselves from lightning strikes by sprinkling holy water around the house, shutting the doors and windows, burning blessed candles, and sticking pussywillows blessed during the springtime holidays above the front door, perhaps even burning a few of the buds from it.

Szent Illés ("Saint Elijah"), also known as Éliás, took over the role of the pre-Christian god of thunder and lightning. When thunder was heard, people said that the sound was his wagon wheels rolling across the sky as he cracked his whip; lightning bolts were sparks from the wheels of his wagon. On or around his feast day (July 20), large storms were certain to come. According to one legend, Illés asked all the other saints in heaven when his feast day was so that he could celebrate by shooting his arrows around the sky. The other saints, fearing the worst, refused to tell him. He had a vague idea of what time of year his feast day fell, but since he couldn't be sure of the exact date, he celebrated frequently throughout the season. If he didn't strike on his actual feast day, he was sure to do so a few days before or after it. In many communities, this festival was a day of work prohibitions; if someone insisted on working, Illés might avenge the disrespect by striking their household with lightning or destroying their crops with hail.

Although today scholars know that many "sky stones" (*mennykövek*, literally "stones of heaven") were chiseled tools crafted by Stone Age humans, the Magyars believed these polished stones had formed from soil that was struck by lightning. Sky stones were wards against future lightning strikes. These stones had many purported abilities, including use in love magic, as financial charms, as cursing tools, and to help women having difficult labors or those who did not have enough breastmilk. They were also valued for their reputed healing abilities. One could run a sky stone along the affected body part of a person or animal in order to cure them. Gently striking the household's milk pitcher with a sky stone or rubbing the stone against its rim would increase a cow's milk production. People lucky enough to be in possession of such a magical object displayed them proudly on their Christmas altars.

Chapter 4
FAIRIES AND NATURE SPIRITS

In the summer months, pilgrims visited sacred spots out in nature. These included clearings, stones, trees, springs, and caves home to helpful spirits who could perform a number of miracles, such as healing the sick, finding a spouse, or ensuring that a woman would soon have a child. Unable to prevent the populace from visiting these sites, the church declared them holy pilgrimage sites; as late as the 1930s, Franciscan monks officially pronounced that "the water from the sacred well is healing for all manner of ailments, if the good Lord wills it so." [30] Chapels and statues were erected in these locations, and visitors were told that the miracles were due to the intervention of the site's patron saint(s).

Sick people wishing for healing left part of their clothing or a lock of their hair at shrines, or they left a cane or glasses in hopes that they were leaving their illness or injury at the site as well. Water from a sacred spring was bottled up and taken home by the pilgrims to be used for healing various illnesses and ridding one's surroundings of evil influences. Many pilgrims would return home bearing green branches, a symbol of the renewal and cleansing of their souls.

Tourists and church groups still visit pilgrimage sites, some of which have shed their Christian associations. For example, in the mountainous region of Pilis, there is a rock formation called *Dobogókő*, meaning the "rhythmically

30. Dömötör, *A magyar nép hiedelemvilága*, 209.

beating stone." A web search in Hungarian for "Pilis" and "*szívcsakra*" ("heart chakra") pulls up dozens of websites on which people proclaim that the area is connected to the planet's heart chakra, and they share their accounts of feeling special healing energy there.

A secular tradition that nonetheless has the makings of a religious pilgrimage is that of visiting Lake Balaton. Many Hungarians and international visitors make the journey annually, and some of them even take up the physical challenge of swimming across it from shore to shore. While tourists visit Lake Balaton annually to the tune of millions of hotel room bookings per year, only a fraction of the visitors are aware of the rich collection of legends about the region. The lakeshore has been continuously settled for thousands of years, so there has been ample time to document the stories of the spirits living in its waters, as well as the giants, fairies, and hidden magical objects in the hills and caves surrounding the lake.

One particularly magical tale describes a young man falling in love with a beautiful water fairy named *Sió*. When she broke his heart with her unfaithful ways, he died of sorrow. His father was a wizard and, in retaliation for his son's death, he cursed the fairy, turning her beautiful hair into writhing snakes. Further stories describe how the fairy eventually made peace with her fate and even went on to help a princess marry her true love.

Legendary Beings

It is safe to say that most modern Hungarians view fairies, known as *tündérek*, as creatures of fantasy instead of living spirits able to affect the world of the living. A number of folklorists interviewed village elders at the close of the nineteenth century about their knowledge of fairies; most only mentioned the *tündérek* in the context of stories, and they never expressed personal belief in (or personal experience with) them.

Almost without exception, fairies were described as having shining gold or silver hair, and they were typically dressed in radiant garments. (Though sparkling creatures who might have been magical and radiant, they were not always paragons of goodness!) Many water sources such as springs, lakes, or wells were said to be inhabited by *tündérek*. Others lived in caves or were imprisoned within trees, most often oak trees. In one common story plot, a witch placed a curse on a fairy, who was then trapped in a tree until the story's hero rescued the fairy. The Transylvanian region of historical Hungary was especially known for its fairy mythology, such as that of the sorrowful fairy *Klára*. She fell in love with a shepherd, but after he disappointed her, she wept so much that a spring bubbled forth from the ground. This spring was subsequently known as Klára's well, and those who drank from it would get a taste of her sorrow.

Fairies remained popular characters in children's stories and literature created for all ages, such as Petőfi Sándor's epic poem *János vitéz*, written in the middle of the nineteenth century.[31] While new creations, these narratives were based on earlier conventions about magical creatures. One of the most well-known fairies in Hungarian literature was *tündér Ilona*. Cursed by a witch, she was only able to be reunited with her beloved Prince Árgyilus after he defeated a number of supernatural creatures.

Óriások ("giants") were treated in a similar way as fairies: while they were reasonably common characters in fairy tales, few accounts of actual *óriások* exist in folk memory. The ones that do were mainly centered on the regions of Transylvania, present-day Slovakia, and the mountains around Lake Balaton, where the locals describe various valleys as the footsteps of giants. Large boulders were said to end up in unusual places because *óriások* were tossing rocks around when fighting or juggling them to amuse their children. Craters were thought to be the imprints of their fists, hills were thought to be *óriás* children's sand castles, and so on. Entire mountains were considered petrified remains of *óriások*, while smaller rock formations were said to be various humans who had been turned to stone by magic-wielding *óriások*.

On the opposite end of the spectrum were the *manó* (a small creature similar to a gnome or elf) and the *törpe* ("dwarf"), humanoid creatures that were either short in stature or much smaller, sometimes no bigger than a walnut. *Törpék* lived in hollow trees or under the ground where they often had complete societies parallel to our own, with cities full of kings, craftsmen, merchants, healers, and families. *Törpék* (or just their king) had access to magical quest items or knew the answers to complicated riddles. They were known for their ravenous appetites and love of material objects, hiding troves of gold, gems, and jewels deep in the ground.

---

31. If you are interested in reading an English translation, Professor John Ridland released *John the Valiant* in 1999, which can be found online.

Once in a while, a *törpe* might befriend a human who impressed them with their wit, generosity, or kindness; they might even share their treasure with such a lucky person. On the other hand, if an individual insulted them, proved themselves to be lazy or dishonest, or used foul language in their presence, they disappeared along with their treasure, or the *törpe* punished them by subjecting them to various pranks.

Professor Szojka claimed that "considered in totality, [dwarves] are friends to humankind."[32] In contrast to Szojka's rather generous view, Kandra Kabos stressed that for all the good that dwarves did for humankind, they often had a dark side, and in some areas, they were believed to be outright malevolent.[33] This latter viewpoint is featured in quite a few fairy tales.

One particularly legendary dwarf-like creature had quite the impressive name: *Hétszünyű Kapanyányimonyók*. He was described as being the height of a child, with a rainbow-colored beard that was roughly thirteen feet in length. He was abnormally strong, with a penis as long as a hoe and testicles as large as human skulls. He was also extremely dangerous and malevolent; only a giant or demigod could defeat him. He stole princesses or celestial bodies, and the hero of the tale would go on a quest to return them. (In some versions, *Hétszünyű* was the father of dragons, and the dragons were the ones to go on to steal said princesses or celestial bodies.) His beard was the key to his defeat: he was usually tied up with it, or when his beard was pulled out, he lost his strength. In one of the most famous Hungarian legends, *Fehérlófia* ("The Son of the White Mare"), the hero followed *Hétszünyű* to the Lower World, where he finally outsmarted the creature. *Hétszünyű Kapanyányimonyók* was so impressive that his name was featured in a Commodore 64 video game, and the Hungarian black metal band Tormentor titled one of their songs after him.

Mining Spirits

The *bányaszellem* ("mine spirit") or *bányarém* ("mine terror") was sometimes described as a giant, sometimes as a dwarf. (Even, at times, a headless one!) A similar spirit was the *kobold*; the word comes from the same German root

32. Szojka, *A természet a néphitben*, 22–23.
33. Kandra Kabos, *Magyar mythologia*, 173.

word as *cobalt*. This was a ratlike, humanoid creature dressed in boots, a cap, and red pants who carried mining tools. While some of these spirits were rather mischievous, they were rarely outright malevolent. They loved fairness, and they could be helpful to those they deemed worthy. However, the *bányaszellem* had various ways of meting out punishments to workers who were lazy, dishonest, or trying to cheat their coworkers, sometimes by means of cave-ins or other disasters. The spirit was also displeased when workers cursed or whistled in or near a cave.

If the *bányaszellem* asked for a ride on the mining cart, the driver had to graciously invite him to do so; his horse would then be able to pull the cart as easily as if it were completely empty. However, if the driver was not as generous, the spirit would hop up on the cart and refuse to move, and he made the cart so heavy that the horse could barely pull it. In another tale, a *bányaszellem* appeared to the women tasked with bringing water to the miners. When the women refused to share their water with him, the spirit was angered. For the rest of the day, any water the miners tried to drink disappeared from the buckets before they had a chance to drink it. The next morning, they brought an offering of a new set of clothes and boots to the spirit, which appeased him; the miners were once again allowed to drink. Tobacco leaves placed on a shovel might also appease an angry *bányaszellem*. If there was a fatal accident in the mines, it was believed that every article of the deceased worker's outfit had to remain in the mine lest the spirit follow the pieces of clothing out and create an accident in a different mine.

Mining spirits sometimes appeared before a tragedy. In these cases, they were not thought to have caused the tragedy, but rather to have tried to warn those who would listen. Before a fire or other accident, miners might see a giant smoking a cigar, a dwarf with a lantern, or a dog or other animal trying to get them to stay out of the mine. Sometimes the spirits forbade the workers to take the coal; if the miners listened, they escaped with their lives, but if they insisted on working that day or scoffed at the warning, they died. According to one story, a group of miners was trapped underground. Several saw a procession of spirits carrying coffins upon their shoulders. Those who saw the procession died, but the ones who did not see the spirits were rescued.

There were many stories about hardworking men who were injured in the mines and unable to support their large families; the *bányaszellem* helped them find ore or outright brought treasure to their doorstep in the night. According to one story, a miner got lost in the mines on Christmas. As he was wandering in the mine, he encountered spirits who filled his hat with gold and led him to the surface. Much to his surprise, the entrance to the cave was right outside his own house's front door, but when he turned around, the cave was gone. He went inside only to discover that he had been missing for a full year instead of mere hours, and the gold he had carried in his hat had disappeared.

Woodland Spirits

Trees were either home to magical creatures or had spirits of their own. One particularly famous tree near the Rima natural spring (located within present-day Slovakia) was home to a spirit known as the *múlt szelleme* ("spirit of the past") which "in gentle whispers, told the stories of the past."[34] Another tree located near what is now Reghin, Romania, contained a spirit known as the *tápió*. People left offerings near this tree and did not dare cut into it, lest it start bleeding; those who wounded the tree would be unlucky. Even human souls could be entrapped in trees. In one account, a tree cried whenever the wind blew. A sinful soul had been tied to it for a hundred years and was fated to remain for a hundred more unless the tree itself was cut down, which would free the soul.

Besides tree spirits, other mysterious creatures inhabited the wild, including:

- A fairy queen who lived deep in the earth, in a cave illuminated by the various shimmering gems built into the walls. If a person should venture down to her lair, they would never see the light of day again, but they would receive a garment made of stones.
- The *kontyu*, who lurked in dark valleys and holes in the ground.
- The *erdőanya* ("forest mother"), who stole the dreams of children.

One creature, known as the *erdei csoda* ("forest wonder"), was vaguely described as eating grass and fleeing from people. The creature was able to perform miracles in some capacity. If an individual had an unfaithful part-

34. Szendrey, "A nép élő hitvilága," 266.

ner, they could go into the forest and pin the heart of a black rooster to a tree. Once the *erdei csoda* found the offering, it would "bend" the heart of the unfaithful partner back to the spellcaster.

The *vadöreg* ("wild old man") was a stocky creature who was covered in long fur and had wild eyes. He wandered along the snowcapped mountain peaks and guarded the forest and the wild. If woodcutters met misfortune, they were said to be shaken by the *vadöreg*. If people annoyed him on purpose or talked about him disrespectfully, he threw rocks at them and made the trees they cut turn to sawdust. To avoid triggering his wrath, woodcutters always left offerings of meat and wine for him on a tree stump at the end of each day to thank him for allowing them to work in peace.

Another creature known as the *vadleány* ("wild girl," also known as the forest girl or the cheerful girl) came after the strongest man in a group and tied him up. She had a pretty face, but her naked body was covered in a pelt of fur, and her long fingers had bladelike nails at the ends. Her footprints were thinner and longer than those of a human, and her feet had claws and fur; even the soles of her feet were hairy. Her voice was a loud shriek. If she was annoyed, she could make a wind strong enough to knock down trees or the shelters of shepherds. The *vadleány* could be caught by placing a single boot along the path she frequented; she would try to put both her feet in the same boot and was thus hobbled.

In various parts of central Asia, travelers created stone cairns at important points along travel routes or on mountaintops. Each person who passed by was meant to place a stone atop the pile. Even modern-day motorists are known to stop by these sites and leave their offerings. According to local legend, spirits who have been imprisoned in the Lower World are prevented from returning to the physical realm because of these heavy stones. Each person who passes by the stone cairns is tasked with keeping the weight heavy lest the wind cause some of the stones to scatter, allowing the evil below to rise once more. Due to the similarity of the evil spirits described in those legends to the legends found in Hungarian lore, it is quite possible that the ancient Magyars also made use of this practice.

Water Spirits

A number of aquatic spirits inhabited the lakes, swamps, and rivers of the Carpathian Basin. One of these was simply termed the *víziember*, "man of the water." (In other places, a similar spirit was called the *süvöltő*, "shrieker," because he was said to have a voice like a squealing piglet.) This spirit was created when a person drowned in a body of water and never had their corpse removed and given a proper burial. The *víziember* was a frightening creature with scaly or furry black skin, the teeth of a fish, and long, curved talons. Sometimes he was rumored to have a palace under the surface of the lake. He would pull swimmers down to him, especially if they annoyed him by being too rowdy or loud, or by tossing stones into the waves.

Other water spirits included:

- The hairy "barrel-headed man" who chased boats
- A child with blackened skin who jumped into boats, grinning and laughing, then jumped back into the water only to disappear beneath the surface
- A man dressed in green clothes who pulled people into the water
- The "water drinker" who drank away the rivers that were supposed to turn the mills

Still another water spirit suddenly appeared in a rowboat as a stiff corpse. If he wasn't harmed, he slowly regained signs of life and jumped into the water again, but if the people on the boat harmed his body or offended him in any way, he sank the boat. This same spirit might appear as a corpse floating in the water; if someone tried to haul him into their boat, he sank the boat and drowned all those in it, taking them to his own home under the water.

Mermaids are known in Hungary as the *vízilány* ("water maiden"), *sellő*, or *hableány* (maiden of the foam). They are often described as beautiful young women who had lower bodies of fish and unusual teeth. Many accounts emphasized their singing abilities; not only were their songs beautiful, but they were able to sing the future into existence. *Vízilányok* were also the ones responsible for teaching people how to sing. When a person drew water from a lake, it was tradition to splash a little back to keep the *vízilány* happy. *Vízilányok* could tempt men into the water, where they would presumably drown; others could climb trees and make a ruckus at night. Mermen were also rumored to exist, but their names were not spoken aloud by fishermen. If the creature heard their name spoken aloud, they would rise to the surface and free the fish caught in the fishermen's nets.

Szent Medárd

After Christianization, *Szent Medárd* took over the role of the *vízek királya* ("king of water"). Natural waters were known as "living water" due to the belief spirits inhabited them, and Medárd was their ruler. On his feast day, June 8, anyone who went bathing or swimming in natural waters was brought down to his underwater castle (and ultimately drowned). On the other hand, horses were encouraged to drink from these "living waters" on his festival day; the water king favored the animals and blessed them with good health, preventing them from having stiff joints in the coming year. Priests tolerated these practices by explaining that the biblical flood of forty days started on *Medárd napja*; for the same reason, it was thought that if it rained on this day, it would continue raining for forty more.

Well Spirits

Various entities lived inside wells; some included the *kokos*, the *vasbába*, and the *kútasszonny* (woman of the well). Many of these spirits were ambivalent in nature, so it was best to stay on their good side; it was forbidden to whistle into a well or otherwise disturb its peace. Well spirits could turn infants into changelings or pull babies into the well, so pregnant women could not sit by wells or nurse their children there. If a woman's baby was turned into a changeling, its mother could implore the baby to be returned; the spirit might oblige.

Despite their danger to children, a well spirit could be helpful to adults. At Christmas, people "fed" the well with various items, such as apples, nuts, garlic, or blessed wafers so that its waters would be healthy and clean/pure. In return, the well spirit might show the people their futures in the water's reflection. A well that had never been gazed in before was thought to be especially potent.

Chapter 5
THE *ROSSZAK*

*R*osszak means "the evil ones." It is a catch-all term that encompassed many subcategories of malevolent spirits. While some of the *rosszak* were nameless, others very much had names, which people nonetheless wanted to avoid using lest they anger or summon the spirits by saying their names aloud. Attracting the spirits' attention in any way could surely bring trouble upon a household; even compliments were rarely given to these spirits. When asked about a taboo activity whose origins were forgotten, people might shrug and say, "The *rosszak* won't allow us to do such-and-such on this day." [35]

When yawning, a person was encouraged to make the sign of the cross in front of their mouth so that the *rosszak* could not enter their body through their open mouth. This may have been specified further, with some saying that the devil would be the one entering the body. Although one might expect that devils, known as *ördögök*, would be chief amongst the evil *rosszak*, this was not necessarily the case. The devils of Magyar legends and folktales were not easily categorized into "good" and "evil." Many were frightening but also ambivalent, and they could help people if the mood struck them. Unlike demons of other cultures, Hungarian devils were rarely pure evil. Kandra Kabos wrote that the devil could "help, take mercy on the desperate, come

---

35. Dömötör, *A magyar nép hiedelemvilága*, 73.

to the aid of those calling him…and offer aid, for which he asks thanks, acknowledgement, and a sacrifice [in return]." [36]

In the centuries after Christianity was introduced, Hungarian demons were conflated with satanic imagery, and some of the stories associated with them took a much darker turn than before. For instance, Bornemisza Péter was a preacher who once described a day full of misfortunes: he got into an argument with a colleague, his children were misbehaving, his wife was annoying him, and even the family dogs chased the hens. He angrily wrote that all of these problems were clearly the work of not just one devil, but a whole regiment of them working against him. [37] One should not assume, however, that every mention of the term *ördög* is equivalent to that of Satan or his minions.

Certain spirits caused (or at least foreshadowed) specific illnesses. In one account, a strange, mute, naked child appeared one day in the village; after this, a great sickness swept through the town, killing many. Other times, the spirit was more nebulous. The *gyík*, for example, caused sore throats; fittingly, lizards (which were known by the same name) were made into various cures for the ailment. The *nyavalya* was responsible for a number of ailments, including epilepsy, and the *guta* caused strokes or paralysis. Even today, there is an expression—*megüt a guta* ("the *guta* is striking me")—that means the speaker is so upset they are likely to have a stroke. *Fene* is the name of yet another spirit which causes tumors or ulcer-like diseases. While today *íz* means "taste" or "flavor," a number of archaic curses such as "May the *íz* eat you up/tear you apart/fall into your throat" hint that there was originally an evil spirit known by the name; Kiss Géza defined the word as something that forces a person to do something against their will—in other words, one of the *rosszak*. [38]

While most archaic curses are no longer used, one that has survived into modern times is "*a fene vigye el*," meaning "May the *fene* take [something] away." Another is "may the *franc* eat it up." As sicknesses were oftentimes attributed to spiritual causes, these expressions might also be used for positive magic, summoning one of the illness spirits in order to drive away an

36. Kandra Kabos, *Magyar mythologia*, 206.

37. Dömötör, *A magyar nép hiedelemvilága*, 54.

38. Kiss, *Ormányság*, 290.

illness, the evil eye, or bad luck. It was considered more effective to fight bad with bad rather than trying to overpower bad with good, so cures for illnesses frequently included obscenities and curses. Curative spells frequently featured chants about dog excrement, for instance, as that was supposed to be a particularly vile substance.

Some of the *rosszak* were spirits who terrorized children in particular; they were aptly named *gyermekijesztők*, or "child frighteners." While some were realistic figures, such as owls, bats, or chimneysweeps, others were supernatural creatures, many of them only alluded to in vague descriptions that went by many names, including the *mumus, bubus,* or the *mókár*. These names were invoked by parents to correct misbehaving children; the spirit was said to kidnap or even eat children. These days, it is less socially acceptable to terrorize a child with *gyermekijesztők*, but the spirits have not been completely forgotten, either. The now-classic *Kököjszi és Bobojsza* is a children's novel in which the two titular *törpék* weave their magic into a young boy's life. In one chapter, the boy, Andris, becomes afraid of the dark after hearing an older relative say that it is full of malevolent creatures. Kököjszi and Bobojsza take Andris to meet the so-called child frighteners who, in a twist on the original tales, end up being friendly creatures with unfortunate reputations.

The *Lidérc*

The *lidérc* (sometimes spelled *ludérc*) was not just one spirit, but rather a category of supernatural creatures that fell into three main subtypes: the pressing demon, the spirit lover, and the evil chicken.

The first type of *lidérc* caused a phenomenon known as the *lidércnyomás* ("pressing of the *lidérc*"), whereby a person felt breathing troubles during the course of the night that they attributed to an unseen spirit sitting on their chest. (Alternate explanations included devils, witches, or the *Szépasszony* sitting on the affected person's chest.) People might also feel the weight of a *lidérc* while out walking in the night, when something incredibly heavy suddenly pressed down on their shoulders.

A second type of *lidérc* was the spirit lover. This malevolent entity entered the house through a keyhole or a chimney and transformed into a humanoid form, usually taking the form of a widow's deceased spouse or lover. It was especially drawn to young people who were mourning their sweethearts, as they could obtain the most energy from them. After engaging in a sexual encounter with their victim—who presumably was tricked into thinking their lost love had returned from the dead—the *lidérc* left the house in the same manner in which they came, often leaving a scorch mark on the wall as their calling card. The spirit returned again and again, and the person they were visiting grew weaker and weaker as their life force was drained from them.

In one account, a woman's husband died, and she mourned him endlessly, crying night after night. Villagers noticed that a shooting star would head toward her house, then disappear. They began to suspect that a *lidérc* was visiting her. The young woman protested that this was not true, but she grew gaunt and weak. Finally, her father advised her that when she was visited by the spirit, she should trick the spirit into revealing his true nature. Since a *lidérc* did not have human feet, the woman was advised to hide one of his boots and see what happened when he could not hide his true form in the footwear. The woman listened to her father's advice. The *lidérc* always left before midnight, but on this night, he looked everywhere for his boot but could not find it. He realized he had been tricked and became enraged, and the woman nearly died of fright. Then he left, and he did not return again. The woman was sick for a long time, but after half a year, she recovered.

To put an end to visits by a *lidérc*, the victim could guard the home with birch branches or cense the house with the powerful *Benedek hagyma* ("Benedek onions," discussed in chapter 9). Both of these techniques were said to keep the spirit at bay. Particularly difficult spirits might require a more elaborate exorcism. In one account, a woman was suffering from a *lidérc*. The townspeople made an altar in her room by setting a crucifix, holy water, and two blessed candles on a table. They also applied garlic to the window frame. Many women gathered in her room to pray over the victim while several men circled the building, keeping watch. At midnight, a black dog ran forth, and the affected woman started screaming and threw herself into a window. Her companions held her down, sprinkled her with holy water, and pressed a holy candle into her hands. A force shook the window so hard that the flowerpots in front of it fell, but the window stayed intact. Subsequently, the woman fainted and fell into a deep sleep, after which she was free from further visits by the *lidérc*.

A third type of *lidérc* had to do with chickens. If a person stole a black hen's egg and held it under their left armpit for a time (sometimes as long as three whole weeks), it would hatch into a *lidérc csirke* ("*lidérc* chicken"). During the day, the *lidérc* took the form of a chicken and asked its owner, "*Mit-mit-mit?*" ("What-what-what?") For this reason, it was also referred to as the *mimitke* or *mit-mitke*. After the master relayed their wishes, the chicken obtained whatever was desired and brought it before its master. Usually, this was money; if a person suddenly became wealthy out of nowhere, people suspected that they had a *lidérc csirke* helper. Even if it shape-shifted into a human, the footprints of the *lidérc* would be those of a bird.

Of course, the *lidérc csirke* would not work for free—it required payment for its services. It ate the first bite of any meal its master ate, or it required an unsalted porridge to be prepared for it, stirred counterclockwise during the cooking process. At night it transformed into a human the opposite sex of its master and required sexual services; at other times, it sucked blood from its master. Eventually, the master would weaken, sicken, and possibly die. The only cure was to get rid of the spirit, which was no easy task. This could sometimes be accomplished by sending the chicken on an impossible quest, such as bringing home water from the river in a colander. A modern solution was to ask the *lidérc csirke* to form a telephone out of sand; the *lidérc* chicken was so engrossed in the impossible task that it literally worked itself to death, and its master would be free once more.

Ghosts

Although a ghost could be one of the *rosszak*, not all were categorized as such. The spirits of the deceased typically live in the *Túlvilág* but periodically come back to visit the living, especially on or around *Halottak napja* ("Day of the Dead") in November. Sometimes they were specifically invited back by their family members, in which case they might be called a *visszajáró halott* ("returning dead") or *hazajáró szellem* ("homecoming spirit"). The family members might symbolically feed them or welcome them home in another manner. Ancestral spirits were likewise honored, though they were not categorized with the *rosszak*.

At times, a spirit might get stuck in the human plane and become a ghost, not wanting to move on to the next world because they were strongly tied to their loved ones. Perhaps someone had mourned them excessively, or they had promised their beloved they would return to them. People were encouraged to help their loved ones move on to the *Túlvilág* through various ceremonies so that they may continue their spiritual journey, but not because the spirits were considered malicious (although they might try to lure their living loved ones into the world of the dead with them).

Another type of ghost was the *kísértet*, which could perhaps best be translated as "ghoul." These restless ghosts were not able to rest for one reason or another. (Perhaps they did not atone for a sin they committed in life, had unfinished business, or sought revenge on someone who had harmed them.) Some *kísértetek* were focused on their own pain and relived it over and over again, while others actively sought out others upon whom they could inflict said pain. A person who had died by suicide, for instance, could not rest until they convinced another person to kill themselves. Some *kísértetek* were so haunted by their own mistakes that they tried to relive the moment when they committed their sin in an effort to right their wrong, while others tried to tempt others to perform the same sin they had done. (A related word, *kísértés*, means "temptation.") These restless spirits generally came out at night and disappeared at the sound of the first rooster's crow.

A *kísértet* might also be created if a person's body was not buried properly. For this reason, it was vital to locate a person's body if they died in places unknown. If someone from the community drowned, a candle was set up on a small platter and set afloat upon the surface of the water; wherever it capsized was where the drowned person's body could be found. In certain portions of Carpathian Basin history, symbolic graves called cenotaphs were created. They had no human remains but all the funerary gifts one would expect to gift to a person journeying to the *Túlvilág*. While scholars cannot agree on the purpose of these graves, one theory is that they were created to appease a spirit whose body was unable to be buried for some reason.

Even if a person had been buried correctly, tampering with the grave (or even behaving offensively in the cemetery) could cause an angry spirit to return. In one story, a young woman mistook a ghost for her lover and playfully stole his hat. The angry ghost ended up haunting her. At the end of the tale, she died, and the ghost said this was so others could use her as an example and not annoy the spirits of the dead.

Some *kísértetek* appeared in groups or as animals such as dogs, cats, horses, and birds. Some were visible, either as translucent or shadowy figures or literally draped in sheets, while others could only be heard (e.g., footsteps in an empty attic, horses' hooves, the sounds of a wagon passing by) or smelled (e.g., foul odors, smell of something burning). A figure riding an invisible horse and a headless monk who wandered the countryside or haunted the dungeons of castles were popular characters in legends. *Kísértetek* might appear as a body part, such as a floating hand or skull. They could sit on a wagon and make it heavier. Murderous spirits could lure travelers into water or the woods with laughter, whispers, or other tricks. The ghoulish spirits found in the wilderness (usually in clearings or in the branches of trees) were able to grow in size and become gigantic.

If a person encountered a *kísértet* but greeted them respectfully, it might allow them to pass while remarking how lucky they were to be allowed to live. If that didn't do the trick, a person could loudly exclaim, "Every soul praises the Lord." The *kísértet* disappeared at once or else responded, "I would too, but cannot." Then they said what action needed to be performed so that they could move on to the next world, which might be as simple as having a Mass said in their honor. Sometimes, a person was able to escape a ghost by trickery or the arrival of the dawn; other times, they returned home with various illnesses or altered mental states, which were then categorized as a type of sickness called *ijedtség* ("fright").

Other times, a person had to address the reason a spirit was restless in the first place. A murder victim needed to see their killer pay for the crime. If something had gone wrong with a person's burial, they needed to be buried again in the proper way. A thief had to see their stolen objects returned to their rightful owners, and those who held on to secret knowledge needed the information to come to light. An aborted or stillborn child needed to be named properly. Sometimes a spirit had to wait a certain amount of time before they were able to move on to the *Túlvilág* (often seven years), such as if they had died by suicide or been executed.

One category of restless spirit was known as the *bolygó*, such as the *bolygó mérnök* ("wandering engineer") and the *bolygó vadász* ("wandering hunter").

These often had some sort of unfinished business, such as righting a wrong they had committed in life, or else they might have had an earthly obsession they valued over going to the next world.

Another category of *szellem* was confined to objects, such as rags, crates, rugs, satchels, clothing, tools, or practically any other object. Although they share a name with a type of ghost, typically these were not associated with deceased individuals; they were closer to the various *ördögök* found in the earth. Most commonly, these *szellemek* were trapped in a glass bottle, in which case the spirit was called a *palackba zárt szellem*, or "trapped-in-a-bottle spirit." While an object-bound spirit was not classified as one of the *rosszak*, it was unwise to place one's trust in them. The *szellem* attached itself to a master when the item it was contained in was bought or found by chance, or when a person cut down a tree in which the spirit had been trapped. Once the *szellem* found a new master, it was able to grant its master wishes, which typically included riches or magical strength. As wishes tend to do, these came at a price: the master lost what they already valued as their wishes were granted. To get rid of this sort of *szellem*, its master needed to destroy the object it was attached to, find another item to imprison it in, or pass on. My cousin and I once found a green glass bottle in a neighbor's yard and spent the better part of the afternoon debating whether or not we should touch it—on one hand, we might get our wishes granted, but on the other, the unleashed spiritual forces might be beyond our control. (We ended up playing it safe and leaving it untouched—who knows what treasures we missed out on!)

The *Szépasszony*

Szépasszony is the name of a destructive, dangerous character, one of the chief villains of the Magyar cosmos. Her name means "Beautiful Woman." It is true that in many legends, she was described as a figure with unearthly beauty: pale, with silver hair, clothed in a white or silver dress. In some legends, such as those told by the Székely ethnic group, she was even able to perform good magic. However, in most cases, her name was less alluding to her otherworldly beauty and was instead a name she was called to avoid angering her or getting on her bad side. The name is a *szépítő*, meaning a euphemistic, beautifying expression—in other words, people didn't want to risk angering her by speaking of her true nature. Pócs Éva describes the *Szépasszony* as "a variation of the Balkan fairy who shares many similarities with witches. But she is not a witch, exactly, because that would make her human. She is more like a fairy, but one utterly lacking any benevolent qualities whatsoever." [39] Still others describe her as the Abrahamic figure of Lilith.

For each of the blessings the *Boldogasszony* gives to humankind, the *Szépasszony* has a harmful counterpart. Whereas the *Boldogasszony* blesses the harvest, the *Szépasszony* causes hailstorms and dances among the destruction. The *Boldogasszony* blesses couples, but the *Szépasszony* seduces men away from their spouses. When a woman gave birth without complication, she was said to be lying "in the bed (or tent) of the *Boldogasszony*"; if she sickened after the childbirth, she was said to be lying "in the bed of the *Szépasszony*."

Wherever the *Szépasszony* traveled, she sowed discontent and danger. She lured men to their doom by dancing them to death, tangled the manes of horses, sickened men and women alike, and stole new mothers' healthy newborns, only to replace them with her own malformed children. When a person contracted various illnesses, they were said to have "stepped into the bowl of the *Szépasszony*." Records from one witch trial stated: "A little girl stepped into the *Szépasszony*'s bowl a little way. If she had stepped in it all the way, she would have died, but luckily she only stepped in a little way and she only got sick." [40] She could even take the form of a storm; when a whirlwind appeared, people said that the *Szépasszonyok* were dancing in the sky.[41] (In the latter case, at least, the term is used not as a proper name but more as a category of malevolent female spirit, akin to saying "evil fairies.")

Like the *Boldogasszony*, the *Szépasszony* also had many places and things named after her. Expressions existed about her bed, spoon, bowl, spit, water, washing water, well, towel, bread, kerchief, porridge, and so on. One of the expressions for the Milky Way was the *Szépasszony vászona* ("the canvas of the *Szépasszony*"), possibly linking her with death or human destinies in some manner. In Transylvania, there is a water source that is still known today as the *Szépasszonyok Kútja* ("well of the *Szépasszonyok*"); if one drinks

39. Pócs, *Fairies and Witches at the Boundary of South-Eastern and Central Europe*, 9.

40. Dömötör, *A magyar nép hiedelemvilága*, 82–84.

41. Pócs, *Hiedelemszövegek*, 164–65.

from its waters at noon or midnight, the fairies are rumored to take them away.[42]

The Noon-Wraith

The *Szépasszony* was most commonly encountered from midnight until dawn; when she was encountered during the day, she was known as the *délibaba*, the "noontime woman" or "noon-wraith." This malevolent spirit was well-known in centuries past. Many Christians referred to this spirit when they referenced the "destructive plague at midday" in Psalm 91, and in Latin, she was known as the *daemonium meridanum* ("the noontime demon"). In Hungary, the *délibaba* was the most prevalent in flat, grassy regions, where the daytime temperatures in summer soared to dangerous heights. The word *délibaba* is closely related to the term *délibáb*, a particular mirage in which one can see the reflection of a large body of water mirrored in the sky. It is quite likely that these mysterious visions—which often lured thirsty wanderers to their deaths—were also attributed to the *Szépasszony* at one time.

The *délibaba* was always female, although she could appear as a mischievous girl, seductive young woman, or elderly woman, dressed in all white or all black. Other descriptions included a woman with the legs of a horse or other animal, a naked woman, or a long-lost lover. Sometimes she was invisible or partially transparent. She could take the form of a woman singing and dancing in a meadow; sometimes, she challenged young women to dance with her. If they pleased her, she rewarded them with dowries. Other times, she used her dancing to attract a young man, then forced him to dance with her until he collapsed in exhaustion, sometimes to the point of death. Dömötör Tekla recorded one woman's account:

> *There was a boulder at the bottom of a certain hill near the village, and a nice green, grassy area by it where the cattle grazed. When [a certain man from the village] was eighteen years old, he went out there one morning, all alone. He was wearing new hide boots, and he decided to sing a song of the Szépasszony:*

42. "A Korondi Likaskő."

Two seeds of wheat, two seeds of rye
I poured them up the hill
They are walking on the hill now
For I poured them up on the hill
And now they're walking on the hill
And if they come down at night, at night
I will bake them on the hill
So it will become a mountain.

All of the sudden, a whirlwind appeared, with three very beautiful young women inside it. They grabbed him by the hands and made him dance endlessly. From around nine in the morning until the afternoon, he was forced to dance. Around four in the afternoon, his employer came out to the field to bring his cattle in for the night. He saw the young man dancing, and the sight was so funny to him that the man just laughed and laughed. Then he called out in greeting, "May God give you a good day!"

After he had called this out three times, the young man was freed and collapsed to the ground. He was unable to talk from the exhaustion. Even when he was given water he could not talk. Then he was given milk, and he drank it all. Then he was able to talk a little, but he was not able to tell the whole story until the next morning. His brand-new boots had been worn straight through to their soles. He warned the others never to sing the song, or else the spirits would come and make them dance until they died of exhaustion.[43]

The *délibaba* could also appear in various liminal places, such as on the road, under gutters, in the cemetery, on bridges, or on a heap of trash or manure. If someone was sitting when the church bells rang out at noon, they had to jump up, for no one was allowed to sit down in the fields at midday or even cool off in a stream—doing so attracted the *délibaba's* attention, and they would be cursed. The curse typically had all the classic signs of heatstroke, including a hurting head and neck as well as dizziness, disorientation, and

43. Adapted from Dömötör, *A magyar nép hiedelemvilága*, 84–87.

madness. Other punishments could include becoming crippled or becoming mute.

It was not only resting people whom the *délibaba* targeted. Sometimes she found her victims working in the fields and taunted them by asking difficult questions. If they were unable to answer, she cut off their heads with her scythe or simply caused them to go mad. When the stalks of wheat started to move like the waves of the sea, she would soon appear, arriving in a whirling dust cloud. When children went flower-picking in the summer, they knew to watch for the *délibaba* and come home before midday, lest she make them disappear in the stalks forever.

Chapter 6
SACRED ANIMALS

Our ancestors, it is said, once knew the true names of the animal spirits. When the humans decided they no longer wanted to be animals, their brethren grew angry. If the humans thought they were better than animals, they should not be allowed to say their true names aloud. Therefore, the people had to use descriptive names for the animals, which were passed down to us. This is why the wolf is called *farkas*, meaning "the tailed one." The stag is *szarvas*, which means "the antlered one." *Nyúl*—from the word "stretch"—is a rabbit, and this name describes the motion the animal makes when running. Some descriptive animal names are borrowed from other languages; the word for bear is *medve*, which comes from a Russian term for "honey-eater."

In *Magyar Mythologia*, Kandra Kabos wrote that in folktales, the most commonly mentioned animals were the frog, mouse, wolf, dove, fish, ant, raven/crow, snake, dog, bear, bee, rabbit, lion, fox, rook, and eagle. These animals were often referred to as kings; in days of old, the word was synonymous for a deity.[44] Indeed, in many stories, these "kings" act as deities, rewarding good deeds or helping the hero in their times of need, for instance by accompanying them on their adventures or giving them magical items. Likewise, various nature spirits such as the wind or sun were also called kings.

---

44. Kandra Kabos, *Magyar mythologia*, 141.

The Magyars lived in close contact with many animals, not only the animals of the plains and forests, but also domesticated sheep, cattle, and pigs. Four animals had special distinction within the nomadic Magyar tribes: the stag, hawk, horse, and canine. As we have seen, the origin story of the Hungarians related that a magical, silvery stag known as the *Csodaszarvas* led the tribes to settle in the Carpathian Basin. We encountered another magical animal, the *turul*, in the legend of *Emese Álma* in chapter 1, in which the mythical bird impregnated Emese while she was sleeping, and she subsequently became the ancestress of the Hungarian people. While it is uncertain what kind of bird the *turul* was, some think it was a raven or vulture, or a bird of prey like a hawk or falcon. Birds were sacred because they served as messengers between humankind and *Isten*, the Sky God.

The horse and the canine were important companions that served alongside people in daily life as well as the hunt and in war. In the distant past, both animals were sacrificed before battles or prior to making important treaties with the intention that the sacrificed animal's spirit would speak on behalf of the tribe, bringing the pleas of the people before *Isten* and the other spirits. When a person died, they were often buried with their animal companions so that the animal's spirit could accompany its master, guide it to the World Beyond, and protect it from any malevolent forces. A letter written in 900 CE to Pope John IX stated that the Magyar people "made godless and Pagan oaths" and sacrificed dogs and wolves to affirm said oaths.[45] The veracity of this (clearly biased) statement is up for debate. However, it is a fact that many burial sites with dogs ritually cut in two were uncovered throughout the region, not just in Hungarian lands but also in those of neighboring nations.

The Magyar's ethnic cousins, the Hanti, live in modern-day Siberia. The author Kunkovács László described a ceremonial reindeer sacrifice he attended in Siberia in such a manner: "First they tie ribbons to the reindeers, then the shamans beat their drums, seeing them off from life."[46] The Hanti also treat the bear as a sacred animal. When one is killed in a hunt, its powerful spirit must be placated. The people decorate its pelt and place offerings of food in front of

45. Vörös, "Kutyaáldozatok és kutyatemetkezések a középkori Magyarországon I," 139.
46. Kunkovács, *Táltoserő*, 32.

it, then dance and sing and tell the sacrificed animal stories about their people and all they have learned about nature. This ritual can last for several days. One can speculate that in ancient days, the ancient Magyars also behaved in such a manner when it came to honoring the spirits of animals.

Small animals such as cats, dogs, and roosters continued to be sacrificed for centuries. The annual pig slaughter still celebrated today is known as the *disznótor* ("the funerary feast of the pig"), and it retains ceremonial movements hearkening back to the old days. With these exceptions, the arrival of Christianity in Hungary ended most animal sacrifices, although animals continued to be associated with the world of spirits. For instance, horse skulls were strategically placed around properties well into the twentieth century to scare away evil spirits.

While horse sacrifice specifically was outlawed for many centuries, there were records of it happening in remote regions much more recently. The scholar Takács György found an elderly woman living in the village of *Gyímesbükk*, now in Romania, who discussed various magic she had personal knowledge about, including mountaintop horse sacrifices to appease sickness demons. According to the spell verses, *Nagy Szent Mária* (Saint Mary the Great, also known as the *Boldogasszony*) sets "a large table" and invites all of the sickness demons to eat the sacrificed horse, with the notable exception of the spirit in charge of the illness the people are intending to eradicate from the village.[47] The spirit will thus become offended and leave, taking the illness with them.

Dogs

Dogs were frequently associated with the supernatural. To call someone a dog was a strong insult, and it is frequently featured in fairy-tale dialogue. Dogs (especially black ones) were treated with a high degree of suspicion; the devil himself was known to appear in the guise of a fearsome black dog. It was said that if a person hung themselves, the devil would take their soul to hell in such a form. Strays might be a witch's familiar, or even a witch herself in shape-shifted form. Quite a few transcripts of witchcraft trials include accusations that witches transformed into dogs and then proceeded to terrorize the good folk of the village or steal milk from their neighbors' cows.

47. Takács, "Nagy Szent Mária egy nagy asztalt terített..." 53.

It was not only supernatural dogs that were feared, of course. To ward off attacks by even ordinary wild dogs, a person could carry a black dog's tooth (or the head or heart of an owl) under their armpit if they went out at night. Canine bones and teeth were also used for various magical potions and as amulets to ward off curses. If a domesticated dog was treated with suspicion, its wild cousin, the wolf, was even more so. Not only was the wolf an objectively dangerous animal, it was considered a physical embodiment of evil, and many fairy tales and religious stories featured a wolf character who antagonized the hero in some manner. Despite the creature's reputation, unprovoked wolf attacks were rare, as the animal tended to avoid civilization. If a wolf did enter a village, the villagers said that it had been sent by witches or the devil.

Birds

Birds were mystical creatures who could carry messages to and from the spirit world. Harming a living bird, whether on purpose or by accident, would lead to misfortune. Even if a bird had built their nest in an inconvenient location, such as a chimney or a roof, knocking it down was forbidden. The consequences for harming a nest or bird varied from having one's cow give bloody milk to the family home burning down. A *szentlélek madár* ("Holy Spirit bird"), also known as a *babuka*, was a carved figure of a bird hung over a table or the family altar. Some communities crafted intricate ones from a single piece of eggshell, adding paper wings. Although many families have such a figure in their home, the original symbolism has been lost to time.

Owls were sometimes referred to as *táltosmadár* ("*táltos* bird") or the *halálmadár* ("bird of death") because of their ability to warn people someone would soon die. They appeared shortly before a person died, so if an owl was spotted hanging around someone's house, a member of the household might soon sicken or die. Dreaming of an owl was a similar sign that the dreamer would soon pass away. An owl might appear when a relative who lived far away died, or it might be watching the living family at the request of a departed soul. It was ominous if an owl hooted three times, as that was considered a warning, and if a person saw an owl during the daytime while away from home, they ought to turn around and return home immediately lest misfortune strike them.

Kakasütés ("rooster striking") was a popular "game" that could take varied forms, all of which included one or more people ritually killing a rooster at seasonal celebrations, when a new home was built, when a new community leader was named, and similar festive occasions. A groom might kill a rooster at his wedding feast, then have the bird cooked and fed to his guests. Young men could compete for the privilege of being the May King by beating a rooster to death or chopping its head off. A community might even declare a rooster to hold all the sins of the village and execute the bird symbolically with a sword. To modern sensibilities, this tradition was an unnecessarily cruel and strange form of entertainment. However, when considered in light of its origins of animal sacrifice, it begins to make sense why the tradition had so much cultural staying power.

With time, the practice of *kakasütés* mellowed into a symbolic act of skill: children shot arrows or tossed beanbags at a rooster-shaped target, or a rooster-shaped puppet was struck with sticks while blindfolded. In one Transylvanian region, a traditional Easter pastime was to fashion a rooster out of white yarn and golden feathers. The participants ceremonially marched to the woods outside the village border and strung the figure up on an evergreen decorated with fruit. Men took turns attempting to shoot the rooster down from afar. The winner was crowned with the rooster's golden feathers and led back to the village as a victor, where he received fruit as a prize.

Bees

Many households kept bees for their honey and useful beeswax. Out of respect for the sanctity of bees, it was forbidden to use the word *megdöglik* about them, and instead the word *meghal* was to be used. While both words mean "to die," the first word is typically used for an animal, whereas the latter is a word usually reserved for humans, who were judged to belong to a higher category of sentient being. (Interestingly, the word for "honeybee" and the word for a woman's womb is the same: *méh.*)

In contrast to countries where bees were predominantly cared for by women, women were not allowed near the Hungarian hives lest they cast the evil eye on the bees; sometimes women weren't even allowed to call the creatures by name. It was unlucky to buy or sell bees; it was better to barter for them or receive a hive as a gift. It was also believed that stolen bees produced superior honey. If, in fact, a household's bees were stolen, its *gazda* (the master of the house) could turn to various magical remedies. In one technique, a person would boil sweet milk, then pour it where the hive had been located before it was stolen. This would make the thief go bald or turn their hair white.

To make his bees strong and able to fight off intruders, a *gazda* could place a horse skull near his hives or sprinkle the blood of a rooster on them. To make the bees sweet-natured toward the members of his own household, the *gazda* could offer them milk or burn pine resin near the hives. To make them loyal, he could offer them his own urine. If a hive got lazy and did not produce well, he relocated the hive over an anthill so the bees could witness the industrious ants and emulate them.

A *gazda* had to be wary of thieves, but bees might also leave on their own accord. To protect against this unfortunate circumstance, the *gazda* could tie as many knots into a *sodort madzag* (a twisted string or cord, often used in magical workings) as he had beehives, then touch each knot to its respective hive. Once he turned around on his heels, the bees were protected and would stay close to home as long as the knots held. Alternatively, the *gazda* could make a plaster of holy water and earth and spread it on the hive, or he could allow the bees to leave the hive for the first time in the spring through the preserved larynx of a deceased wolf.

Ladybugs

People from Germanic areas especially revered ladybugs as sacred creatures that transported messages from humankind into the skies. The ladybug was favored by various pre-Christian goddesses of love and clear, sunny days. Later, these goddesses were conflated with the image of the Virgin Mary, but the ladybug kept its associations. The creature was said to bring good weather as well as to bring the souls down from the World of Spirits into newborn babies. It was forbidden to harm the animal; if a ladybug landed on one's finger, it was allowed to fly off—if it flew toward the sky, a variety of blessings would ensue, ranging from good weather to a new baby to sweet treats. When I was young, I learned a similar variant: if a ladybug flew from your finger into the sky, you would be lucky in love, whereas if it flew downward, your love would hurt or betray you.

Snakes

Although snakes were a necessary addition to the ecosystem because they kept pests away, they could also be dangerous to both humans and animals. The superstitions surrounding these creatures was likewise ambivalent: while snakes were associated with healing magic and good luck, they were also seen as omens of death and destruction; certain poisonous snakes were even called *boszorkányos-féle kígyók* ("witch-type snakes"). It was a lucky omen if the first snake of a season appeared on a person's right side; if it appeared on the left, the person would likely face trouble.

A snake in the yard could indicate misfortune to come. Others kept a *házikígyó*, i.e., the "house snake." While this term could simply refer to a snake that made its home on a person's property, some believed that it personified the protective spirit of a home. If the *házikígyó* was harmed or chased away, it might chase away a house's good fortune—or worse. In one story, a woman beat the *házikígyó* to death, and her daughter soon died.

While one superstition stated that if a snake approached a sick person, the patient would recover slowly, if at all, people also agreed that snakes had many healing and protective qualities, especially the snakes caught in early spring, before *Szent György napja*. One could use a powdered snake for healing, light snakeskin for censing, or bury a snake in one's yard in a specific manner to protect the members of the household from gunshots. Sewing snakeskin into a hat's inner lining saved the wearer from a headache. Snake fat was a remedy for gout and weak vision, and censing a sick person with smoke from a burnt snakeskin would drive the illness out.

For luck, a person could carry a snakehead in their wallet or tie a snakehead to a fishing net. Stuffing a snake into the barrel of a new gun would give it the power of straight shooting, and a dead snake tied to the harness of a horse would make it a fast runner. Tying a dead snake to a plow's yoke would guard the cattle against snakebites and curses, while placing a dead snake into a watering trough would keep birds of prey from taking the chicks.

To curse one's enemy, a person could place snake bones in their bed on a full moon. If someone stepped on the skeleton of a snake, their leg would dry up. Even seeing a snake could prove dangerous; if a child saw a snake and cried out in fear, their teeth would fall out.

A *miskakancsó*

Snakes were also used in various magical spells and potions. To understand every language in the world, a person could grind a dried snake into a powder, mix the powder into water, and drink it. Sometimes, the magic was thought to transfer to another object that had touched the snake: if a young man touched the young woman he liked with the staff used to kill a snake, she would not be able to resist his advances. And sometimes, snakes themselves were able to purposely enchant an object through their own free will: if one or more snakes (sometimes up to fifty or even one hundred snakes) *ráfújt* ("blew onto") a stone, it became a *kígyókő*, a snake stone. A person could search for one of these egg-shaped stones around *Szent György napja* in the springtime; the larger the stone, the more snakes had breathed on it, and the more power it would have. Holding one of these in one's mouth would cause invisibility, and a body part (especially a cow's udder) could be healed by gently rubbing the stone over it. Some snake stones had a hole through them; milking a cow through one would make the cow immune to curses.

Due to the ability to shed their own skin, snakes were also symbols of renewal and rebirth. As such, they were typically depicted in a circular form, with the head eating the tail. Decorative snakes were used on ceramic wine pitchers called *miskakancsók*. These ceremonial pitchers were used to serve wine to the poor after a funerary feast, during healing ceremonies, and during a baptism. Dömötör Tekla theorized that these customs hinted at ancient spiritual associations with snakes that have largely been forgotten. Snakes were carved on the staffs of shepherds to keep real snakes in the grass at bay, and they were decorative finishes on gates for protection against evil. Blacksmiths also frequently integrated snakes into their metalwork.

Frogs and Toads

Frogs and toads were associated with both positive and negative magic. Nailing a frog to one's front door was protective from various dangers. If someone saw a frog and *megcsodálta* (i.e., was impressed by it or stared at it) with their mouth hanging open, their teeth would end up falling out in retaliation. If a frog or toad showed up inside the home, it was an omen of death in the family; one hanging around outside the house was an indication that someone was jealous of the family's luck. It was especially bad luck to have a frog show up at one's wedding or wedding feast; this was a sign that the marriage was ill-fated. Dreaming of a frog was usually a bad sign too, although in some cases people were rumored to come into unexpected fortune after dreaming of a frog.

Witches were thought to have the ability to shape-shift into toads, so if a person noticed a toad around their property that was perhaps behaving in an unusual manner, it was advisable to injure or maim the frog in some way. When the witch turned back into a human, she would have the same injury that had been inflicted on the toad.

Frogs were used in many love spells, some of which could be quite cruel to the poor frog in question:

- A young woman who wanted to go dancing sewed a frog into the bottom hem of her skirt so that the target of her affections would dance with her all night and pay attention to her alone.
- A person might shut a frog in a jar. When it died and dried up, its body was ground up and mixed into a drink, which the spellcaster could offer to their love interest.
- A frog was placed in a stolen, lidless ceramic container, which was buried inside an anthill. Then, the spellcaster ran away. If they lingered, they would hear the frog scream, the sound of which would deafen them. After a few days, the ants would have eaten the frog, leaving its bones behind. The sharp bones were stuck like pins into the clothing, collar, or hat of the spellcaster's love interest to bind the couple together.

Dried and powdered frogs were also used for more benevolent magic, such as in healing potions prepared for particularly bad colds or warts. Bandaging a toad onto an infected body part was thought to heal the wound. If a pig or cow was sick, a dried toad might be ground into their food. Powdered toads were even thought to be useful for healing diseased crops, and they served a protective function by guarding against birds, which damaged the fields or gardens.

Dragons

The *sárkány* ("dragon") is one of the most common—if not the most common—mythical figures featured in Hungarian fairy tales. They were represented as almost exclusively evil—or at the very least, antagonistic, an embodiment of the challenge a hero had to overcome in his journey. Fairy-tale *sárkányok* lived in palaces situated in the sky (e.g., hanging from the stars, situated on the Tree of Life, or simply floating in air). Many of these magical palaces were described as spinning on the tail of a rooster or on the feet of various birds. By the time I was a child, many fairy tales described these palaces as *kacsa-lábon forgó* ("spinning on the foot of a duck"). The palaces were generally constructed of glass, copper, silver, gold, or diamond; the stronger the dragon, the more radiant their palace. The more heads the dragon had, the stronger they were. Stories frequently featured three dragons—typically brothers—and each subsequent *sárkány* had more heads than the one before it. Some rode a magical horse called a *táltósparipa* (a shamanic steed) and had magical weapons or fighting abilities. The dragons kidnapped maidens (especially princesses), who then had to serve their every whim.

A seven-headed dragon, commonly featured in fairy tales

According to Magyar tradition, *sárkányok* were formed when an ordinary animal (such as a snake or rooster) spent a specific number of years—usually seven—out of sight of humans; for example, underground or in a swamp. The ordinary creature then transformed into an extraordinary one. Hungarian dragons were scaled, crocodilian reptiles with long tails and bat wings that helped them reach their lairs at the tops of mountains or in the sky. One kind of dragon called the *tarajos csúszó* (or the *tarajos kígyó*) was a large, winged creature with supernatural strength. Its long, scaly body looked like a horse in the front and a snake in the back. It had talons and fangs and could breathe fire. Some dragons emerged from wells or a hole in the ground called a *sárkánylyuk*, or "dragon hole." One account stated that the villagers tied sticks end-to-end to see how deep a chasm in the ground was, but it seemed to be without end; they knew, then, that it was a dragon hole. In another story, as late as the nineteenth century, the citizens of Sárrét showed visitors holes in the ground that they referred to as *sárkánylyukak*, which they believed to be the homes of living dragons.

Some *sárkányok* could control the weather, unleashing storms, hail, lightning, and even whirlwinds and tornados. When it was cloudy, people said, "What a large cloud—surely there is a dragon in it!"[48] A weather mage known as a *garabonciás* could control these storm dragons, encouraging them to cause storms. *Garabonciások* were also able to ride dragons through the countryside. "A dragon is not a gentle thing...but the *garabonciás*...pets him and talks to him [and tames him]. He loves most to ride it through the dark clouds [and] dark woods [and] the hidden caverns which are difficult to approach."[49]

Some *garabonciások* were born with their magical talent, although many were said to have learned their magic through formal study. While not all *garabonciások* were evil by nature, they were frequently associated with chaos and danger. There are many accounts of a *garabonciás* knocking on a door in the guise of a beggar, asking for milk, sour cream, or eggs. If householders were stingy with their offering, the visitor took out a book and started reading spells, summoning a violent storm to wreak havoc on the village and surrounding countryside. Then, the *garabonciás* either summoned a dragon to do their terrible bidding or rode a dragon off into the clouds.

Despite their association with storms, not all dragons were destructive. In one account, a dragon was reported to live in Baranya county, near the village of Szentmihályhegy. Locals said that it was "a very rare, peaceful, gentle animal which protected the village."[50]

48. Diószegi, *Az ősi magyar hitvilág*, 205.
49. Pócs, *Hiedelemszövegek*, 401–9.
50. Fáy, "Harry Potter magyar sárkánya."

Part II

DAILY LIFE

Folk religion was experienced differently in the small communities throughout Hungary than in the bustling urban centers and market towns. In the village, or *falu*, folk traditions and beliefs were the core of everyday life instead of an afterthought. Those living closest to the land felt the changing of the seasons in a unique, personal way, and a city dweller did not rely on traditional healing practices, agricultural magic, or protection from evil spirits to the same extent. To understand folk religion, one needs to first understand the setting in which it thrived the most. So, with that in mind, let's take a look at what daily life might have been like in a traditional household, in a traditional village, somewhere in the Hungarian countryside.

Chapter 7
THE VILLAGE

While a small group of households could technically be considered a *falu* ("village"), most villages had a few dozen households and public buildings, most commonly a church, a school building, a general store, and a *kocsma* ("tavern") or *fogadó* ("inn"). Most businesses were run out of private homes; only larger towns had dedicated stores and services. Households shared resources and provided physical and emotional support to one another. Clusters of villages were grouped together in administrative regions known as *járások*—the literal translation for *járás* is "a walk," and true to the name, a person could frequently walk from one community to the next to celebrate festivals, trade, or find employment or spouses.

It was not unheard of for a person to stay within the bounds of their home village for their entire life, or to only travel to a nearby city a few times in their lifetime; families remained in the same village or *járás* for generations, even centuries. It is not surprising, then, that people might have referred to the village they were born in as the *világ közepe* ("the center of the world"), or the *világ szíve* ("heart of the world"). This was a metaphysical concept more than a physical one; some legends describe a chasm located in the *világ közepe* that goes down into the Lower World; at other times, it is the location from which the World Tree grows, or where golden apples landed as they fell from the celestial realms. This concept is still alive and well today: the local Facebook group of one of my ancestral villages, for example, is named "Zámoly, a világ szíve!"

The Household

The main unit of the village was the household. At some points in Hungarian history, extended families lived together in patriarchal households; grown sons often stayed in their parents' households for life, and daughters joined their husband's household when they married. These households could grow quite large, with up to thirty or more members consisting of multiple generations living together alongside various hired employees. In other eras, nuclear families were the norm. Most marriages were for life; divorce was almost unheard of, although a woman might sometimes return to live with her parents if her marriage was irreversibly broken.

Whether families were small or large, male and female gender roles were distinct and firmly separated. Men worked the fields, made tools, did basic carpentry, traded, and cared for the livestock, while women worked with fabrics and did the cooking, washing, gardening, and childcare. The eldest male in a household was known as the *gazda*, and his wife was known as the *gazdasszony*; together, they were responsible for the members of the household. This not only entailed practical matters, such as allocating wealth and resources; the *gazda* and *gazdasszony* were also responsible for the spiritual well-being of the family. They performed certain magical rituals throughout the year to attract good fortune and to keep malevolent forces at bay, led the family in worship, guided the children's spiritual development, and passed down family lore and knowledge about the ancestors.

The *gazdák* who lived in the village made the community decisions together. The larger and wealthier his household was, the more say a *gazda* had in the village governance. The leadership was headed by the *bíró*, who was a cross between a judge and a mayor. Besides practical matters of maintaining law and order, they also had to be familiar with the traditions of the village, as they were in charge of organizing community gatherings such as the summer solstice bonfire, harvest festivals, or the annual tradition of border walking, all of which will be discussed in part 4.

While infants and toddlers were carefully supervised, children from about the age of three tended to roam around the village in the company of their peers. When school was not in session and the weather was fine, they played largely unsupervised in the village square or streets, sometimes with everyone together, other times dividing into smaller groups. Girls often separated themselves and played quieter games or made crafts instead. If there were chores to be done around the village that they could help with, children went where they were needed. Common activities included weeding gardens or supervising small animals as they grazed.

Men socialized as they worked alongside one another in the fields or when drinking in taverns after working hours. Once they became mothers, women tended to stay close to home, rarely venturing out in public unless they went to religious ceremonies, community work events, or village festival days. Before they got married and took on the full responsibilities of adult-hood, young people had the chance to socialize more extensively at dances and festivals. This will be discussed in more detail in chapter 24.

Further opportunities for mingling could be found at communal work parties, often known as *kaláka*. In the autumn and winter months, young people would gather together in private homes to do labor-intensive jobs, such as de-feathering poultry or shucking corn. The atmosphere at these work parties was festive, with music, singing, dancing, refreshments, storytelling, games, and other entertainment. The parties typically lasted into the early morning hours, and the workers were rewarded with fruit and nuts to take home with them. Sometimes magic was even woven into the festivities, such as using the shucked ears of corn for divination: whichever young person found three red corn cobs in one evening was sure to marry within the year.

The *Fonó*

A very important social institution in a traditional village was the *fonó*. This was a gathering place for older girls and unmarried young women, where they worked alongside one another spinning, sewing, weaving, and doing other such handicrafts while singing, telling stories, gossiping, putting on plays, and planning their eventual marriages—all the while adding a few magical twists to their work. Lajos Árpád described many aspects of this social phenomenon in his book *Este a fonóban* [*Evening at the Spinnery*]; most of the information presented here comes from his research.

The spinning season lasted from the autumn harvest until late winter. Even in the roughest weather, the *fonó* was open most nights, with the excep-tions of days when women's work was prohibited with a *tilalom*. A young woman had little choice but to attend the *fonó*. If she did not show up for several meetings, the other girls sent a gang of boys to bring her in forcefully in a wheelbarrow.

In the *fonó*, the *nagylányok* (the young women of the community) performed very necessary work for the community, and in return, they were afforded the rare opportunity to be away from the watchful eyes of the rest of the community. Young men visited the *fonó* on certain nights to dance and play games and pranks. It was not unusual for young people to flirt or even kiss at these parties, and young women openly sat in the young men's laps; older villagers largely overlooked the antics. It was important that the visits were on the girls' terms—any young man who showed up without an invitation was cursed with a verse promising to "spin away their mustache." If, on the other hand, young men were expected at a gathering but did not show up on time, there were several methods by which the girls could magically make them appear:

- One girl took a broom and stood in front of each girl present, sweeping the air toward them while asking which young man should be swept to her. When the girl called out a name, the asker tapped the broom in front of her.
- The young women took their trash outside, gathered it up into a heap, and stood upon it. Then they whistled. Whichever direction had the loudest barking dogs was the same direction the boys would arrive from.
- In the same way a chicken scratched the yard, the girls "scratched" the young men to the spinnery by going outside and scratching at the building's outer walls.
- Young women went to a bridge and tossed string onto the ground while miming urinating as a man would, then threw the yarn backward, through their legs.
- The girls turned wall hangings and decorations to face the wall while chanting, "In the name of the Father, Son, and Holy Spirit, let the young men visit us!" [51]

---

51. Lajos, *Este a fonóban*, 136.

The quality and quantity of the girls' work determined how much others respected them both at the spinnery and in the village as a whole; producing well increased their chances of landing a good husband. A particularly industrious or talented young woman might have a reputation that spread beyond her own village. Spinning lots of yarn also benefitted the girls' household in other ways. It was said that the longer the skeins of yarn a girl spun, the longer the links of sausage in her future household would be. Spinning was so important to a woman's life and future marriage prospects that when a girl was ready to start learning the craft, her mother went to a mill and threw the first ball of yarn she had spun into the millstone while it was in motion. This ensured that her daughter would spin as quickly and enduringly as the wheel of the mill was turning.

Downsides to Village Life

A traditional village was built upon human relationships and social connections. Being shut out of the village social life was one of the worst sanctions a person could go through. Anyone who opposed the social norms risked being publicly called out for their behavior. Violations were quite varied, from refusing to go to church to gossiping, acting haughty, doing shoddy work during community efforts, falling pregnant out of wedlock, or even having a romantic relationship with a large age gap. No one was immune to social criticism.

Some people simply chose not to deal with the social expectations of community life. Outlaws generally lived outside the village borders. *Betyárok*, much romanticized in popular culture, were young men who refused to go into military service or were fugitives from the law for one reason or another. They hid out alone or, more commonly, in groups. They harassed the nobility and stole from the rich, but they also avenged the injustices done to the poor. The poor returned the favor by bringing them gifts of food and hiding them from the authorities. Stories about famous *betyárok* were passed down through the generations; after many retellings, stories developed supernatural features, such as witches gifting the heroes with various supernatural powers.

Like *betyárok*, thieves also lived together in groups—but unlike *betyárok*, they did nothing positive for the community, and they were greatly feared.

Groups of thieves robbed and stole, and they also performed various crimes for hire, up to and including kidnapping or even murder. They had their own forms of magic, which often included unsavory ingredients such as the body parts of unborn children, the rope used to execute a criminal, or the ashes of a frog that was burned alive.

The Church

The church played a vital role in the life of the community, helping the poor and needy as well as providing moral and spiritual guidance. The community monitored who attended church and who did not, and social hierarchies were visibly affirmed and reinforced based on where a family was allowed to sit in the pews. If an individual broke a social taboo, they might be forced to stand at the back of the building instead of having a proper place to sit in the pews. Although townsfolk were encouraged to attend church as frequently as possible, this could not take place at the expense of the building's purity, which could be defiled by a number of actions or substances. For example, menstruating women were advised to stay away from churches. They were warned that if a drop of their blood defiled the building, their bleeding would not cease. If the church became sufficiently impure, *Isten* might express his anger by striking the church with a bolt of lightning.

Church bells were traditionally rung at different times of the day, often in the morning, at midday, and in the evenings. One could recognize a witch in the community if they saw a woman who appeared to be bothered by the bells; some witches were rumored to struggle with their magical brooms, which might try to fly away at the sound. Bells were also rung to keep away violent storms or other dangers that threatened the community. Evil spirits causing a storm would flee from the tolling of a blessed bell. (If the bell was rung at the funeral of someone executed for their crimes, the bell would lose its ability to banish hail.) Certain spells were only performed during the ringing of the church bells; one involved a young woman eating sugar or honey while the bells tolled so that she would appear sweet to potential suitors. The physical bell itself was also magical; a thread from its rope could be swallowed to cure a sore throat.

In addition to being a spiritual haven, church was also a physical refuge. During invasions, the fortified buildings served as fortresses against attackers. If someone sighted the enemy, they rang the church bells, summoning the villagers to barricade themselves inside. During invasions, villagers sometimes buried the various treasures of the community, including hiding the church bells in swamps or lakes. Some legendary bells were never recovered and remain hidden to this day. According to legend, these hidden bells rang out once more in times of danger to warn the villagers to take refuge in the church. In one village, a bell rang every seven years from the bottom of Lake Bogdány. In another, the church bells rang out from their hidden location whenever an enemy force threatened the village it protected—this was reported as recently as the first World War.[52]

Not all religious worship took place in the church itself. People prayed "in the morning, in the evening, before and after meals, when the church bells rang…and also during work. When traveling they would recite their prayer beads….On Saturday and Sunday afternoons [the people] gathered to pray and sing."[53] Not all prayers were sanctioned by the church; some were passed down through the generations. These frequently contained foreign religious elements such as trance-inducing repetition and pre-Christian symbolism. Despite the priest's disapproval, these prayers were said in private homes through the centuries. All in all, prayer was an integral part of daily life, and a reminder of humankind's place in the cosmos.

52. "A kezdetek…(Legendák és a feltételezett valóság)."
53. Bálint, Népünk ünnepei, 32.

Chapter 8
THE HOMESTEAD

The nomads of the Eurasian steppes traveled in yurt-like tents; various historical reenactments include these tents in their festivities. The Hungarians who settled in the Carpathian Basin no longer lived in yurts, but in many ways, the architecture of their homes reflected these tents in function if not form. Early Hungarian homes were permanent one-room structures with a center beam holding the roof up. This beam, often ornately carved, was called the *Boldogasszonyfa*, the "tree of the *Boldogasszony*." People typically linked this post with the imagery of the World Tree: just as the beam held the roof up, the World Tree was believed to hold up the sky's canopy.

As you read this book, you may notice that many spells had to be performed on or near the front doorstep. This was because to the Magyars, the entrance was a symbol of transition, and such liminal locations had intrinsic power, connecting the physical world to the unseen world of spirits. Many properties were fenced in, especially in villages, and front gates were treated in a similar manner as the front doorstep. The *székelykapu* was a highly ornate gate decorated with various carved or painted symbols. It is especially popular amongst the Hungarian minorities living in present-day Romania; the custom highlights the longstanding tradition of honoring the threshold between private and public realms. One traveler wrote, "I was surprised to see that…a house was still being built, but the carved *székelykapu* was already standing by the side of the road." [54]

54. Abkarovits, "A Székelykapu."

The Quadrant System

Activities of daily living were designated as *tiszta* and *tisztátlan*, either "clean" and "unclean" or "pure" and "impure." This was a holdover from nomadic times, when different activities of daily living were located in different parts of the travelers' yurts. *Tiszta* ("clean") tasks were things like sewing, whereas unclean tasks such as cooking had the potential to make a mess; however, the designations came to have spiritual significance as well. Before homes had interior walls that separated the different rooms, a house was divided into four quadrants, each known as a *sarok* ("corner"). These designations determined which tasks could be performed in each area of the home. Faint echoes of this quadrant system were passed down through time, such as spells in which the caster throws walnuts into each corner of the room while invoking the directions. An accompanying verse the thrower can say is, "My dear four corners, I cannot give more than this small gift, so please accept it!" [55] One old custom was to make a sign of the cross in each of the room's four corners before going to bed; I myself was taught that when going to bed in an unfamiliar room (such as while traveling), we could not fall asleep until we looked at and acknowledged each corner, one by one.

The most important quadrant, spiritually speaking, was the *szentsarok* (the sacred corner). This was where the family's *oltár* ("altar"), holy objects, family heirlooms, and artwork were located. Church altars were typically oriented toward the east, the direction of the rising sun; likewise, the holy quadrant of many houses was also located in the east. (In other homes, the focus was again on the east, but it was the front doors and beds that would be oriented toward the sacred direction "so at no point did a person go to bed without their head placed in the direction of the sunrise." [56]) No unclean work or item could be brought into the *szentsarok* lest it desecrate the sanctity of the space. In many homes, family members largely avoided spending time in the *szentsarok* except during prayer or a great storm (since lightning was unlikely to strike such a holy spot). Opposite the sacred *sarok* was the hearth, containing the family's fire. Of the remaining two corners, one served as a sleeping area, and the other had a table as well as storage chests, benches, and shelves.

55. Manga, "Szlovák kapcsolatok a palóc karácsonyi szokásokban," 98.
56. Kovács, *Szeged és népe*, 345.

The Hearth

The brick fireplace known as the *kályha* or *kemence* had a special place of honor in the family home. The magical oven was featured in many regional legends and fairy tales, such as the familiar tale of Hansel and Gretel, known as *Jancsi és Juliska* in Hungary. In real life, too, the oven was a sacred spot. The household members not only cooked in it, but also spent the bulk of their time near it when inside the house. The hearth was the heart of the *tiszta* area of the house. Unclean tasks including combing one's hair were forbidden near the oven (or while sitting on its bench) because it was said that "God's body was baking inside the oven."[57] Scolding the fire, throwing garbage into the fire, or spitting into it was especially blasphemous; this would result in a person's mouth erupting in sores.

A brick oven known as a *kemence*

57. *Magyar Katolikus Lexikon (MKL)*, "Tűztisztelet."

Different objects were thrown into the oven to produce various magical effects. It was acceptable to dispose of blessed objects such as the leftovers of holiday meals, eggshells from Easter celebrations, or the remnants of candles by throwing them in the oven. Objects people wanted to send to the *Túlvilág*—such as items for deceased relatives or food for the ancestors— could be sent via fire as well. Various festivals throughout the year (such as *Florián napja* and *Nagypéntek*) had a custom of ritually lighting or extinguishing flames. The spatula used to bake bread was also associated with a number of seemingly unrelated magical techniques, including healing rites, beauty magic, and turning changelings back into humans.

When someone baked bread, a piece of the dough or a sprinkling of flour was thrown into the fire for various spirits, including those of deceased family members, the souls in purgatory, or even various angels. If some food dropped during cooking, it was likewise tossed into the flames. If a fire burned unevenly, people would soon start to bicker in the household unless someone threw a little flour into the fire to appease it. Despite the general prohibition against spitting into a fire, an out-of-control fire might be deliberately insulted with phrases such as "Go to the neighbors' house instead!" Another practice was to throw salt into the flames while chanting "Into the mouth of the evil one" three times. All of these practices would avert arguments.[58]

House fires were one of the greatest calamities a family could face. They were often explained as a divine punishment that a family incurred when household members broke religious taboos, behaved immorally, or had done a taboo action (for example, injuring a bird or its nest). When building a fire in the hearth, the *gazdasszony* made sure to sprinkle water in the shape of a cross inside, outside, or in the general direction of the oven before lighting the flames. Hanging up a wreath made on the summer solstice, placing a picture of Saint Florian on the wall, keeping blessed wafers or bread in the attic or on the beams of the house, and taking seven buckets of water into the house were some of the methods used to prevent fires.

If fire did break out, it was the *gazdasszony*'s duty to run around the house while holding a loaf of bread or to lift up her skirts, revealing her bare backside to show the fire spirit that she was not intimidated by its presence. Alter-

58. Bosnyák, "A moldvai magyarok hitvilága," 56.

natively, the members of the household could throw symbolic items into the fire, such as blessed bread, eggs, milk, or even a cat; some even specified using a tricolored cat for this purpose.[59]

The *Tisztaszoba*

Over time, houses evolved, and even simple houses had multiple rooms, including kitchens, sleeping rooms, and storage rooms. In recent centuries, more well-off households popularized a room known as the *tisztaszoba*, which can be translated as "the clean room" or perhaps "the room of purity." Thematically, it can be seen as a version of the sacred *sarok*. As such, it was not to be used for activities of daily living. The *tisztaszoba* housed the family's religious art as well as their heirlooms, and it had one or more beds used for momentous occasions such as giving birth or—on the other end of the life spectrum—dying. Honored guests were housed in this room, and a young woman might be allowed to spend the night in the *tisztaszoba* with her groom-to-be. When the sacred bed was not in use, the household's extra bedding was piled up on it, typically in full view of the windows facing the main street. Embroidered bedding was expensive and tedious to make; having a good amount of it added to the household's status.

Nowadays, for the most part, *tisztaszoba* can only be found in very traditional or historically recreated houses. My childhood home was built hundreds of years ago and still had a *tisztaszoba* which opened to the street. This room did indeed contain family heirlooms and religious art, but its spiritual purpose was rather muddled by the time I was born, seeing as how my cousins and I were sent there in the evenings to watch movies, hardly a sacred activity. In some semblance of tradition, we were strictly forbidden from bringing any food or drink into the *tisztaszoba*, including water, even though the room opened right off the kitchen. Once, I asked if I could watch a show while husking the corn harvested from our garden, but I was told no since it wasn't "clean" work and, thus, couldn't be taken into the *tisztaszoba*.

59. Berki, "Babonák a tűzről – Mivel csillapítsuk a tűz éhét?"

Furnishings

Both house layouts and the furniture within varied by region and time period. Some pieces of furniture were universal, however, such as the table, bed, and storage chest known as the *láda*. These were familiar additions to the home even before the Magyar settlement, and they were featured in numerous legends and fairy tales, often with magical properties such as always being full of riches no matter how many times the hero emptied them of their contents. The magical chest was even a euphemism for reproductive organs: one community custom was to ceremonially tease the groom about opening the bride's *láda* on their wedding night![60]

As time went on, there was more and more furniture and household objects in a typical home, all of which served practical and magical uses. From tablecloths to oven tiles, chairs to vases, pitchers to wooden spoons, all items were decorated with symbolic art, including floral patterns that recalled the *Boldogasszony*, sacred animal motifs, and geometric designs. The kitchen table served as a sort of altar. In one of her articles, Pócs Éva explored some ways in which the kitchen table was a magical piece of furniture.[61] Not only did the table serve as a central feature of the Christmas festivities and magical rites, it was forbidden to place an impure item, like a comb, on such a sacred spot.

Spirits of the Home

Besides containing a household's possessions, the structure of the house itself was akin to a spiritual entity. It was able to provide physical *and* spiritual protection. As explained in later chapters, a family could stay protected from various evil forces when they remained secure in their home, especially after darkness fell. When a house was built, certain rituals ensured its lasting good luck. *Kőmíves Kelemenné*—a legend that is still included in the national Hungarian school curriculums at the time of this writing—describes a tower that would collapse each day as it was being constructed. It was not until the foreman's wife died and was buried under the rubble that the tower was able to be built. Even though people might no longer believe that a human has to

---

60. Paládi-Kovács, *Magyar néprajz nyolc kötetben*, vol. 7, 65.
61. Pócs, "Az asztal és a tűzhely, avagy hol van a szentsarok?"

die in order for a building to be completed, the notion that a sacrifice was required has been a long-standing one. It was encapsulated in the saying "A new house demands a sacrifice."[62]

The first living creature to sleep in a newly built house would die first, so the eldest member of the family spent the night before the rest of the family did, or else the family tried to outwit the house spirit by shutting an animal in for the first night. (Other versions of this belief were that the first person to make a fire in the hearth or to turn off any lights in the new house would be the first to die.) To avoid this fate, the family might sacrifice a chicken on the front doorstep and sprinkle its blood throughout or around the house. Alternatively, an animal (or something coming from an animal, such as an egg) was walled into the foundation of the building, although this practice had become rather rare by the start of the twentieth century. Another method of tricking the house spirit was to measure the shadow of a terminally ill person, then place the measuring stick inside the house walls. Over time, it became increasingly likely that money, holy water, or prayer beads would be encapsulated in the wall.

Priests blessed each house in the village annually, although the dates of the blessings varied regionally. Some blessings took place during the Christmas season, others during the springtime months. The most common day was that of *Vízkereszt* (known to English speakers as Epiphany, but literally meaning "water christening" or "water blessing") in January. The *gazda* and *gazdasszony* set up a table with food, feathers, and wheat. After praying and chanting, the priest censed the house with sweet-smelling herbs or frankincense, then sprinkled blessed water in the corners of the house and on any other buildings, like the barn, to protect them from storms, lightning, fire, and witches. He also sprinkled holy water on all the members of the household as well as any pets or livestock, then poured a little holy water into the well. When the blessing was complete, he made a protective mark on the gate or doorpost of the house with blessed chalk. Before leaving, the priest had to sit down for a time so that the hens would also sit well upon their nests.

Sometimes the house itself was able to lend its protection to the family who lived in it. A *babona* my family took very seriously was that if a person

---

62. *Magyar Néprajzi Lexikon (MNL)*, "Építőáldozat."

had already left the house and realized they had to run back inside for whatever reason, they should always sit down for a moment before exiting the house again. I never could figure out the reasoning behind this *babona* growing up, but I followed it faithfully—and often catch myself doing the same even today!

To protect a home from malicious spirits or witches, a number of techniques could be employed, such as:

- Standing an upside-down broom near the door
- Rubbing the doorframe with seven cloves of garlic
- Sprinkling salt or poppies over the front door's threshold
- Laying a broom across the threshold
- Sticking a knife into the doorframe at nighttime
- Making the sign of the cross in each corner of the room before going to sleep
- Decorating a home with birch branches

If a house was already under spiritual attack, a blessed object could drive the spirits out. First, the house had to be completely cleaned. Then a blessed candle or incense was burned, or holy water was sprinkled throughout the home. The latter practice was described in a fight against two malevolent house spirits known as the *rekegő* ("creaker") and the *kopogó* ("knocker"). These types of spirits infested a house and frightened its inhabitants, warning them that bad fortune was about to come. In one account, a woman got so desperate to rid her home of a *kopogó* that she performed a cleansing ritual, which was described by her friend as such: "She sprinkled the house [with holy water], all four corners of it, east, south, west, south [sic], etc. and the bed and the walls." [63] The rite worked for three days to keep the entity at bay, but after that, the creature unfortunately returned.

It was important to care for the house physically and spiritually. Every item in a home—the cooking utensils, furniture, bedding, curtains, tablecloths, and even the very walls of people's houses—could be infused with blessings if they were decorated with floral patterns, which were symbolic of the divine femi-

---

63. Pócs, *Hiedelemszövegek*, 153.

nine. But it was no use to decorate a dirty, untidy home—helpful spirits were repelled by filth and clutter, while malicious ones were attracted by the same. The floor had to be swept daily before the sun set; women swept the dust outward, toward the front door; sweeping toward the center of the house was only done if there was a dead body being prepared for burial. (In some areas, the opposite custom was practiced: sweeping inward kept fortune in the home, while sweeping outward swept fortune away.) Any trash had to be disposed of before dark as well; if an item was disposed of after dark, or even merely forgotten outdoors, a witch could take it and cast a spell on the family. While housekeeping tasks were to be done every day except Sunday, more intense spring and autumn cleanings purified the home in preparation for holidays.

While the concept of house spirits was not as ingrained in Hungarian culture as it was in neighboring Slavic lands, there are some records of helpful entities that helped take care of cattle or horses. One household entity was the kitchen witch, the *konyhaboszorkány*, or *konyhaboszi* for short. These were small figurines in the shape of a witch hung up in one's kitchen, often shown flying on a broomstick. The figurine's job was to work magic for the family by frightening away witches or bad spirits who could harm the food or cause an oven fire to break out, instead allowing the *gazdasszony* to complete her cooking in peace. For its service, the kitchen witch was left gifts of food and spoken to kindly by the family members. Although the tradition has faded somewhat, kitchen witches can still be found in novelty shops today, and many families still follow this custom, even if it is seen as only a pleasant superstition.

I have a hazy childhood memory of going into the city with my mother one summer day to procure one of these witch figures. The process itself was quite magical in its own way; we went down a small, cobblestoned alleyway until we found the nearly hidden shop, which we entered by going down a set of stairs until we had descended under street level. The shop was filled with gifts and trinkets, including a wall of kitchen witches. The one we chose still hangs in my mother's kitchen. When I moved into my own household, I got a *konyhaboszi* of my own. There was no mysterious gift shop involved, however—mine was shipped directly to my door through the magic of the internet.

Home Purification

Once the family home was physically clean, a good housekeeper then went on to beautify and bless the space further. A bucket or metal cone was filled with water, and the woman held her finger over a hole in the bottom to control how fast the liquid came out. Women made patterns on the ground with various swinging motions. Sometimes dyes, soil, milk, or even cow dung were mixed into the water so they left behind designs as they dried. Alternatively, women could fit a paper stencil into a sieve and fill it with sand, tapping the sides lightly to leave a sand imprint of the desired shape; this was referred to as "making a sand rose."

House walls were freshly whitewashed in the spring and autumn, and sometimes before festivals. This had to be done during a waning moon so that the pests in the home would wane as well. (For added luck, the spoon used for whitewashing could be thrown into the neighbors' yard—that way, any household bugs would follow it.) If furniture had to be moved for this deep cleaning or painting, the shape of the object was traced in its usual spot so the item wouldn't "forget" where it belonged. Women traced various designs onto the wall, which were visible even after the whitewash dried. These designs could be geometric shapes or other sacred motifs such as flowers, grapevines, or geometric designs. This process was called *pingálás*, or sometimes *cifrázás*. A children's song still popular today references a palace called a *cifra palota* (i.e., a building that had gone through the process of *cifrázás*). While *pingálás* usually referred only to decorating houses, *cifrázás* could also refer to decorating other household objects: furniture, ovens, doorposts, and so on.

Magical Pest Control

Magical methods were employed to help keep vermin such as rats, snakes, and bugs at bay—and many of them required a lack of clothing. For instance, if someone had a rat infestation, the *gazda* could run around the house, unclothed, three times in succession. Alternatively, he could go out at midnight—once again, naked—and sweep the entrance of the rat's home three times. If that still didn't work, he had yet another opportunity to undress on Christmas Eve, when he could chase the rats away from the house by cracking his whip and yelling at them. Later spells instructed the caster to write a message instructing the rats to get out, with varying degrees of politeness. Then, the piece of paper was thrown on a departing automobile; the rats would, in theory, go as far as the car did.

Gardens and Livestock

All but the most humble houses had access to a small kitchen garden. While men were generally in charge of the fields and orchards, women were the ones who took care of the gardens where the majority of the family's vegetables were grown. Seedlings were started indoors on *Bálint-nap* (Valentine's Day) so they sprouted in time to transfer into the gardens during the springtime; *Szent Bálint* was asked to bless the growing plants. The Ice Saints (*Fagyosszentek*) were said to come for one last visit in the middle of May, after which summer planting could officially begin. There were a variety of other ways to "wake up" nature. People shook fruit trees so they would wake up from their winter slumber and hopefully bear much fruit in the coming months. If the trees did not behave properly, it was possible to remedy the situation through sympathetic magic. The *gazda* could go out into the orchard with an axe and threaten to chop down the tree, explaining that it was not producing well. His partner in magic would stand behind the tree and speak on its behalf, apologizing and promising to produce more fruit.

Not all households were able to keep livestock, but since dairy was such an important part of the Hungarian diet, most tried to keep at least one cow for milking. Wealthier individuals had several cows as well as horses, sheep, and pigs. Countless magical techniques were employed so that the animals would be fertile and healthy. From the time they were born until the time they were butchered, animals received special treatment to protect them against witches, spirits, and other curses. To protect his animals from wolf attacks, for instance, a *gazda* could take a pair of scissors and tie it closed with string, believing the wolves' jaws would likewise be tied. The barn where the animals lived was carefully guarded, both physically and magically, in the same way as the house the family lived in. To keep the animals from wandering away, a broom could be laid across the barn's threshold.

In the springtime, animals left their winter barns and were driven out to the fields, where they would spend the warm season grazing. This activity was marked by various rituals, such as driving the animals over an egg as well as an iron chain that had a closed lock attached to it. These objects ensured that the cows would return home as round as an egg and that the jaws of any predator would remain shut. The herdsman would use a fresh, green elderberry branch to drive the animals so that they would not get lost nor fall into the clutches of witches. Alternatively, branches from a pear, birch, or hazelnut tree could be used. Afterward, the branch would be fastened above the barn doors.

Even if they did not have the funds for larger animals, most households were able to keep some poultry (chickens, ducks, geese, and, less frequently, turkeys) for eggs, feathers, and meat. Women were traditionally in charge of the poultry, and there were many ways in which the *gazdasszony* could magically encourage and protect her hens, such as:

- Feeding them leftover desserts from the holiday meals
- Poking the hens' bottoms with a stick on *Luca napja* in December
- Hanging an empty sack in the kitchen with its mouth toward the floor
- Sitting on the floor while her daughter swept the floors toward her from all four corners of the room to make the hens lay well
- Placing a barrel hoop on the ground and tossing the poultry's food inside it so they would stick close together and not run away from the barnyard
- Burning the fur of a skunk near the chicks

If a woman broke a work prohibition, she was often warned that the spirits would cause her chickens to get sick or die as a result.

Black hens were an especially prized—and feared—addition to the henhouse. They were considered magical, and their livers were saved, dried, and crushed into powder that was then mixed into various healing potions. Black hens were sacrificed before a person went out to seek buried treasure, and if a *gazdasszony* wanted to curse someone, she could serve them a black hen for dinner. If one had the egg of a black hen in their pocket and went to church on Easter Sunday, they would be able to identify any witches in the congregation. Upon leaving the church, the person had to quickly rid themselves of the egg or else the witches would carry them off.

One folktale with many variations dealt with an unfaithful woman who wanted to be rid of her husband so she could be with her lover. She prayed for a supernatural being to aid her, but her husband was hiding nearby as she prayed. Disguising his voice, he told her to cook a black hen for her husband every night, which would supposedly blind the man. The woman did as she was told. At first, the husband feigned blindness, so the wife carried on openly with her lover, thinking her husband was none the wiser. In the end, her husband revealed that he had been able to see all along.

Chapter 9
SACRED FOOD AND DRINK

With its rich black soil and temperate climate, the Carpathian Basin was ideally suited for growing wheat, and it quickly became the most important Hungarian crop and a staple of most meals. For much of Hungary's history, grain was consumed on a daily basis in some form, whether in breads, small-grained pasta known as *tarhonya*, or porridges, often called *kása*. Wheat itself was sacred, and many blessings and rituals mentioned an abundance of wheat as a primary blessing. Each stage of the growing process, from sowing the seeds to gathering the harvest, had numerous spiritual rites associated with it to ensure divine blessings. A *gazdasszony* could even cast spells on the crop after harvesting; while baking bread, she could twirl around to show the bread to rise as high as her skirts lifted.

Pork, chicken, sheep, and beef were the most common meats consumed in Hungary, along with fish. Wild game was available to some members of society. Ham was featured on many holiday tables, and the annual pig slaughter had ceremonial movements associated with it; we'll take a closer look at this tradition in chapter 22. Pork was also made into various products like *kolbász* ("sausage") and *szalonna* ("bacon"), both of which made special appearances at various festivals throughout the year. Although the wealthy had access to plentiful meat and fish, most commoners ate plant-based meals the majority of the time, with the exception of holidays and Sundays. (For centuries, all members of society fasted from meat on Fridays in remembrance of Jesus, who was crucified on that day of the week.)

The Carpathian Basin was home to a wide variety of fruits and vegetables. Dishes incorporated a range of flavors, with the cuisine of many regions emphasizing spicy and sour flavorings. Herbs and spices were used generously, as they were believed to promote good health in body and spirit as well as provide a pleasurable eating experience. Garlic, for instance, was widely known for its protective qualities. Eating garlic, hanging strings of garlic from rafters, or rubbing it on gates or doorways kept witches, bad spirits, and even wolves from entering a home. Both garlic and onions could be blessed for ritual use. One way of blessing them was to place freshly picked onions on a rooftop for seven days and seven nights so that they could be touched by the sun, the moon, and dew. The resulting blessed onion would be known as *Benedek hagyma* ("Benedek onion"), since the time for picking onions was around *Benedek napja* (March 21).

Even foods that were not specifically blessed might have magical or spiritual qualities. A man who wished to increase his virility could eat soup made out of a rooster, as the bird was associated with manliness.

Bread

Bread was considered the holiest of foods, representing the bounty of the earth itself (and, for Christians, the body of Jesus). Out of respect for bread's sacred qualities, a woman tasked with baking bread might be forbidden to speak during its kneading. Szendrey Zsigmond wrote, "Even today, the main food of the Hungarian person is bread: if one has this, they have everything." [64] My great-uncle often said that if you didn't eat at least one slice of bread with your food, it did not count as a meal.

A person who failed to show bread the proper respect and appreciation quickly learned their lesson through losing their sustenance. It was a widespread belief that if a piece fell on the floor, it had to be ritually purified to avert divine retribution. Many families—including my own—always blessed a loaf of bread before slicing into it for the first time by drawing the symbol of the cross on its underside. After the bread was sliced, it was immediately covered lest it become spiritually unclean. The most important decoration on a Christmas tree was a slice of bread. My family always had a slice of bread

---

64. Szendrey, "A varázslatok eszközei," 387.

hanging on our Christmas tree, and even if it was dry or moldy, the bread was never thrown in the garbage. Instead, it was burned or placed outdoors.

Bread could be used to heal, such as by rubbing a slice around a person's affected body part, then throwing the bread into the road so birds would eat it and carry away the illness. A healing verse could be inscribed on a piece of bread before feeding it to a sick person. Bread was carried in pockets by those traveling at night to protect against evil spirits, and it could be placed under pillows before going to sleep. A new dog or pig would be fed a piece of bread that had been already chewed by their owner so they would never roam far from home.

Kalács is a rich, soft, braided bread that resembles the Jewish challah loaf in shape. Today, it is customary for families to make one on Easter, but in the past it was a staple of every holiday table. Wealthier families were able to provide a weekly *kalács* for their Sunday table. The *kalács* included the richest ingredients a family could afford; these were usually sweet, but they occasionally included savory ingredients like sausage or eggs. Some *kalács* were formed into elaborate braided forms at various festivities; at weddings, a bride (or her relatives) personally prepared an *örömkalács* ("*kalács* of joy") to be publicly presented during the wedding feast. This could be enhanced with nuts, fruit, flowers, ribbons, or candles. Even family members who did not attend the wedding got a piece sent to them so they could partake in the feast.

Another type of special bread was a biscuit called the *pogácsa*. Hungarian children grew up hearing fairy tales in which the main character received some *pogácsák* at the beginning of a long journey. In the stories, the *pogácsa* often had magical powers baked into them. In real life, too, *pogácsa* were baked for practical reasons (they were easy to carry while traveling) and for magical purposes. Later on in the book, there will be mention of several ways in which the *pogácsa* could be utilized for magic, such as in divinatory rites, to feed the dead, and for various spells. The *pogácsa* was a truly versatile and magical food, and it is still a popular snack today. It is even given to young adults when they graduate as a symbolic present.

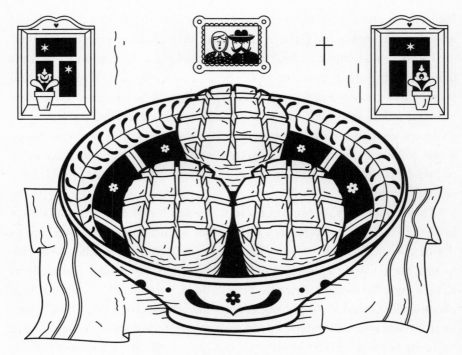

Biscuits known as *pogácsa*

Both wheat kernels and flour were blessed as a versatile ingredient for spells and rituals. One spell to chase away rats from a place went, "Not nine, not eight, not seven, not six, not five, not four, not three, not two, not one, let there be not even one!"[65] The charmer then had to take a pinch of flour and scatter it where the rats would walk. Flour could also be used directly for healing—the flour found on the bottom of loaves of bread, for example, was thought to be especially potent for certain rashes. There were many methods for an ill or injured person to partake in flour's healing properties, such as rolling a person in a pile of flour or stuffing the patient into an empty flour sack.

Apples

Golden apples were found in countless legends and fairy tales. The hero or heroine was sent on a quest to obtain them, frequently from the courtyard of a celestial palace, or more generally from the "Kingdom of the Sun," a land

65. Bosnyák, "A moldvai magyarok hitvilága," 45.

where even the grass, trees, and flowers were made of gold.[66] (The center of the world was often said to be where the golden apples landed as they fell from the heavens.) After many trials, the character obtained the golden apples, which had magical healing properties and might even bring people back from the dead. Although it was never explicitly stated that the "fruit of knowledge" in the biblical story of Creation was an apple, many people equated the two, so apples were found in many religious allegories and artworks. One song's lyrics reference the baby Jesus lying in a golden cradle, holding a golden apple in his right hand.[67]

Apples did not have to be golden to be considered magical. Even common red apples could be used for various magical techniques, including divination:

- Apples were tossed into the sacred midsummer bonfire so that they would travel to the world of the dead to make the spirits of deceased children happy and content.
- Engaged couples gave one another apples at their betrothal ceremony, and they also displayed apples at their wedding feast. The fruit was touched to the bride's face for beauty and health.
- When a person visited a newborn, they could bring along an apple as a gift for the child.
- A person could curse another by throwing an apple representing the victim into a crossroads. (The original text does not elaborate on this method, but it's possible the victim's name or likeness was carved into the apple, or a slip of paper with their name was stuck inside, etc.)
- Apples were blessed on *Kisasszony napja* (Maiden's Day) in the autumn; if an animal got sick in the following year, the blessed apples would be fed to them in hopes they would make a full recovery.
- To cure a wart, a person could cut an apple in half and rub the inside of the fruit on the wart three times before dawn. Then the two halves would be placed together and buried under the gutter. As the apple rotted, the wart would disappear.

66. Bosnyák, "Napkorona, aranyalma, pásztorbot, suba," 7.
67. Versényi, *Bányák, bányászok, hagyományok*, 84.

Milk

Milk was a sacred food due to its life-giving qualities and its link to motherhood. Many folk beliefs, healing techniques, and magical lore included milk as an ingredient. Some curses did as well. A curse might have instructed the caster to pour milk into a fire or onto the hearth; this was considered a blasphemous act, as milk was a symbol of life and nourishment. If a person wanted to curse their neighbor, they could take some of the neighbor's cow's milk, place it in a boot, and hang it in the chimney over an open flame until the milk boiled and started smoking. This would curse the cow and not allow her to give any more milk. Even someone accidentally sticking a sharp knife into a cup or bucket of milk caused the same sort of damage to the cow. The cow could also dry up as punishment for someone from the household performing a wicked deed, such as knocking down a bird's nest.

The milking bucket had to be covered before being taken out of the barn, and if one had to take milk outside at night, it needed to be salted lest bad spirits fly into it. Another method of keeping milk safe from curses was the use of wild rose. Bornemisza Péter, a famous professor and Protestant preacher who lived in the sixteenth century, recorded a method by which a person placed wild roses into a vat, then poured milk from a cursed cow onto the branches. The milk was stirred with a branch from the wild rose bush and then poured onto the ground in front of the barn doors in order to reverse the curse.[68] (Various tools associated with dairy products were crafted from wild rose branches; it was thought that the milk would be of higher quality and more plentiful.) In other accounts, the *gazda* burned the branches of the wild rose to cense the barn, stuck the branches to his gateposts, or struck the cows gently with the supple branches so that witches and evil spirits would stay away from them.

The first time a cow was milked was a significant event. A woman had to milk the cow while she was unclothed, then place a silver coin or head of garlic in the milking bucket. After she had finished milking, she then spit on the cow. This "first milk" was thought to have special properties, whether it was consumed raw or used to bake a special flatbread called a *lepény*. Many people were invited to partake in this magical milk, especially the neighborhood chil-

---

68. *Magyar Néprajzi Lexikon (MNL),* "Vadrózsa."

dren. While the children were eating or drinking, someone poured water over their heads from a sieve; when they finished, they needed to jump up and down or run around the garden. (While the original texts do not elaborate on why these actions were done, this seems to be a technique by which a cow would be encouraged to produce plenty of milk in the future. The active children would aid the cow, or her future calves, in being lively and healthy.) The *gazdasszony* might also send the milk to a neighbor or friend; the person making the delivery was sprinkled with holy water (or simply doused with a bucket of water) while blessings were said.

Alcohol

The most common alcoholic drinks were wine and *pálinka*. The latter was a very strong drink resembling schnapps or moonshine, distilled from various fruits rather than grains. Making *pálinka* was a popular method of using up leftover, fallen, bruised, or unneeded fruit from the orchard so that none of the fruit was wasted. It was considered a drink that could strengthen both the body and the spirit, and treasured family recipes were guarded and passed down through the generations. *Pálinka* was used to toast people after working together or after holiday observances, and it was given as a remedy when one was ill or weak. It was also drunk on various festivals to increase a person's health.

Wine was featured at rites of passage and at holiday meals. While the grape harvest, or *szüret*, is still a part of rural Hungarian life, for centuries it was celebrated as a major holiday—even deployed soldiers and those working in foreign lands were allowed to come home on leave to help their families and villages with the harvest. Many of the traditional *szüret* festivities hearken back to festivals in honor of the Roman god of agriculture and wine, Bacchus, who was honored throughout Europe at the height of the Roman empire. The entire community, from youngest to oldest, went into the vineyards together, wearing bright colors (often the red, white, and green of the Hungarian flag). They sang, shouted, played music, or beat rhythms on empty barrels; even young children were given rattles and noisemakers. The racket frightened birds away as well as any evil spirits who would cause the grapes to turn sour.

After all the grapes had been picked and loaded into carts, the villagers headed back into town to continue their celebration. Girls prepared a large wreath from the grapevines, and two girls dressed in white carried it at the head of the procession, while other girls scattered flower petals along their path. After the wreath came a wagon carrying a life-sized "Bacchus figure" sitting on a barrel, surrounded by empty cups or gourds. Young men followed, performing special acrobatic dances with intricate movements. The final wagon carried musicians seated on barrels of wine. Once in town, the celebrants went to a hall decorated with colorful ribbons. An enormous pile of grape clusters was placed in the middle of the room, next to two chairs decorated as thrones for a young couple who dressed up as king and queen. When the procession arrived at the hall, the two girls in white presented the wreath to the queen, while a young man presented to the king a staff decorated with grape leaves. After this rite, the feasting could begin.

All evening and throughout the night, musicians played lyres, zithers, and tambourines. There was plenty of freshly pressed grape juice as well as wine from the previous year and an extensive selection of food. Guards were appointed to make sure no one stole any grapes from the king and queen; guests played along and tried to swipe a cluster here or there. If they were caught, they were humorously punished for their transgression. The guests could play games of chance or skill to win the bounty. Guests wore masks or dressed in the clothing of the opposite sex and played all sorts of pranks and tricks on one another.

While the grape harvest was the major wine-related holiday, several other minor festivals throughout the year were also related to wine. During the Christmas festivities, on *Szent János napja*, new wine was brought to church and blessed to imbue it with mystical healing properties. This wine was said to be especially effective for stomach ailments. Small amounts of this blessed wine were poured into barrels of common wine in hopes that it would keep wine from spoiling and turning into vinegar. People still remember *Szent János* as the patron saint of wine; the last drink of the evening is often toasted to him.

Szent Orbán was another patron saint of wine; many villages in wine-growing regions had a statue of him. Villages that did not have a permanent statue sometimes made a temporary one from straw or bundles of sticks on his feast day. If it promised to be a good grape harvest that year, community members crowned the statue with wreaths of flowers and splashed wine at his feet, then dried and saved those flowers for magical purposes. On the other hand, if the springtime weather promised a poor harvest, the people abused the statue in various ways: by throwing rocks at it, spitting on it, beating it with sticks, splashing cold water on it, or even burning it.

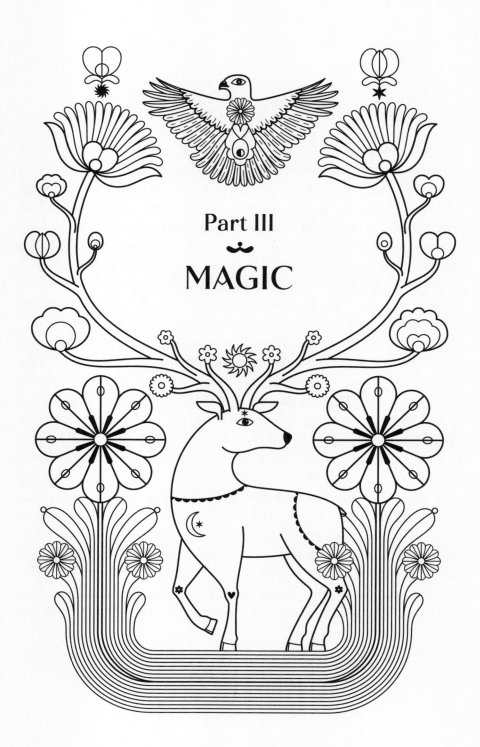

Part III

MAGIC

Throughout this text, it is a recurring theme that in the traditional mindset, there was very little division between "real life" and the fantastical—they were very much one and the same. One did not have to be a witch or magician to lead a magical life; life itself was magical. Even the most pious Christians believed in fairies and spirits and witches and knew countless *babonák* (charms or superstitions) and believed in numerous *hiedelmek* (superstitious beliefs). There was little doubt that unseen spiritual forces affected every aspect of life. Magic constituted a body of knowledge (much like scientific theories do today), and knowledge of nature and supernatural forces were woven together and difficult to separate from one another.

Everyone practiced magic in some form, whether it was by eating special lucky foods on the first day of the new year, stepping out of bed with the right foot, or interpreting various divinatory signs in daily life. There was a correct way to perform daily tasks, and one's surroundings had to be ordered in a specific way to bring luck. Still, even though magic was accessible to the average person, certain individuals specialized in learning about the world of spirits. These included *táltosok*—spiritual cousins of central Asian shamans—as well as the descendants of pre-Christian priestesses who, over the centuries, were transformed into witches known as *boszorkányok* or *bábák*. Other magical folk included the *garabonciások* ("wizards"), *látók* ("seers"), and various types of *tudósok*. *Tudósok* can be translated as "the wise ones" or "the knowing ones," but in folk tradition it means that the person had special diabolical helpers or powers.

In this section, we will examine some of the magical techniques practiced by common folk, as well as some of the more advanced magic users of the day.

Chapter 10
THE WITCH

The *boszorkány* ("witch") was sometimes merely a form of evil spirit, one of the *rosszak*. While flesh-and-bone humans were accused of witchcraft, the term *boszorkány* could just as well refer to a nebulous, vague concept not always tied to humans. When something unfortunate happened to an individual or a community, the harm could be blamed on *boszorkányok*—but there was not always a rush to find a guilty individual. Saying that "witches" had ruined something was akin to saying that bad luck had befallen the situation. If one ate late at night, the *boszorkány* was sure to "press them" in their sleep; i.e., they would have a restless night. In other situations, however, witches were considered very much human, at least in their physical form.

The witch was an almost universally known archetype in Europe, and Hungary was no exception. The image of the Magyar *boszorkány* is familiar to us: old, evil, and powerful; haggard, with a hooked nose, iron teeth, and a unibrow. Possibly, she was a transgender woman; in one witch trial, the witness stated that over the course of a night with the accused, they were surprised to find "large testicles and a penis, like those of a bull" between the supposed witch's legs.[69] In legends and stories, witches were described as cannibals, wanting to eat the heart, liver, or little finger of their victims so as to absorb their vital forces and grow in their own power. Another one of the witch's powers was taking control of people's dreams; most frequently, they

69. Tóth, *Boszorkánypánik és babonatéboly*, 272.

invaded young men's dreams and ordered them to dance all night long, to the point that they woke up in the morning exhausted.

Witches preferred the nighttime hours to daylight and were accompanied by animal companions such as snakes, toads, or chickens that they treated as familiars. They were master shape-shifters and could transform themselves into objects or animals (often a cat, frog, horse, dog, or raven) or plants such as a pumpkin vine or a berry vine. They could fly through the air, sometimes on magical objects like brooms and fireplace pokers, at other times simply by applying a magical salve called *repülőzsír* ("flying lard") or *boszorkánykenőcs* ("witch ointment") under their arms or on other parts of their bodies. (It was said that the crucial—and horrific—ingredient for this ointment was the rendered fat of an unbaptized child.) They could also become invisible, see in the dark, and contort their bodies to fit through keyholes.

Witches held power over nature and could cause hail or whirlwinds. Witches also had power over animals and livestock. If a herd scattered, it was usually attributed to the work of witches. Many witchcraft trial charges related to milk; the accused were rumored to be able to either decrease the amount of milk an animal (or human mother) could make or turn it bloody. (They could also cause milk to appear from wells, gates, or the Christmas tablecloth.) Witches could even change horse manure to butter. Pócs Éva recorded an incident in which a witch visited a family. When she was dismissed, she begged the generous *gazdasszony* for merely a handful of salt, which she agreed to give. When the *gazdasszony*'s husband found that she had given the witch the salt, he scolded her, saying, "Why did you give her any? We won't have any milk, any butter, or anything else now! She took it all along with the salt!"[70]

One of the worst ways a person could be attacked by a witch was for the witch to *megnyergel* (put a saddle on) them. The victim felt as if a heavy weight was on their shoulders, and their diabolical rider directed them to perform actions they could not refuse. In such a state, the victim might be forced to carry the witch to distant locales, such as to their coven meetings. One account detailed the struggles of a young lad who worked as a blacksmith's assistant. When the lad went to bed at night, the blacksmith's wife

70. Pócs, *Hiedelemszövegek*, 359.

snuck out to his quarters and threw a bridle and reins on him. He turned into a horse, which she rode until morning. After several nights of this, the lad turned her into a horse instead through the same method, then told the blacksmith there was a strange horse outside. The blacksmith nailed horseshoes on the horse. In the morning, the blacksmith found that his wife had horseshoes nailed to her hands and feet.

People did all they could to guard against the witch's magic. General deterrents against evil spirits typically worked against witches as well. Countless protections were woven into everyday tasks, such as washing out milk jugs with special herbs, placing thorny branches at the entrance of the barn, or taking out trash only during the daylight hours. Wearing a strand of garlic deterred curses, as did sprinkling poppy seeds behind oneself if walking outside at night: witches would be compelled to pick up the seeds and would thus be distracted from their pursuit.

On certain nights, such as *Szent György napja*, *Luca napja*, and Christmas, witches traveled to sabbat gatherings at various caves, mountaintops, or forest clearings, usually by flying. (Gellért Hill, overlooking the Danube River, was said to be a popular gathering site for witches. It was named after a missionary called Gellért who was martyred by being rolled down the mountainside in a barrel after he angered the locals by passionately preaching against Paganism.) Over the centuries, rumors about the witches' sabbats became more and more detailed and elaborate. Likewise, the descriptions of the covens themselves became more complicated; witches were said to have hierarchies similar to military ranking systems.

People locked away their broomsticks on nights when covens were believed to be meeting and burned incense from blessed herbs. Prudent individuals took extra precautions on full or new moons, or even on Tuesdays and Fridays throughout the year, nights when witches were rumored to meet. Those who did not travel far distances might also gather brazenly in the village itself, in the main streets, the tavern, the mill, or outside private residences. After the witches arrived at their coven meetings, they proceeded to eat and drink out of bowls and cups made from human bones and had orgies—sometimes including intercourse with the devil.

How did someone fall into such a life of debauchery? Some witches inherited their powers through lineage, while others learned witchcraft through an apprenticeship. It was believed that an elder witch was unable to die without passing on her powers to someone; this could be done by holding hands with a protégé or by giving them a magical object such as a broom. Those who could not find a witchy mentor had another option: the devil himself. If one formally renounced their faith in God, the devil was sure to appear to them in short order and teach them all the forbidden knowledge they wanted to know—after the would-be witch proved themselves by passing various tests. In some versions, the devil appeared in the form of a wasp that flew into the person's nose when they were being initiated. In other versions, a fly itself could be turned into a witch if it survived the winter; if a person saw a fly after the new year, they would have to swat it to prevent this from happening.

When a witch did finally die, they paid the price for the evil deeds they had done in life. Their coven members appeared in spirit to torture them, and after their soul had left their earthly body, there would be a terrible, destructive storm. The coffin of a witch was either much heavier or much lighter than expected. If it was heavier, it was because of the weight of their many sins or because the devil was riding, unseen, on top of the coffin. If it was lighter, it was because the devil had already taken the witch's soul—and perhaps their body—as payment. Those witches who were not taken directly to hell were punished in other ways. For example, in a folktale called "The Witch and the Hunter," a witch pays for her crimes when a band of devils cuts her into pieces and cooks her, then pieces her back together.

There were numerous methods to help villagers figure out who the witch in their midst was. One of the most famous was to use a *lucaszék* ("Lucy chair") crafted shortly before the winter solstice. (This technique will be discussed in greater detail in chapter 22.) Other methods included:

- Drawing a magic circle with blessed chalk in a crossroads; standing within it made the caster invisible and able to see any witches traveling upon the road
- Lighting a fire in a crossroads on Christmas Eve, with kindling collected on *Luca napja*
- Looking through a wooden spoon with a hole bored through it on *Luca napja*

- Growing a bulb of garlic from the head of a snake, then sticking the sprouted garlic in the brim of the hat one wore to church so any witches in attendance would be uncovered

Even though witches were feared and hated for the harm they were thought to cause, members of the community sought them out when in need of aid, as they were said to know various healing techniques and magic spells. The witch's knowledge of love magic was especially sought after.

The Witch Trials

In Hungary, as in elsewhere in Europe, the church and government did their best to uncover and eradicate witches in a systematic manner. English speakers talk about "witch hunts"; in Hungary, the phenomenon was known as the *boszorkányperek* ("the witch trials"), even though the accused included other types of magicians as well. Between the fifteenth and eighteenth centuries, over forty thousand individuals were tried in Europe for witchcraft and related crimes; over fifteen thousand of the accused were executed. Unlike in other European regions, where the trials were led by various church leaders, the trials in Hungary took place (for the most part) in civil litigation, much like any other criminal case. In Hungary alone, there are records of more than a thousand witch trials, over four hundred of which were held near the city of Szeged. The most dire incident was a mass execution held on July 23, 1728, when thirteen individuals were first tortured and then burned at the stake. The location of this atrocity is still referred to as *Boszorkánysziget*, or "Witch Island."

During their trials, the accused were charged with making pacts with the devil and causing all manner of harm to community members, from minor inconveniences such as spoiling their milk to outright causing their children to die. Witches were accused of causing injuries, disease, disability, and death; taking bones out of people's bodies; and causing men to become impotent. They were said to suckle the breastmilk out of nursing mothers and to transform content, healthy newborns into deformed changelings. They caused strokes and heart attacks, and they could cause emotional and mental difficulties, nightmares, anxiety, and sleep paralysis. Other charges included cursing people, livestock, and weather; making happy couples fall out of love;

herbalism; and falsely purporting to heal others or tell fortunes for money. Even something as mundane as a wagon getting stuck on the road, or bread or butter not coming out right, could be blamed on a witch.

Widows, people living unconventional lives, the mentally ill, and midwives and those who knew the healing arts were among the most frequently accused, but no one was safe—even nobility, at times, were accused of consorting with the devil. Many victims were summoned to court, but others went to the officials voluntarily to be absolved from rumors about their involvement in witchcraft. The accused often underwent extreme torture, and some made radical confessions due to the extreme torture they underwent.

Beyond witches, other magical folk were also tried. Professional midwives, known as *bába*, were first in line to be accused of witchcraft. On one hand, they were treated with a certain leniency because they were providing essential services to the community by helping women deliver infants. On the other hand, they were treated with a great deal of suspicion. Midwives had practical and esoteric knowledge about starting (and ending) pregnancies, herbs, spells, potions, and various magical techniques to bring a baby safely into the world. If something went wrong with a birth or if an infant was born sick, the attending *bába* was often accused of performing evil magic. Even a person's criminal activity later in life could be blamed on a midwife placing a curse on the innocent child at birth! Before priests took over the role of blessing babies, midwives were the ones who initiated women into motherhood and welcomed their infants to the world.

The Hungarian *boszorkányperek* started and ended later than witch trials in the majority of Europe. While many individuals were tried in Hungary, relatively few were executed; less than two hundred were actively burned at the stake. The Austro-Hungarian ruler Maria Theresa finally outlawed the practice in the eighteenth century. With time, Hungarians came to view witchcraft as a superstitious anachronism, and the crime was no longer prosecuted in court. In rural areas people continued to be accused of witchcraft well into the twentieth century, although no formal government action was taken against them. In an ironic twist, trial records have kept alive various *babonák* and spells that would otherwise have been forgotten. Through studying the witness statements from the trials, researchers have been able to learn about a variety of specific magical techniques and superstitions as well as general beliefs about the abilities and qualities of magical persons. Many trial records have been made public or are published in academic texts; more recently, they have been digitized into searchable databases online.

The *Bába*

The Hungarian word for a midwife is *bába*. Midwives were associated with witchcraft throughout central and eastern Europe, but the powers of the *bába* spread beyond midwifery. The Slavic Baba Yaga is probably the best-known example of this type of entity. In Hungarian mythology, fairy-tale heroes wandering through the woods could meet a *vasorrú bába*, "the hag with the iron nose," who put them through various trials. (A less common variation of this figure was the *vasfogú bába*, "the crone with the iron tooth.") If they passed the tests, the hero might be reluctantly rewarded but would most likely simply be let go, free to live another day.

Many *vasorrú bábák* had supernatural strength or other feats of strength, such as the ability to jump far or climb impossible walls. Some had dragons as sons, and they vowed revenge if their children were slain. These crones attacked heroes, but if they were flattered, tricked, or overpowered, they might impart knowledge or magical items to help the hero on their quest. By the end of the story, the witch had usually been defeated or killed in a violent way. Sometimes she was simply a victim of her own hatred, exploding in anger or bursting into flames.

Chapter 11
OTHER MAGICAL PERSONS

A person who was destined for a life communing with the spirits may have been born in the caul or with physical markings such as prematurely erupted teeth, a furry pelt, wings, feathers, or an uneven number of bones—typically extra fingers or toes. (Regional artwork about shamanism depicts this phenomenon, such as a ceremonial glove with seven fingers, a metal hand depicted with six fingers, and statues carved with six fingers.[71]) The mother might have had an extraordinarily long pregnancy, nursed her child in an unusual manner or for an unusual amount of time, or perhaps the child had nursed from a non-human animal. Some magical children were able to talk and walk directly after birth; one legend even speaks of an infant who fought off dragons from his cradle by releasing a stream of urine on them from afar.

Sometimes these children simply had an auspicious future, such as being untouchable by a bullet. Most often, though, it was expected that the spirits would call them in some manner. Markings only signaled the child's potential—they did not seal a child's fate or guarantee power later in life. Typically, a marked person had to pass certain trials, receive special training, or obtain an item with magical qualities before they could unlock their full potential. Their destiny could also be thwarted in certain situations, like if their parents pulled

71. Diószegi, *Sámánizmus*, ch. 4.

the extra (or prematurely erupted) teeth from their mouth, or when they lost their virginity.

If someone was not born with any special markings, they might still have a chance of obtaining magical knowledge. While some learned magic from books or human teachers, others volunteered their souls in exchange for learning the magical arts from witches, the undead, or the devil himself. These teachers put the seeker to the test, frequently at a crossroads. The devil might enter their body in the form of a fly or wasp, or the teacher may tell them to stand within the protection of a magical circle, then send a variety of threats (such as devils, wild animals, or—in more recent years—a speeding car or train) their way. Some tales describe how those seeking forbidden knowledge had to tolerate being in a cave or cellar while various bugs and other creatures crawled over their unclothed body. If the seeker maintained their composure, the impressed teacher would take them on as a student, offering them the necessary knowledge in exchange for their soul.

The *Táltos*

The *táltos* was a shamanic figure, the descendant of central Asian practitioners. *Táltosok* could talk to spirits of animals, weather, and nature, as well as to ancestral spirits. They could interpret dreams, cure illnesses, remove curses, and aid wandering spirits. Some owned magical weapons to use against ethereal enemies in the spirit planes, while others specialized in making various potions and incenses. In the words of one writer, "The craft of the *táltos* is to make wind, storm, ice, fire, and flood, to become invisible, to shape-shift into an animal, and to curse people. The *táltos* knows the secrets of the herbs… the herbs speak to him in human language."[72] Many shamanic practices dealt with sending one's spirit forth to climb up and down the World Tree in order to meet the various spirits in the sky and lower realms beneath our feet; other times, the *táltos* invited another spirit into their own body to channel their knowledge. Since spirits were not constrained by time and place in the same manner that humans were, the *táltos* could access knowledge from distant times or locations by consulting them.

In some eras, the *táltos* held a high rank in society, and they are mentioned in several origin legends. Göncöl was a famous historical *táltos* who had a

---

72. Róheim, *Magyar néphit és népszokások*, 15.

potion that was the cure for all disease. (The constellation now known as the Big Dipper is called the *Göncölszekér* in Hungarian: "Göncöl's Wagon.") The role of the *táltos* shifted once the Magyars settled in the Carpathian Basin and accepted Christianity. Since the outward practice of Pagan rites was forbidden, the community no longer looked to *táltosok* for religious guidance—although several kings continued to keep a *táltos* among their court advisors, despite papal disapproval. According to one account, the king's head *táltos* ritually killed a sheep to divine the future: "He stuck a knife in the lamb's neck…and studied how much blood was shed, and how quickly? What color was it, and how fast did it congeal? How long did the lamb live? How much did he sigh?" [73]

Of course, far more *táltos* lived in humbler circumstances than advising the ruler of the land. They passed their techniques down from generation to generation, sharing how to heal illnesses and curses, talk to the dead on the community's behalf, control the weather, or tell the future. Like the witch, the shamanic *táltos* figure was both feared and needed. At some point during their formative years—often around their seventh birthday—a potential *táltos* was tested with some sort of a trial, such as their spirit being made to climb to the top of the World Tree. The trial could also take the form of an illness, which might include long periods of unconsciousness as the spirits dismantled the child's astral body to make sure they had an uneven number of bones, then put the spirit back together. A spirit might also appear to the sick child in the form of a bull, bear, or horse, which the child's spirit had to physically fight. If they survived, the spirits offered knowledge so that the child could learn to heal or make prophesies, talk to the spirits, and travel between the worlds at will. If the child turned down their mission, they would become crippled or paralyzed in some manner.

Many *táltos* had animal spirit helpers. In fairy tales, this animal was usually a horse, a magical steed called a *táltos paripa*, but bulls, pigs, bears, and other creatures could also be spirit helpers. These animal companions had magical powers, were able to talk, could advise the hero, and transported them from location to location, flying and defeating opponents through various feats of strength. In real life, the shamanic *táltos paripa* was likely a euphemism for items that helped the shaman enter a trancelike state known as *révülés*. These items could include hallucinogenic herbs or instruments

73. Diószegi, *Az ősi magyar hitvilág*, 55.

such as rattles and whistles made of wood or bone, which produced a noise similar to the sounds of various animals. The instrument most often associated with the *táltos* was a drum of animal skin stretched over a circular frame, decorated with symbols and inscriptions, and beaten with a leather-topped drumstick. The louder the drum sounds, "the faster the horse gallops in the otherworld."[74]

Central Asian shamans directed animal sacrifices and dressed up as animals, wearing animal skins and headdresses with feathers or antlers. The *táltos* of the Carpathian Basin gave up these practices, but the symbolism remained in folk memory: both witches and *táltosok* were believed to duck or twist their heads or bodies when entering doorways so they could fit their invisible antlers inside the doorframe. Those who could "see" the true nature of witches through various techniques could see them with antlers or feathers as well, further linking the witch and the *táltos* figure.

Even though *táltosok* were typically men, there are records of women *táltosok* as well. During the witch trials, some of the accused vehemently denied that they were witches, protesting that they were healers instead. In 1725, the following dialogue took place during the trial of Bartha Andrásné:

Questioner: Who taught you your healing magic, when and where, and was it easy to learn?

Accused: I learned it from my elder brother, who is a *táltos* as well. And another girl, she is twelve now. She was born with two teeth.

Questioner: Did you teach others? Who and in what manner?

Accused: I did not teach anyone how to be a *táltos*. It is God who forms the *táltos* in their mother's womb to be one.

Questioner: If you are a *táltos*, tell me, what powers does a *táltos* have?

Accused: They fight in the heavens [to see who is the strongest]…God himself takes them under his own wings, and gives them wings of their own, as if they were birds.[75]

74. Róheim, *Magyar néphit és népszokások*, 10.

75. The source for this dialogue is Ortutay, *Kis magyar néprajz*, 106–7. The text has been adapted slightly for clarity and brevity.

Over the centuries, the influence of the *táltos* waned. By the start of the twentieth century, only a handful of *táltosok* remained. Generally located in isolated regions, they were reputed to know weather spells and had little in common with the *táltosok* found in older lore. In recent decades, there has been renewed interest in reviving shamanic techniques as well as coming up with new ones based on the traditions of their ancestors.

Seers

A figure closely related to the *táltos* was the seer, known by the name of *látó*, "one who sees," or as sayers, watchers, or talking women. There were both male and female seers. Often, their visions began to manifest during adolescence when they, like the *táltos*, had to battle a challenging illness. During the course of their illness, supernatural beings appeared to them and led them on a journey to the world of the spirits.

While many seers were able to control when they went into a trance, others were contacted by spirits at random—at least initially, before they learned how to use their powers. A seer, filling the role of a shaman, was able to contact the spirits at will, going into a trance known as *elrejtőzés* ("hiding oneself"). Some were able to go into this trance state for more than an hour, during which time their soul walked around the world of the spirits, seeking the information they were after. Some *látók* were able to channel healing powers during their trances; others only conversed with the spirits and asked them questions. *Látók* with especially famous reputations were valued and might receive visitors from faraway lands.

The reasons that people turned to *látók* varied from minor to profound. If a *gazda* lost a cow, for instance, he could visit a *látó* and ask them where the animal had wandered off to, and if it had been stolen or eaten by a predator. Seers who specialized in talking to the dead, called *halottlátók*, were even rumored to be able to locate the bodies of murder victims so they may be put to rest. Grieving family members consulted *halottlátók* to ask the deceased about their preferences for their funeral, such as which clothes they wanted to be buried in.

Shape-Shifters

In prehistoric times, shamans used costumes, masks, gestures, and sounds to transform themselves into animals, deities, archetypal characters, ancestors, ghosts, etc. The purpose could be religious, educational, or simply entertainment. Over time, these magical transformations were no longer limited to shamans. Dömötör Tekla wrote that through sacred role-play, "benevolent spirits, forces of nature, or deceased ancestors were given physical form [which in turn increased] fertility" of various kinds. She continues, "Their essence was…ambivalent; though they brought blessings, they were, at the same time, fearsome."[76] During the course of the year, there were several occasions for people to don masks or costumes in parades, pageants, or costume balls; some simply chose to dress up and go from house to house, asking for donations. Beyond human transformations, quite a few supernatural creatures in Hungarian lore also had shape-shifting powers. Witches were especially notorious for turning into animals (a phenomenon discussed in greater detail in the previous chapter).

One of the oldest-known spirits was the *beng* (plural *benga*). This was an evil spirit, one of the *rosszak*, at times synonymous with the devil himself. The *beng* could appear in a number of forms, as it was able to shape-shift. It was described as a dragon, a headless man, a horse, a donkey, an old woman, a shepherd offering chewing tobacco, a giant, a dog, and a cat, among other forms. If multiple people encountered a *beng* at the same time, it might even appear as a different spirit to each of them. Seeking out or conversing with a *beng* could very well cause one to lose their life. It often guarded treasure or hid in cemeteries; one might hear an otherworldly music when approaching it. If a person was walking along a roadside at night, the *beng* might try to lure them off the road and into the wilderness. The spirit was also accused of causing sickness or stealing unbaptized children. An old curse that could be heard into the twentieth century was *A beng vigyen el*, or "May the *beng* take you." One could protect themselves from the *beng* with a cross.

Another creature famous for its shape-shifting powers was the werewolf, known variously as the *farkaskoldus* ("beggar wolf"), *küldött farkas* ("sent wolf"), *prikulics* (a Romanian entity that appears as a handsome man during

76. Dömötör, *A népszokások költészete*, 63.

the day and transforms into a shaggy dog at night), or the *Csordásfarkas* ("the herdsman wolf"). If a bloodthirsty wolf stalked a flock of sheep, sometimes a human was blamed for the losses. During the witch hunts, alleged werewolves were tried alongside witches. The accused were mostly social outcasts; many belonged to the Roma ethnic group, were criminals, or were not trusted by other shepherds for some reason.

The typical werewolf was a shepherd who was either cursed with the ability to turn into a wolf or one who deliberately sought out the knowledge. They transformed by passing through magical hoops fashioned from the branches of a silver birch, usually three times, but sometimes seven times in succession. A midwife could pass a newborn through such a hoop shortly after birth; the child would gain the powers of shape-shifting at will when they turned seven years of age. It was more usual, however, for a person to learn how to shape-shift as an adult.

There were female werewolves as well as male ones. In one account, three wolves came into the yard of a wise man. He forced the animals to run through a birch hoop, at which point they turned into young women. They had been sent from the next village to steal food to take back to their *fonó*. Since they had been on a mission, the villagers called the young women *küldött farkasok*, meaning "sent wolves."

Transformations did not always happen smoothly. If the process of transforming was interrupted, the person only partially transformed. This might happen if a bystander brandished a crucifix, which stopped the transformation. It was possible to get stuck in wolf form, thus having to wander around forever as an animal. Even if a person properly transformed, there might be some telltale sign of a human within the werewolf, usually an article of clothing (such as a belt) that had not been removed. Other times, werewolves retained a piece of their wolf form when they changed back into a human, perhaps having shreds of their victim's clothing caught between their teeth.

There are scattered records of people transforming into other types of animals, not just wolves. Some of the most common forms were dogs, boars, goats, horses, snakes, cats, birds, and fish.

The Diabolical Professions

The word *tudós* (or in the case of women, *tudósasszony*), literally translated, means "someone who knows." A wise man, an advisor at court, a professor, or a teacher could all be called a *tudós*. Even today, the word is used to refer to an expert in a field, such as a scientist. But in years past, saying someone was a *tudós molnár* ("wise miller"), for example, did not merely mean that they were learned in their craft—it implied that the individual was receiving help from a supernatural force. The term was often used interchangeably with the adjective of *ördöngős*, meaning "aided by devils," or having the qualities of a devil themselves. Usually, those accused of this sort of magic were people who stood out of the typical peasant lifestyle in some way by specializing in a profession, such as being a coachman, hunter, or musician.

Like a witch, a *tudós* could not die without passing on their knowledge. The devil himself informed the servant exactly how long they had to live so that they may pass on their knowledge before time was up. Teachers could pass on their cursed knowledge via direct teaching, by shaking their successor's hand, or by giving them a magic book or charmed object. This object followed the successor throughout their life and contained their power.

It was nigh impossible to steal such an object from a *tudós*. Many legends related the ways in which the *tudós* foiled the would-be thief's plans. Sometimes the *tudós* met the thief and stated aloud that they knew what they were bent on doing. Other thieves became paralyzed when touching the object (or stuck to the object) and not be able to move until the *tudós* undid the curse. In stories in which a thief did manage to take the magical object, the item would harm them instead, or they were not able to use it (such as a stolen gun not being able to fire for anyone but the intended owner).

Chapter 12
MAGICAL TECHNIQUES

This book keeps returning to a common theme: in traditional life, magic was not something certain people performed at certain times; rather, the supernatural was just a part of everyday life. People watched for omens and practiced divination, and they put as much faith into healing spells as we do today into the modern care we receive at the hospital.

Simple spells and wards were considered basic home remedies. If a person failed to achieve their desired outcome, they turned to an expert who had received further training in the magical arts and sought their guidance on more complicated incantations and spells. When a young person was training for a specific profession, their education included learning magical techniques from their mentors. Still other magical techniques were passed down within families, from generation to generation, shrouded in great secrecy—it was thought that if any outsiders learned of the magic, the technique's power would dissipate.

The most important spiritual principle was that of sympathetic or analogous magic. In the words of the researcher Szendrey Zsigmond, "*A hasonló előhívja a hasonlót*," or, "What is similar evokes that which is similar," or, more simply put, "Like attracts like."[77] Actions, words, and even unspoken intentions had the power to make things happen in the physical world. Folklorist Ortutay Gyula wrote about the principle of *cosmic unity*; when one

77. Szendrey, "Tiltások és tiltott cselekvések," 248.

considers this type of thinking as a desire for wholeness, it starts to make sense why people believed in sympathetic magic, for instance, or in divination through omens.

Healing, fertility, farming, wealth, and love magic were all popular themes in spellcasting. A lot of the time, magic had to be performed alone and silently so that the person could focus their willpower on their goal; if a person spoke their intentions aloud, they released the power prematurely. Sometimes the person placed something in their mouth (a seed, a stone, an apple core, holy water, etc.) to remind themselves to be quiet. Magical techniques where one had to be silent included some forms of divination, breaking curses, planting seeds, collecting dew, healing, and collecting magical treasure. For example, if one wanted to cure a headache, they could splash river water on their head silently before the sun rose. Sometimes hand motions were used to emphasize spells; other times the magic was done entirely through various orchestrated gestures.

Another category of spells, known as *ráolvasások*, demanded the exact opposite: these spells depended heavily on incantations that often took the form of repetitive, rhyming verses. Some had the speaker directly state their wish. Others threatened whatever they meant to banish or invoked a higher power (such as the moon) to aid them in their task. Still other spells were nonsense words or a combination of word roots. A seventeenth-century spell intended to cure epilepsy, for instance, instructed the caster to chant the nonsense syllables *elim, melim, relim*. This same spell was being practiced as late as the twentieth century, when a woman was recorded saying that the only way to remedy a snakebite was to chant these syllables at dawn the day after the bite.

Even faithful Christians cast spells, which many would preface by asking for help from God, the Virgin Mary, or other saints, who then made their magic more powerful. In the sixteenth century, the famed Protestant preacher Bornemisza Péter wrote disparagingly about many of these spells; he believed in them even though he deemed them to be of the devil. Reciting prayer beads or other formulaic prayers during or after the magical working was another popular method of utilizing energy, as the repetitive, familiar prayers put a person into a meditative, trancelike state. Some prayers themselves were not unlike magical spells. Folk healers included terms such as

"Blessed Be the Sunshine" in their workings, or they referenced the infant Jesus "as beautiful as the shining sun, full moon, or the red dawn."[78]

Many spells required the practitioner to purify themselves by fasting prior to performing the ritual in order to increase the spell's power. *Böjtölés* ("fasting") was an important spiritual practice that could help a person achieve a goal such as finding a spouse, getting pregnant, or having a loved one heal from an illness. Entire communities might fast on anniversaries of tragedies to prevent them from happening again. "Fasting upon an intention" (variously called *ráböjtölés*, *kiböjtölés*, or *megböjtölés*) involved spells that specified how long one was supposed to fast for a specific purpose. To get revenge on an unfaithful lover, for instance, one was instructed to fast for nine days on bread and water alone. The intended result was that after the fast was complete, the cheater would die. Cursing through fasting could backfire—if the curse was unjust, the faster would be the one to die instead of the intended victim.

The line between positive and negative magic could get blurry in all types of magic, not just fasting. Sometimes cursing was a method of performing positive magic, where the spellcaster cursed one of the *rosszak* or attempted to nullify a previous curse or illness. Many spells, in fact, were forms of curses. Singing an *átokdal*, or "song of cursing," was one method of cursing. These songs could get very colorful and descriptive. Even folk songs often had elements of curses. For instance, according to the lyrics of one version of the folk song "Fehér László," the singer wishes that their target's washing water turns to blood, their garments catch on fire, their bread turns to stone, and "the Sky" (i.e., God) never blesses them again.[79]

Other curses invoked the *rosszak*, saints, or even *Isten*. Quite a few curses were structured in such a way that they would not be activated unless someone earned the punishment in them, such as touching forbidden treasure or betraying a lover. A fire might appear in the location where a curse had been cast, or where it had landed. Some recorded methods of cursing included putting a spell on an item belonging to the target, such as their hair or scraps of their clothing. The curser could also blow smoke in the target's direction, lick

78. Kovács, *Szeged és népe*, 345–46.
79. Olosz, "Fehér László."

their forehead or eyes, or use sympathetic magic to "measure" their luck away from them. It was risky to curse someone else; the curser might fall sick from the evildoing, or the curse might return upon them if their target was more powerful, more innocent, or had spiritual protection.

Although some spells featured exotic ingredients like powdered frog, coffin nail, or the noose of a hanged man, most spell components were readily available to anyone, found in the household or abundant in the natural world. Water, salt, candles, and herbs were all blessed for ritual use and kept at hand. People jumped across sacred bonfires, burned effigies, bathed in natural waters, sprinkled blessed dew on one another, decorated their homes with greenery, and struck one another with supple branches. Noisemaking was also a common magical technique, performed throughout the year to frighten away bad spirits.

Throughout the year, individuals, households, and communities performed various cleansing rituals. Many were connected to certain times of the year (such as the first day of the new year, early springtime, or the solstices) or to activities (such as the first day the livestock were sent to their summer pastures). Scourging was often performed on various festival days throughout the year to purify people and spaces with specially crafted whips.

Frequently, the four elements were used in some manner. Many magical workings feature water. The source was usually specified. Different rites involved well water, rain water, holy water, dew, water from sacred springs, or ritual baths with certain items placed within. A person could drink the water, wash with it, bathe in it, throw something in it, or sprinkle it on or around something or someone. Water could cleanse a person, heal a sick animal, or rid a place of malevolent spirits. A person was ritually bathed when they were born and ritually washed when they died, and several holidays included sacred water rites. Dew was collected in the spring and summer for various magical purposes. Water drawn at midnight on Christmas, as well as at dawn on various holidays (such as New Year's Day, May Day, and the summer solstice), had special powers and was called *aranyvíz* ("golden water") or *életvíz* ("life water"). Another form of water magic was bathing in natural waters like lakes and rivers on special days for health and vitality.

Fire was another primal element many cultures regarded as divine, or at least as the home of spiritual entities. Muslim contemporaries wrote that the Magyars worshipped fire. (To be fair, the scholar Dienes István pointed out that Muslims of the day referred to followers of any non-Abrahamic religion as "fire worshippers," so this might not be particularly descriptive of the Magyar faith itself.[80]) Whether or not fire was considered divine in its own right, it was commonly regarded as a symbol of the Creator, and many old traditions could well be remnants of a pre-Christian culture that treated fire as a sacred being.

Bad spirits (such as those causing storms) could be frightened away by flames, and a bride jumped over a bonfire at dawn to bless her new marriage. If a person found an object they believed was cursed, burning the object in a fire could neutralize the threat. A person could yell their wishes into a fire, especially if asking for a specific marital partner. Whispering one's sins into the flames cleansed them from guilt. One sacred form of fire was the *új tűz* ("new fire") built in the traditional manner, such as by rubbing two sticks together or by using a flint stone. Sacred bonfires were lit on the summer solstice as well as in springtime.

Censing, called *füstölés*, was done to spiritually purify a space or entity. Censing was thought to protect against both physical and spiritual threats as well as to heal illnesses and curses. If a household feared witches were about, a member of the family could walk around the house, censing it with protective incense. Church officials often used frankincense for religious ceremonies, but laypeople tended to burn a variety of blessed herbs, spiderwebs, or the remnants of holiday meals to get the desired smoke. Sometimes, a censing rite did not require special ingredients, but for the ingredients to be sourced from a specific place, such as dirt from a grave or a sliver of wood from a front door. As with other magical techniques, censing could be used for both positive and negative purposes. For instance, certain herdsman knew techniques for keeping their flocks together by throwing skulls or hooves into a fire and letting the smoke reach their animals; this same technique could be utilized to scatter the herds of their rivals.

---

80. Dienes, *A honfoglaló magyarok*, 47.

Binding

Kötés, or binding/tying, was an extremely popular form of magic. It could be utilized for positive or negative intentions; even strong, malevolent spirits and curses could be made powerless through this method. Although locks could be used for binding magic, it was more typical to tie a knot in rope, thread, or twine while visualizing energy being wound around the target's body or spirit. Records from the *boszorkányperek* ("witch trials") show that suspected witches were accused of using yarn, string, hair, pins, horsehair, feathers, and many other materials for their binding magic. Although some spells indicated that the caster should tie a knot near the intended target of their magic, powerful witches, wizards, and *táltos* were able to bind from a distance.

Knots were commonly used in healing and health-related magic. Binding could be used to quell fevers, stop bleeding (including internal bleeding or excessive menstrual or postpartum bleeding), or remove warts. Midwives could use knot magic to help women who were having trouble giving birth, healers could use it to cure impotence, and if an animal could not urinate, knots were tied and loosened several times in a row under its belly. At the other end of the spectrum, knots could dry up a mother's breastmilk or cause impotence, kidney stones, and urinary blockages. When someone died, all knots in their vicinity had to be undone to allow their spirit to freely journey to the *Túlvilág*.

If a person wanted to make sure that a woman would not marry after her husband passed away, they could tie knots on her clothes. A wife could ensure that her husband would remain faithful by cutting a knot off of his pants and burying it under the home's threshold. Even weather such as rain or wind could be bound up and loosened at will. A famous example of this was the legend of the *Szélkötő Kalamona* ("Wind-Binding *Kalamona*"), in which a monster locks up the winds in a kingdom as a form of blackmail.

Casters could leave the bindings for the desired amount of time, then loosen the energy by untying the knot—this loosening was called *oldás*. Some children's games reflected this sort of magic. In one form, children would sing a song to bind the passage of birds. The birds would circle helplessly until the children sang a different song to loosen their way. If someone suspected a witch had tied a harmful knot, the suspected caster was asked, forced, or bribed to loosen the knot in order to nullify the binding.

Surrounding

Kerítés or *bekerítés* ("surrounding") was a magical method by which the subject of the spell was encircled within a protective barrier that did not permit evil spirits, curses, or energies to pass through. The surrounded area would then become a space full of positive blessings. On the other end of the spectrum, an evil spirit or illness could be contained within the magic circle and not allowed to spread further. *Kerítés* could be accompanied by chanting or the use of incense. Some examples of *kerítés* include:

- A *gazda* could walk around a barn seven times in a row—starting at three in the morning on Good Friday—to ensure that only female calves would be born that year so the household would have more cows for milking.
- After sowing, a naked woman could run around the garden plot to protect the seeds against birds.
- A shepherd placed a cooked egg in his pocket when taking the sheep out to pasture, walked around the herd three times in a row, then ate the egg. His sheep would grow round and their coats would be as smooth as the egg.

Spitting

One way to ward off the evil eye, witches, bad spirits, sicknesses, or other misfortunes was *köpés* ("spitting"). A person could spit once, twice, or three times in a row. Healers spat on the person they were trying to heal, and the sick person "spit their sickness away" by spitting into a well or moving water. If someone visited a newborn, they spat on the baby and said, "May I not give you the evil eye!" A baby was also spat on during their baptism to get rid of the devil inside them.

Spitting was more than a way to ward off harm—it was also a technique for bringing good fortune into a person's life. If a person opened a business, the first coin they received in payment was spat on. A person might spit on cards when gambling, or a fisherman might spit on his first catch of the day.

This custom is still alive and well in some form. Whenever my mother found a coin on the ground, for example, she mimed spitting on it and then said, *"Apád, anyád idejöjjön!"* ("May your mother and father come to me!") In other words, if the found coin represented a small amount of financial luck, she was bidding a larger amount of wealth to materialize in her life as well.

Taking Up Tracks

Nyomfelszedés is translated as "taking up tracks." The general idea was for a spellcaster to secretly gather dust from their target's footprint, but there were many variations on this basic format, such as taking dust from nine footprints or from the left footprint, or by pouring wax into the footprint to make a mold, or by carrying the dust from the footprint next to one's body for three days. Throwing the dust from an intended victim's footprint into a grave could cause a person to develop a deadly illness, while hanging the dust inside a chimney caused a parching illness. On the other hand, some healers were paid to take a sick person's footprints and ritually turn them around so that their health would likewise take a turn for the better.

Taking up tracks could be used to bring love into one's life. Dust from the intended lover's footprint could be buried under the caster's front door. This tied the target's tracks to the caster's house—and they would keep visiting until they fell in love. Another way of using tracks to cast a love spell included pouring molten wax into the impression left by the target's foot. When it cooled, it could be thrown into the oven as the caster chanted, "May your heart burn for me like this wax melts in the oven!" [81]

If someone wanted to chase away a spouse, the caster could make a wax impression of the spouse's foot approaching the home, then turn the wax print around to show them leaving the home instead.

Twisting

Sodrás was a traditional craft made by twisting strands of yarn into a multicolored cord. The resulting *sodort madzagok* were used as decorative elements for clothing, traditional satchels, pillowcases, or fabric projects within the house. More than simply being decorative elements, *sodort madzagok*

---

81. Szendrey, "Nyomfelszedés."

were also protective spiritually: someone who laid their head on a pillow decorated with a *sodort madzag* was said to be protected from nightmares, and if one tied a *sodort madzag* around the handle of their front door, a witch would not be able to enter the house.

Sodrás, the process of making such a craft, was also a form of love magic. The person making the *sodort madzag* needed to concentrate on their love interest while making the craft in order to bind that person to them. These *sodort madzagok* could then be given as love gifts.

A *madzag* could also be used in cursing. Throwing one into a fire would bring harm to the caster's intended victim. Some of these *madzagok* were made out of unusual materials, such as the intestines of wolves, which could be buried in a roadway to bind a horse from traveling over it.

Chapter 13
TALISMANS AND BEYOND

While some magical techniques could be accomplished with only words or gestures, others used certain objects, either found in nature or blessed. Coins with holes in them protected against illness, curses, and the evil eye. Small magical talismans made of metal, stone, wood, bone, or leather were carried in a pouch or pocket or worn around a person's neck, wrist, ankle, or waist. These amulets were often carved or inscribed with names, runes, or magical words. Some amulets were incredibly simple, such as a strip of red cloth nailed to the front door to keep ill will out.

An *akasztott ember* ("hanged man") could provide several useful magical objects, including the rope with which he had been hanged (called the *akasztott ember kötele*), a satchel made out of his clothing, and various parts of his body. Thieves valued the *akasztott ember kötele*, believing it enhanced their sneaking abilities. If an animal was rubbed with this rope, the animals would become fat and healthy. Likewise, if the string from the man's underwear was rubbed on a horse, its coat would gleam. If a tavern-keeper put the criminal's genitalia under or into a barrel, his establishment would have plenty of customers.

Clovers, though small, contained powerful magic. They could uncover a cheater and other subterfuge. If a person wanted to find out which villagers were witches, they could get up early on Sunday morning and find a four-leaf clover. If they stuck the clover in the heel of their shoe or boot, they were able to see any witches who were in attendance at church services that morning.

The guilty party would be facing away from the altar, although to all other eyes they seemed to be sitting properly in the pews.

Some of the most common types of talismans were religious items. Some were consumable, such as wine, candles, herbs, water, or the remnants of holiday feasts, known as *morzsa*. Priests blessed each of these items on specific days so the community had a ready supply on hand in the coming months. Herbs and flowers, for example, were blessed on the festival of *Úrnapja* in the springtime; if one did not wish to wait for the holiday, they could simply place the leaves or blossoms between pages of a prayer book or the Bible for a few days. (I've personally seen many a prayerbook that wouldn't shut because there were so many dried flowers and holy cards placed between its pages!)

Other sacramentals were passed down through the generations, becoming more and more powerful with each passing year. These included prayer books, holy cards with pictures of saints, and prayer beads. These items, too, had many uses. One of my grandmother's neighbors set up an entire shelf of holy cards facing her front door; she was convinced the saints represented on them would watch over her home and keep it safe from robbers. The members of the household could also bring offerings to the saint in question for help with a specific task, such as finding a spouse. Prayer beads could be worn or placed somewhere malevolent spirits were likely to attack, such as inside the swaddle of an infant. Rosaries even had some magical uses that had nothing to do with prayer: hunters could use the beads from a rosary to shoot at witches, a whirlwind could be thwarted if a rosary was thrown into it, and a set of prayer beads could be tied onto a door handle to keep witches from attacking in the night.

Holy water could be bottled from sacred springs believed to be blessed by the saints (or woodland spirits) directly. Ordinary water could also be transformed into holy water through the blessing of a priest. Each household had a supply of holy water, which had countless uses, including:

- Sprinkling onto seeds before sowing to ensure a plentiful harvest
- Protecting newly hatched chicks from predators and disease
- Being shot out of a hunter's gun to remove any curses placed upon the weapon that might be affecting its aim

- Protecting a newborn and their mother from evil spirits by sprinkling the postpartum bed or the newborn's cradle
- Curing blisters, earaches, sore throats, rashes, and eye ailments, and healing in general
- Sprinkling holy water around the home during storms so that lightning wouldn't strike the house
- Anointing oneself, one's wagon, and one's horses with holy water before going on a journey

The *ostyák* ("wafers") used during church services were believed to either symbolize or legitimately transform into the body of Jesus, who was worshipped as a god. Understandably, these *ostyák* were believed to be very powerful magically. For instance, hunters could place a wafer in their gun and use it as ammunition to ensure that the weapon would always hit its target. As the *ostya* was such a holy thing, if a witch placed one in her mouth, she would not be able to swallow it, holding it in her mouth until she could spit it out after Mass. If a priest dropped an *ostya*, it was believed that the person whom he had been trying to give it to was a witch, and the *ostya* had flown out of his hand rather than go to the witch. Witches were known to carry *ostyák* to the devil for his nefarious purposes. In one witch trial, the accused allegedly mixed a communion wafer with wax and choked an unbaptized child with it. Another story related how a woman did not eat her *ostya* but instead placed it in a satchel each time she went to church. When she died, she was buried with the satchel. Her body would not decompose, and for a year following her death, a mysterious flame blazed on her grave every midnight.

Skulls and bones had magical abilities. Powdered skulls could be mixed with *pálinka* or added to a person's food to cure illnesses. Epilepsy could be cured by burning a skull and grinding it into powder, then mixing the powder into a person's food and water for sixty days. (The powder could also be mixed with oil to prepare an infusion or distilled into alcohol to make a tincture.) If an alcoholic drank from a skull, they would be cured of their addiction. Skulls might also be placed into healing ritual baths, and placing a salted skull into a horse's drinking troughs would ensure their health and strength. Even the mere presence of a skull could be protective; fastening the skull of a horse to a gatepost or placing it in one's attic would protect the homestead from witches and curses.

Other parts of the body also had magical curative properties. For instance:

- Touching a corpse's hand three times in a row cured goiters and lymphedema.
- Human bones could be rubbed against rheumatic joints to heal them.
- Male infertility could be cured by a potion containing powdered human bones.

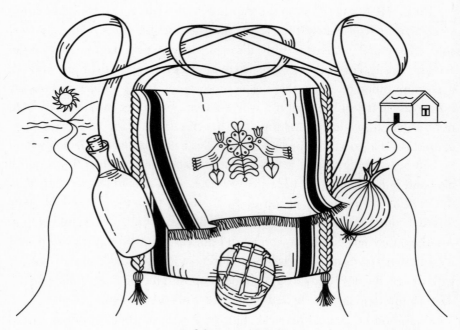

A fabric *tarisznya*

In fairy tales, clothing was often described as having magical powers. Wearing a belt, cloak, or vest could impart one with special powers. Special weapons and armor were gifted to the hero or heroine by fairies, witches, or devils. Even in the real world, people were rumored to have accessories with magical powers. A *tarisznya* was a type of traditional satchel made from leather or heavy fabric. A common feature of many fairy tales involved the main character's mother gifting them with such a satchel at the start of a journey. Many times, the *tarisznya* contained unlimited food and drink to sustain the hero. In the real world, the *tarisznya* was sometimes used for healing magic: a parent could place salt, bread, a slip of paper on which a priest had written a healing verse, and garlic inside the satchel, sew it shut, and then hang it around their sick child's neck. (Other healing agents placed in the satchels included black pepper, wheat kernels, incense, or coal.)

Today, many people associate the satchel with the *ballagás* ceremony of young adults at the end of their school years. The celebration of this ceremony varies from school to school, but the graduating students are traditionally gifted with a decorated *tarisznya*, complete with various sentimental and symbolic items—including salt, a small pouch of earth to represent connection to their homeland, coins, sometimes a flask of wine, and a *pogácsa*—inside. In our family, we give a *tarisznya* as part of a young person's coming-of-age ceremony.

Number Magic

Numbers may seem like a strange addition to this chapter, since they are not tangible items, but sometimes physical objects had to be grouped in certain numbers to be considered magically effective, prayers (or spells) had to be repeated a specific number of times, or the way in which an act was performed the first time would magically affect what followed it. The numbers one, three, seven, nine, and thirteen were most significant.

The first time an activity was performed, or the first time it was performed in the year, was often accompanied by certain actions to ensure a lucky outcome. One common belief was that the way in which a cow was milked for the first time would affect whether that cow would be a good milker or not in the future. The *gazdasszony* was obliged to use the milk to draw a cross upon the animal to ensure that it would continue giving milk. She would then invite the neighborhood children over to consume the milk. They sat on the floor in a circle and spooned the milk from a shared pot.

There were superstitions and *babona* about the first animals encountered in a year, such as:

- The first bat of the year could be nailed to a shop's door to ensure many customers.
- When a man saw the first sparrow of the year, he should lift his hat and greet it politely so that he might have good luck that year.

- If a person saw the first frog of the year on dry land, they would have good fortune, but if the frog was swimming in the water, the person's wealth would soon be washed away.

Spells were chanted three times in a row. Many rites were repeated three times (such as in the morning, in the evening, and at midnight) or performed on three subsequent nights. Sometimes, only a part of a ritual had to be repeated thrice; for example, part of a shape-shifting ritual involved lighting and extinguishing a candle three times in a row. A shepherd could walk around his herd three times to protect them. A horse taken out to the woods for the first time had to be brushed three times from head to tail with an evergreen bough. Many fairy tales featured three trials for the main hero, and a popular saying even today is *Három a magyar igazság*, "Three is the Magyar truth," meaning that significant events repeated in threes, or that an event was not finished until it had been completed three times.

Seven was also a powerful number. The seventh child in a family was thought to have special powers, such as being especially strong or able to commune with spirits, having healing powers, or being able to find magical treasure. Fairy tales are said to take place in the seventh kingdom past the speaker (which is a general way of saying very far away). Some descriptions of the cosmos said that it was split into seven layers from the lowest to the highest (other variations said that there were either nine heavens above ours, or nine layers of the Lower World, or that there were seven locks on the gate of heaven). Other people claimed that seven devils (or kings of devils) existed, or seven evil forces. In traditional healing, there were seventy-seven categories of illness.

The number nine was frequently used in healing magic. In one collection of Hungarian spells compiled by Pócs Éva, dozens of spells mention the number nine: either an action had to be performed nine times in a row (such as striking a child's shirt onto a threshold nine times in a row to heal their illness), a prayer or spell had to be recited nine days in a row, or nine ingredients had to be gathered for a cure. These nine ingredients could be nine dried fleas, nine types of herbs, dried mud from nine footprints, dirt from nine graves, or flour from nine different houses. In yet another curative spell, an egg yolk had to be divided into nine parts before being buried in specific places to heal the patient's illness.

Thirteen was typically seen as a number related to witchcraft or the devil, so it was lucky in mystical workings but generally unlucky for God-fearing people.

Criminal Talismans

Criminals had their own forms of dark magic, and many of their spells involved hard-to-source ingredients, such as nails taken from coffins. An especially dark talisman for thieves was the finger of an unborn child; it was said that this finger would light up on its own, like a candle.

To open locks, a thief could use the herb *Verbena officinalis*, which they knew as *vasfű* ("iron herb") or *zárnyitó fű* ("lock-opening herb") or *vérfű* ("blood herb"). If an honest man touched this herb, he would be compelled to become a thief. There were two methods to source the magical plant. The first way was to pick it on the one night of the year it grew, which was the evening before *Szent György napja* in April. The second method was to shut a baby turtle into a locked chest. Its mother would try to free it by bringing the herb in her mouth. The person could then simply take the leaves from her mouth.

To use the herb, the thief had to put his hand in scalding water and place the herb under his skin as it healed so that it became part of his own hand. A gentler method was to cut one's palm and drip dew from the plant into the wound. Whichever method the would-be thief used, once he was healed, he would be able to open locked doors with a mere touch—and perhaps even have the power of invisibility.

A thief could also sprinkle the powdered ashes of a tree frog (or just its powdered skull) onto a lock to open it. Both of these techniques have a long history, with written records noting them as far back as the 1600s.

Sacred Plants

Many plants were thought to have spiritual or magical qualities that made them ready components of spells and rituals; some plants were simply thought to enhance a person's environment for the better by serving as a reminder of the Divine. If you look at any sort of traditional Hungarian artwork, clothing, or household decorations, chances are you find many floral motifs. The symbols not only beautified a home (or person), they also warded off storms, bad

spirits, and negative energy. Flowers were also mentioned in songs and stories, often in reference to fairies or spiritual beings. Many folk songs, including those already sung in medieval times, refer to roses and tulips.[82]

In his book about the flowers most important to the Magyars, Rapaics
Rajmund listed fifteen, among them roses, carnations, tulips, violets, daisies,
rosemary, lily of the valley, marigold, geranium, and chrysanthemum.[83]

Roses were revered throughout Europe, and they had an especially strong
following in Roman times due to their associations with the sacred feminine. Although many early Christians adopted the flower as a divine symbol, others were not quite so eager to do so. The influential Christian author
Tertullian wrote emphatically about the dangers of the so-called "rose cult,"
and Bishop Clement of Alexandria declared decorating with roses a sin.[84]
The symbol of the rose remained popular enough that the church, facing a
losing battle, stressed that the rose was sacred to the Virgin Mary. Now, she
is often depicted surrounded by the flower, and although the prayer beads
dedicated to her—what English speakers know as a rosary—are traditionally
called *olvasók* ("readers") in Hungarian, they are also known as *rózsafűzérek*
("string of roses") even when they are made from materials such as wood
or metal. Roses remained popular symbols of love in Hungary and beyond;
both men and women in Hungary have traditionally addressed their sweethearts as "my rose."

The lily was another popular flower. It was a symbol of purity and youth.
In many folk songs, lilies symbolize young women, and sometimes the
Boldogasszony herself.

Carnations also had mystical associations. Most of the carnation varieties
known to the Magyar people tended to have either five or seven petals, both
of which were sacred numbers.

The tulip was known throughout Eurasia as a sacred flower. It was
believed to be sacred to the *Boldogasszony* because it represented feminine
beauty, love (both platonic and romantic), and grace. The tulip was especially
popular with brides; many a dowry chest was painted or carved with tulips.
Depictions of the *Életfa* often showed tulips growing from its branches.

82. Viski, "A tulipán szó történetéhez."
83. Rapaics, *A magyarság virágai*, iii.
84. Rapaics, *A magyarság virágai*, chap. 3.

Of all the trees known to the Magyar people, elderberry, known as *bodza*, was probably mentioned the most frequently and in the most spiritual contexts. It was both edible and poisonous, depending on which parts were consumed and in what manner. The traitorous apostle Judas was said to have hung himself from an elderberry tree, and it became cursed as a result. While sometimes, *bodza* was used to decorate gateposts to keep evil spirits at bay, planting it near the house might cause lightning to strike the home. If someone wished to curse another, they could cut three branches from the uppermost part of a *bodzafa* and place the branches under the eaves of the victim's house. Then, the caster had to throw a handful of dust upon the home while chanting the curse. Despite these negative associations, elderberry also had magical healing powers. The water from a child's first bath could be poured on a *bodzafa* to protect the child from skin rashes. If animals (or even people) were struck with *bodza* branches in the early spring, they would be free of disease in the coming months. The plant could even heal from afar: if an animal had larvae in its wounds, a *gazda* placed elderberry branches on the ground at sunrise and stomped on them to make the larvae fall out of the animal's wounds.

Although not as commonly used in folk art, the *vadrózsa* ("wild rose" or "dog rose," not to be confused with the garden rose) was another important plant. According to legend, Jesus, Mary, and Joseph rested under a *vadrózsafa* as they were fleeing Bethlehem. Mary dried the infant Jesus's diapers on the thorny branches, so to this day, the flowers have a sharp smell. Springs under *vadrózsa* trees were thought to have healing qualities. Threatening creatures would get caught in its thorns (either physically or symbolically), which warded them away or neutralized their power, so *vadrózsa* trees were placed around the homestead and at the corners of fields. The plant was an especially useful guard against witches in particular; magical spells to protect against witches often included the curse "May there be a *vadrózsa tüske* [thorn] in her side."

Another plant, known as *Árvalányhaj* ("Hair of the Orphaned Girl"), appeared as light, straw-colored grass that grew in wild places. It had an interesting origin story: according to legend, the Virgin Mary was in the forest and sat down to comb her hair. The strands that fell to the ground became the first *Árvalányhaj*.

Chapter 14
DIVINATION

Divination, known as *jóslás*, involved spells, rituals, and other magical techniques that helped people gain esoteric knowledge about the future. There were many active forms of divination (such as the act of baking magical *pogácsa* or looking into mirrors by candlelight), though one could simply pay attention to various signs in the environment. Omens (as well as the more deliberate love- and death-related divination methods discussed later in this chapter) were known throughout the Hungarian-speaking population, with countless regional variations. Many are still shared from one generation to the next.

Many people today are familiar with the superstition of a black cat or a broken mirror signifying bad luck; I did not come across these specific omens in Hungarian literature, but I did come across many similar ones. Seeing a falling star meant someone was dying; comets meant war was on its way. When a person went to the market, they would be lucky in their trading if on their way they ran into someone carrying a full bucket. Many divination techniques had to do with weather. For instance, fog on *Pál napja* (January 26) meant a plague would soon arrive, and a Christmas Eve with a southern wind meant that animals would die from disease.

The body also communicated via various signs, which often depended on the side of the affected body part:

- If someone's left palm itched, they would soon receive money. If their right palm itched, they would soon have to spend money.
- If someone's left cheek blushed, someone was praising them. If someone's right cheek blushed, someone was scolding them.
- If someone's left eye itched, they would soon be joyful, but if their right eye itched, they would soon cry.
- If a person's nose itched, they would be irritated soon.
- If someone's left ear rang, they would soon hear good news; if their right ear rang, the news would be unfortunate.
- If someone sneezed, the last sentence they had uttered was confirmed to be the truth.

Love Divination

One of the most common purposes of divination was to unveil the mysteries of love. Young people were curious about who their future partners would be, with most love divination techniques being performed by older girls and young women. Some were solitary spells whereas others were communal activities, whereby sisters or friends performed a ritual together. As with other magic, the spellcaster was often advised to perform certain actions before performing the rite, such as fasting, not bathing, or avoiding going to church.

Sometimes it was enough to discern which direction a potential mate would be coming from; listening for dog barks while standing on top of a trash heap was one method for this type of discernment. Whichever direction barking originated from would be the direction where the young woman's future groom lived. Other times, someone wanted to know more details about their future match. In that case, performing an *öntés* ("pouring") was a good choice. A young woman poured lead or wax into a bucket of cold water; this produced shapes that could be interpreted. Sometimes the shape took the form of the letter that the future husband's name started with; it could also resemble a tool, which showed what profession he was trained in.

Inducing a dream or vision of the future lover was a common theme. In one variation, if a young woman washed her face in the well at midnight on

Christmas Eve, then went to sleep, her future spouse would dry her face in her sleep. Alternatively, she could place an item of male clothing under her pillow, and her future spouse would be revealed as she slept. Another version involved baking an unsalted *pogácsa* and placing it by her bedside with a glass of water. Her future spouse would come to her in her dreams, and the two would share the meal. Eating fish on the eve of *Szent György napja* in the springtime would also cause a young woman to dream of her future spouse.

Some divination methods included naming various potential suitors and narrowing down one's options. Popular methods included the following:

- A young woman wrote the names of her eligible suitors on slips of paper, then made a *gombóc* ("dumpling") around each slip. She threw the *gombóc* into boiling water. Whichever rose to the surface of the water first contained the slip bearing the name of her future husband. (Alternately, the girls would write their own names on the slips; the order in which the dumplings rose to the surface indicated the order in which they would marry.)
- Nine branches were cut from various fruit trees. Each was labeled with a different potential suitor's name. Whichever branch sprouted first bore the name of her future spouse.
- Twelve potential suitors' names were written on twelve slips of paper. In the following days, she threw one of the slips of paper into the fire, one slip each evening. The last remaining slip contained the name of her future husband.

Love divination was a popular activity that girls would do when they got together at the *fonó*. In one method, the girls formed several figures from tufts of wool and designated each tuft to be a potential suitor. Another figure was made to represent the seeker. The seeker was placed in front of a male figure, which was then lit on fire. The way the male figure burned determined how the suitor in question thought of the seeker: for a long time, for a short time, or not at all. Fire and wool had other divination uses. A young woman could light a piece of wool on fire and throw it into the air. If it stayed lit as it fell, someone would ask her to marry soon. If the flame went out, she would remain unmarried.

Apples were often involved in love magic and divination. For instance, to divine the name of her future husband, a young woman could take one bite out of an apple each day. When the core was small enough to fit into her mouth fully, she placed it there. Without swallowing any piece of the apple, she walked through the village while holding the fruit in her mouth. The first man she met on the street shared the name of her future husband.

In other cases, the identity of the potential husband was not as import- ant as the qualities he might have. A young woman could pick a stick from a stack of kindling at random. If the stick was short, the man would also be short, and if it was long, he would be tall. If it turned out not to have bark, the diviner's future groom would be poor; the more bark there was on it, the more wealth he would have. Additionally, if the cottage a girl lived in had a roof of thatched plant material, she could strike the ceiling with a broomstick while holding her apron aloft to catch the falling seeds. She could divine who her future husband was depending on the seeds she caught. The material that fell out of the roof foretold whether she would marry a wealthy or poor man (wheat kernels versus chaff, for example).

Death Divination

Another common purpose of divination was to find out when someone was going to die. Such divination methods included:

- Filling an empty walnut shell with water and placing it on the window- sill. If the water evaporated from it by morning, the asker would die within the year.
- Standing slabs of firewood upright overnight; each family member chose one slab to represent them. If their wood fell before morning, they would die before the year was over.
- Baking a *pogácsa* for each member of the family and sticking a white goose feather in each. If the feather stayed unburnt throughout the baking process, the person it represented would remain healthy, but if the feathers charred during baking, the person would not live to see another year.
- Tying a key to a string, then wrapping it into a Bible. After the book was shut, the person twisted the key and counted. However many

turns the key made before the string broke was the number of years they would live.

Other times, people did not have to perform a ritual themselves—they simply had to be watchful. On a husband and wife's wedding night, whoever fell asleep first would die first, and when someone heard the cuckoo for the first time that spring, the number of times the bird called out was how many years the person had left to live. A number of dreams warned of impending death, such as walking in a cemetery, digging a hole, or giving a gift to a dead relative. If a person dreamed of their teeth being pulled out, someone close to them was about to die; if losing their teeth was a painful process, it would be a close relative who died, but if it was painless, it would be a distant relative.

The family home, especially, could communicate with the members of its household by sharing omens of future misfortune, especially the impending death of family members. Some warnings included:

- If furniture creaked as if someone was using it
- If a shingle fell off the roof in front of the front door
- If a picture fell from the wall on its own
- If a plant grew through the walls of one's house
- If the ground outside the door cracked
- If there was a knock on the window, but no person was seen
- If the crust of a bread cracked or burned while it was baking

Some omens about death were suspiciously specific; for example, if a strange white horse ran into a yard, the master of the house would die unless he spit on the horse three times in succession. Other death omens involving animals included:

- A pig digging in the dirt in front of one's front door; pouring salt water into the hole prevented a grave from soon being dug for a member of the household
- A mole tunneling within the home's immediate vicinity, ants building an anthill inside the house, or wasps building a nest on the home

- Having a skunk or ermine on one's property
- If a bat flew down the chimney
- If a white *halálpillangó* ("butterfly of death") flew around the house
- If a dog whined with its head down or scratched under the table
- If a cat scratched at a sick person's bed
- If a rabbit showed up at a funeral, a relative of the deceased would soon die

Crime and Judgment

When a crime was committed in the community, people often turned to supernatural methods to determine who the guilty party was. *Kulcsforgatás* (key-spinning) and *rostaforgatás* (sieve-turning) were popular ways to uncover a thief; both methods involved taking ordinary household objects and rotating them in such a way that they indicated the guilty person when they came to a stop. Other times, *Isten* himself was said to miraculously unveil the guilt of a person; it was believed that if a murderer was brought in the presence of their victim's body, the wounds on the corpse would start bleeding anew.

When disagreements that could not easily be resolved arose, they had to be settled to avoid upsetting the equilibrium in the community. Many times, people left the matter up to fate or God. If a crime had been committed and the perpetrator was unknown, the suspects drew lots; the person who "won" the contest by drawing the stick of a different length was deemed to be the guilty party.

Istenítélet is translated as "the judgment of God," and it usually involved a battle of skill. Contestants believed that whoever triumphed was also the winner of the argument, determined by *Isten*. Some contests were harmless, such as seeing who could stand with their arms stretched out in front of them longer. Other times, *istenítélet* was used to decide grave matters, such as choosing rulers or deciding whether a person was guilty of a crime. In the latter case, the accused was placed in an extremely dangerous situation; if they survived, it was believed that God himself had delivered them from the danger to prove their innocence. One could prepare for such a trial by fasting and praying, or by sleeping in the church the night before.

One method of *istenítélet* was trial by fire, of which there were several variations. One involved having a priest pray over a fiery piece of metal, ask the accused to make a testimony, and vow that they were not being aided by any demonic forces. Afterward, the accused had to pick up the heated metal and carry it into the church. The person's hands were then bound up in bandages. If their wounds healed in three days' time, the accused was considered innocent. Otherwise, they would face further punishment.

Trial by fire was not the only type of *istenítélet*. Trial by food involved filling a person's mouth with a piece of heavy food, such as cheese or bread. The accused had to eat the food without choking. Trial by water was used in witch trials; it was also known as *boszorkányfürösztés* ("bathing of a witch"). Suspects were placed in water with their hands and feet tied. The guilty floated, while the innocent sank; it was believed that witches had lost their soul, making them lighter than average. Other women accused of witchcraft were thrown off mountaintops to see if they survived the fall. If the woman perished, she was cleared of all charges.

Chapter 15
HEALING MAGIC

W hile cities had trained doctors, it was uncommon for villages to have a doctor of their own. If a villager was seriously ill and could afford the costs involved, they could travel to a city for medical treatment. For the most part, however, people either consulted local healers (like a midwife or *táltos*) to diagnose and treat their illnesses and injuries, or they were forced to go it alone. As with all other spheres of life, there was no clear distinction between the physical and spiritual realms, so magical healing rites were considered just as reasonable as other treatment plans. One researcher noted that during the witch trials, it was often fellow healers who accused their rivals of practicing witchcraft, even when they themselves practiced very similar forms of healing techniques.[85]

The best cure was preventative—people did what they could to ensure lasting good health. This was done by eating certain foods on certain days, such as consuming blessed wafers with honey and garlic on Christmas. On holidays, they bathed in natural waters like ponds or rivers, or they washed themselves with dew. During the first storm of the spring, people would hit their heads with stones so they wouldn't get headaches that year, then roll around on the grass so their backs wouldn't hurt.

Breaking taboos (such as working on a holiday) could cause illness within the household. If a woman failed to wear her head cover, for instance, she

85. R. Várkonyi, "Közgyógyítás és boszorkányhit," 403–4.

might get headaches. Eating beans or lentils during certain springtime holidays would make the family develop ulcers. Spitting in a river would cause a person's livestock to get sick. Sometimes these taboos could be broken on purpose as a means of cursing another person, such as pouring a drink from a hand held backward to make the other person sicken.

Performing a routine task incorrectly on purpose, such as doing the task backward, could confuse malevolent spirits who might be inclined to curse a person with illness. Since the spirit world was seen as the mirror (or opposite) of our physical world, the spirit became confused and thought they were lost or had lost their power. Those who feared witches might try to enter their house left an upside-down broomstick by the door, as seen in the folktale *A táltos ökör* ("The *Táltos* Ox"). Parents dressed their unbaptized infants in inside-out or backward clothing to keep them safe, and wearing inside-out shirts might cure a patient from illness or bad dreams or aid them in spellcasting. I remember being told as a child that if someone accidentally wore a shirt backward, they would instead have an unexpectedly lucky day. In a similar vein, one writer stated that "the *alvilág* ["Lower World"] is a backward world, a left-hand world [so] to protect against forces from the *alvilág* one must use the left hand." [86]

Despite all their precautions, people did, inevitably, fall injured and ill. The first step in healing a person was to figure out what was causing their illness. Performing an *öntés* ("pouring") was one diagnostic test employed by traditional healers. The reader would hold a bowl of water over a person's head, then drip wax from a blessed candle into the water, then interpret the resulting shapes and forms. Wax was especially effective for *öntés* since the material was produced by honeybees, which were a sacred symbol of the Virgin Mary (who was, of course, linked with the *Boldogasszony*).

Many illnesses (especially those without an obvious cause, like epilepsy, neurological disease, or paralysis) were thought to be due to the evil eye, which was the curse of a ghost, witch, or other evil spirit—or simply of another person with no specific magical affiliation at all. In Hungarian, the term for the evil eye is *szemverés*, which can be translated as "beating with the eye." Pócs Éva explains that "besides witch- and ghost-beliefs, this was

---

86. Bosnyák, "Napkorona, aranyalma, pásztorbot, suba," 9.

the sphere of traditional popular beliefs and popular mentality that survived the longest—until today, in fact. In many village communities, even members of the younger generations believe in the harmful effect of the evil eye."[87]

Those who were blessed with youth, good health, or exceptional beauty were most at risk of *szemverés*. Anything that was weak was also vulnerable: newborns, young animals, sprouting plants, rising bread dough, churning butter, or milk that could sour. While witches were especially talented at casting powerful *szemverés*, anyone could do so, sometimes even unintentionally. The evil eye was not always caused on purpose; simply being envious of someone's fortune could place a curse on them. Anyone who became emotional about a situation, *megcsodálta* (meaning marveling at a thing), or even praised something excessively might cast the evil eye. People with crossed eyes or bushy eyebrows were rumored to have especially strong abilities.

Some cures were focused on neutralizing the threat itself, while others tried to return the malevolent energy to the person who originated it. Various amulets and incantations could protect a person from the effects of the evil eye; examples include a red ribbon tied around one's wrist or pearls worn around one's neck. Garlic was also a potent remedy; wreaths of garlic were hung on walls and over doors, windows, and beds. One cure involved cooking nine dumplings. The victim was bathed in the cooking water, while the dumplings were fed to a dog the same sex as the victim. Other cures were based on disgusting the spirit who had been attracted to the victim and thus involved vile elements such as spit, excrement, or urine. For instance, a child who had been cursed with the evil eye could be washed with their mother's urine.

Some magical cures involved simply denying it: The healer ritually announced that the person in question suffered from a specific illness. The person being cured replied, "You are lying. I do not have it." It was even possible to transfer pain to another person. A child's teething pain could be transferred to another person by having the child chew on an item, then throwing the item into a road where someone was liable to step on the object or pick it up.

87. Pócs, "Evil Eye in Hungary," 205.

As wheat and related grains were so sacred, many forms of them—such as pieces of bread or barley—could be used for healing. The grain would be pressed to the body part the healer wanted to heal, then fed to the birds or simply thrown away, either over their shoulder, into a well, or into a crossroads. It was considered especially effective if the healer told the grain, "you will never sprout. Likewise, may my trouble never return!" The healer might also use kernels to surround a patient in a healing circle.

It was generally easier to prevent being cursed than to remove an existing curse. To do the latter, one had to convince the caster to remove it—through threats, violence, pleading, or payment—or get a stronger caster to counter the spell. It was thought to be more useful to fight fire with fire, i.e., chanting extremely offensive verses to counter the evil of the curse. For instance, one counter-curse went, "If it was a man who did the cursing, let his testicles split open. If it was a woman who did the cursing, let her breasts split open!"[88]

The cures for *szemverés* were often similar to the cures for *ijedtség* ("fright"), meaning the person had been "terror-struck" in some manner that caused their good health to be scared away. *Ijedtség* could manifest as sudden fear, crying, or uncontrollable shaking. This was considered an illness (or a group of illnesses) just as real as other physical ailments. Sometimes it took years between a causative incident and the subsequent feelings of terror. It was usually children who were terror-struck, but adults could fall victim to it as well. Adults were most likely to be terror-struck by souls of the departed visiting from the *Túlvilág*, whereas children were commonly frightened by chickens and dogs—both were animals that had connections with witchcraft and the devil.

There were a number of remedies for a terror-struck individual. The mother of a cursed child could bake a pretzel large enough for her infant to pass through, and the child could be *átbújtatva* ("passed through it") at sunrise, after which the pretzel was fed to dogs. The most frequently utilized remedy was taking a healing bath in water, often with coal or ashes in it. The water, in this case, would be called *szenes víz*, "coal water." Another popular cure had to do with pouring lead into water; the water was then known as *ónos víz*.

88. Dömötör, *A magyar nép hiedelemvilága*, 147.

Gentler cures included being sprinkled with holy water, hanging a blessed candle around one's neck, or having one's nose pulled several times in a row. Gentian tea was also a cure; in fact, gentian was known colloquially as *rettegőfű* ("terror herb"). Another method of cleansing required visiting nine distinct molehills, gathering two handfuls of dirt from each of them, and adding all of them to the ritual bath. (The method of bathing in this instance would be to simply pour the water on the victim—they did not have to immerse.)

Rather than try to lift a curse, a person could seek out the caster and ask them to voluntarily remove it; if they refused, the curse could simply be sent back to the perpetrator. To uncover the guilty party, a person could throw three, seven, or nine pieces of coal into a basin filled with cold water. Each time one was thrown, the name of a possible perpetrator was called out. The one that sank first was guilty. Alternatively, four pieces of coal could be designated as a man, woman, boy, and girl. The piece of coal that sank first described who had cursed the individual. Possible suspects could be narrowed down in this fashion until the guilty party was determined. Afterward, the water was poured in the four corners of the home to ward off bad spirits. Sadly, many witch hunts were sparked when desperate family members tried to find out who was responsible for cursing a sick child.

If the perpetrator could not, in fact, be established, it was still possible to return a curse. Instead of naming a specific person, the victim could instead chant, "Blue eyes, brown eyes, green eyes, black eyes, yellow eyes, mixed eyes." [89]

Though most illnesses were thought to be caused by humans or spirits, some were caused by animals that had managed to crawl inside a person. If someone fell asleep outside, a snake (or sometimes, a frog) was likely to crawl into them through their mouth; they were then able to feel the creature wriggling around inside. (It's possible that parasites were the actual culprits of these stomach ailments.) Drinking *pálinka* or consuming blessed horseradish was thought to cure the person. Sore throats were known as *torokgyíkok*, "throat lizards." The mentally disturbed were thought to have bugs inside their heads; ulcers were thought to be frogs in the stomach; brittle bones

89. Pócs, *Magyar ráolvasások I*, 54.

were caused by gnawing beetles; toothaches were attributed to a biting insect under the gum.

Besides finding out the origin of an illness, a healer had to determine which category of maladies it belonged to. In traditional healing, diseases were classified into various categories. One popular way of classifying illness was by color; the remedy needed to be in the same color category as the illness. For example, a number of diseases were known as *sárgulás* ("yellowing diseases"); these were frequently thought to be caused by contact with the dead or by looking in the window of a house where there was a dead body. Cures for this category of sickness included:

- Making a cup out of yellow beeswax, dropping a golden ring into it, pouring water in the cup, letting it sit, then giving it to the patient to drink
- Carving a cup out of a carrot, putting the patient's urine in it, then placing it in the chimney; as it dried, the sickness would pass
- Tying a pendant of yellow beeswax on a yellow string—preferably silk—and wearing it around the neck until cured
- Having the patient eat an egg yolk or yellow sugar
- Covering the patient with a yellow cloth

Sometimes, the color had to be associated not with the illness itself, but the patient. One cure for a cough included drinking warm water with the hair of a cat; if the patient was blonde, the cat's fur had to be from a red or gray cat. If brunette, the cat's fur had to be black.

Healing spells often specified *who* was to perform the ritual (for example, the child's godmother), *where* it was supposed to take place (such as in the garden, the home's threshold, or by the hearth fire), and *when* it was supposed to take place (e.g., a healing bath had to be taken directly before sunrise). Potions were more effective if the herbs used in them were gathered at specified times or prepared in certain ways. A remedy for a hurt foot required a foot bath made with the spiny rest-harrow plant, but the healer had to steep exactly nine leaves after the sun set and pour out the water before dawn.

Baths, teas, and censing an ill person with blessed herbs were universally popular methods of healing magic. Other methods for curing sickness included:

- Scolding or threatening the sickness while ordering it to depart from the victim
- Making gestures or other motions above the body to sweep away the sickness
- Touching various blessed objects or amulets to the patient
- Having the patient ritually deny their illness
- Touching an object to the patient to absorb the illness, then throwing away the object, burning it, burying it, or tossing it into moving water
- Having the patient cross a river in a boat, take their clothes off, leave them on the opposite shore, and come back across the river—thereby leaving their sickness behind with their clothing, symbolically

The magical technique of *bekerítés* ("surrounding") was also a popular healing remedy. There were a number of variations of it, such as:

- A healer tracing a circle around the edges of a wound or skin lesion during the course of a spell to contain the ailment
- A healer walking around a patient, possibly censing them with the smoke of blessed incense
- A laboring woman's husband walking around her to help her release the baby

There were times when a person simply appealed to a higher power to heal them. An old remedy for a sore throat advised the suffering person to kneel upon the earth, repeating "Mother Earth, I tell you, my throat is sore" three times, kissing the ground after each repetition. This was then followed with a Christian addition: instructions for the person to say the Christian *Miatyánk* (known in English as the "Our Father" prayer) while still kneeling. Another healing spell had the healer ritually describe how an eye ailment was caused by the patient walking in the Garden of Eden; they then asked "my lady, my *Boldogasszony*" to lay her blessed hands on the patient.[90] Whatever the method utilized by the healer, it was forbidden to thank a healer for their medicine before the patient was fully cured, or else the cure's potency would be thwarted.

If an entire community was in need of healing, such as in the case of a contagious disease or pandemic, the villagers might join together to perform various rites. One involved having seven women weave linen and prepare a shirt from it. Then, a villager who did not share a name with any other villager carried the shirt to the edge of the town. If the spirit of the illness took the shirt before morning dawned, the plague would leave the town.

90. Gönczi, "Az emberi betegségek gyógyítása a göcseji népnél, második közlemény," 129.

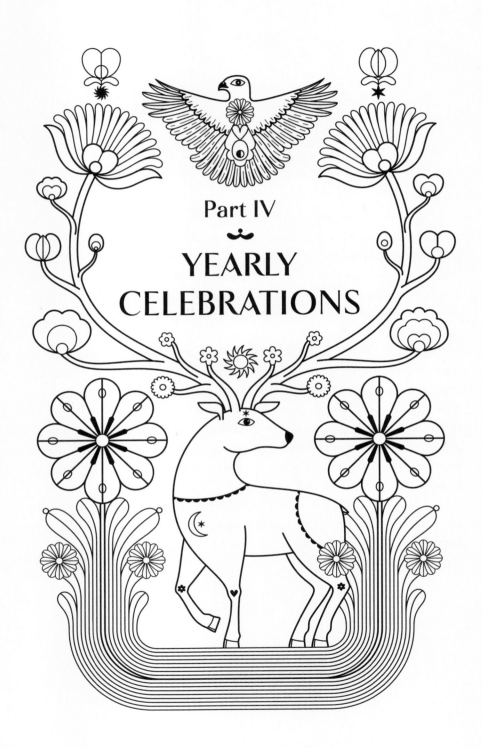

Part IV

YEARLY
CELEBRATIONS

Readers of this book may be familiar with the Wheel of the Year, in which eight equally spaced holidays are celebrated throughout the year on the solstices, equinoxes, and cross-quarter days. Many cultures had celebrations on these days, often themed on what was happening in the natural world. Summer holidays typically had to do with the harvest, springtime holidays had to do with fertility, and so on. Hungarian festivals were no exception to these patterns.

Besides the major holidays like Easter and Christmas, Hungarians also celebrated dozens of smaller festivals called *jeles napok* (which can be roughly translated as "signpost days" or significant/meaningful days) with greater frequency. Not every community celebrated every *jeles nap*, of course, and the traditions varied by region, but many customs were shared through almanacs and formally taught to children through the public school system. As a result, many customs have stood the test of time, and quite a few are still celebrated today!

In this section, we will take a look at the various highlights of the Hungarian year—both the larger holidays and some of the more influential *jeles napok*.

Chapter 16
SACRED TIME

Going from house to house and singing, reciting verses, or performing tricks was common on many *jeles napok* throughout the year.[91] Sometimes children were the main participants, but just as often the participants were young men and/or women, and sometimes grown adults. Performers might wear costumes or bring along noisemakers, blessed branches, or brooms. Many productions included an element of noisemaking, either to wake up good spirits or chase away harmful ones.

When the performers arrived at a home, they had to ask the homeowners for permission before getting started. Some festivals required the participation of the family being visited, such as exchanging answers back and forth or having the *gazda* ceremonially beat the visitors with brooms. If they were given permission, they performed. Many performances included various blessings upon the household. In return for this good magic, performers were rewarded with treats such as money, sweets, fruits, nuts, or pantry staples such as flour or bacon. Young men were often gifted alcohol. If, on the other hand, the performance was not permitted by the homeowners, or if the reward they were offered was scanty, the performers played tricks on the household or said various threats or curses before leaving, such as, "If you do

---

91. In the United States, we still have similar practices: children dress up in costumes on Halloween, go house to house, and collect candy, and in some communities, Christmas carolers still go from house to house.

not give me bacon, I will knock your house beams down," "May a wolf take your pigs!" or "May the bread you bake not rise!"

Name Days

Most of us are familiar with St. Valentine's Day and St. Patrick's Day, but in Hungary, almost every single day of the year was named after a saint.[92] When naming children, parents were allowed to choose from a relatively modest list of possibilities, which were typically the names of the saints. Village birth registries documented how child after child was named Péter, Pál, Mária, Anna, and other religious names. Full names were typically only used on official documents; the community referred to individuals by countless variations or nicknames to distinguish them. (Today, Hungarian officials still publish lists of names parents must choose from when naming their children, but they have many more options and are no longer limited to biblical names.)

Individuals were thought to have a special connection with their saintly namesake and their fellow villagers with whom they shared a name. Various magical rites urged the spellcaster to call on the aid of several villagers who shared a name. For instance, erysipelas, known colloquially as *Szent Antal tüze* ("Saint Anthony's fire"), is a rash that was very common in days past; it was thought that the only way to heal it was to get someone named Antal to cast a curative spell on the skin.

Névnapok ("name days") held as much cultural significance in Hungary as birthdays do in American culture. Although birthdays are also frequently celebrated nowadays, traditionally, family and friends recognized a person on the day associated with their name. For example, everyone named Anna was celebrated on *Szent Anna napja* ("St. Anne's Day"). On name days, special greeting verses called *köszöntők* were recited to the celebrant; these were lighthearted and often humorous, and they blessed the recipient with various forms of good luck. A popular one (which is now also recited on birthdays) is *"Isten éltessen sokáig, füled érjen bokáig!"* which means "May God grant you a long life, until [you are so old that] your ears reach your ankles!" Others were more sentimental, such as the following: "I wish for you many beau-

---

92. Just like Americans shorten St. Valentine's Day to Valentine's Day but do *not* shorten St. Patrick's Day to Patrick's Day, some name days use the *Szent* prefix while others dropped it.

tiful things; may your life be a joy to you. May you bloom on your name day as the lily of the valley blooms in the forest depths!" [93] *Köszöntők* are still popular today, and books and websites publish many examples of verses to use.

Since there are so many name days to keep track of, there are websites and radio stations that proclaim the daily name each morning, and planners and wall calendars are printed with the same information. If you are interested in finding out when your own name day is celebrated, you might have luck pulling up the results with a quick web search of your name and the word *névnap*. If you do not have a Hungarian name (or one with an obvious Hungarian equivalent), there is a good chance that your name does not show up on these lists. You wouldn't be alone. These days, with there being ever-increasing name varieties on the official-approved baby-naming list, as well as having increased cultural diversity, not all names are associated with specific days. Most people in this situation choose a name that either sounds similar to their own or one that has a similar meaning and pick that as their special day to celebrate.

Weather Omens

Americans study the groundhog in early February to see if spring will soon be on its way. Likewise, the Hungarian calendar was filled with folk teachings about weather divination, such as:

- If Mátyás (Saint Matthias) found ice on the ground on his day (February 24), he would break it. If he found none, he would make it. (A colder February predicted a shorter winter.)
- A popular rhyme still heard today goes *Sándor, József, Benedek, zsákban hozzák a meleget!* Literally translated, this means that the saints Sándor, József, and Benedek are bringing warmth in a sack; i.e., the weather turns warm around mid-March.
- Rain on *Margit napja* (June 10) was scorned and was said to be the result of the saint urinating on the earth. If it rained on this day, forty more days of rain would follow, and the harvests would rot.

93. *Neved napjára kívánok sok szépet*
  Legyen számodra boldogság az élet
  Mint gyöngyvirág az erdő közepén
  Úgy viruljon az életed, névnapod ünnepén!

- If the stars shone brightly on the eve of *Jakab napja* (July 25), the weather would soon turn hard. If the Milky Way showed as a light gray, the winter would be short; if it was a dark gray, there would be a lengthy cold season ahead.

- In some regions, they said that if Saint Martin rode in on a white horse (i.e., it snowed) on his festival on November 11, it would be a long winter, but if he rode in on a brown horse (i.e., there was no snow) the winter would be short. In other communities, the exact opposite belief was held, and a clear day predicted a harsher season to come.

Modern Pagans consult tables of correspondences and moon phase charts before performing certain actions. Likewise, the Hungarians believed that there was a right and a wrong time to perform tasks. In this book, a recurring theme is that historically, there was no clear delineation between what was magical and what was not, so even tasks that many would consider to be quite mundane had a "proper" time that they needed to be done.

The differing qualities of nighttime and daytime dictated which activities could take place during each time period. Daytime was for attending to practical, rational matters; nighttime was the domain of the spirits and magic. The sun was regarded as a symbol of goodness whose light kept evil spirits away; at the first crow of the rooster, the ghosts and witches who wandered the countryside dissipated into the mists. Water drawn from a well or river at dawn on a holiday was called *aranyvíz* ("golden water") and was a source of luck and magic. The first rays of the sun were greeted with prayer and were known for their healing qualities, which were utilized in some restorative spells. If someone had a high fever, for example, a close relative could wrap themselves in the patient's bedsheets and run out to a hillside to meet the rising sun, then trample the sheets while shouting various commands to make the fever leave the patient.

Many actions that were safe in the daylight were unsafe to do after dark, when the protection of the sun had dissipated. It was true that criminals and predators both tended to prefer the cover of darkness, but the danger was more than physical. In the nighttime, evil creatures like witches and ghosts roamed the countryside. It was best to stay in the borders of the villages and to avoid wandering outdoors alone. And yet, even though people were more at risk of falling under a curse in the night, these hours were also a time when beneficial magic was more potent as well: spellcasting, divination, and picking herbs for magical use were all activities that were best performed under the light of the moon.

The Days of the Week

Different days of the week were thought to be auspicious for certain tasks and unlucky for others. Almanacs passed down these bits of wisdom to the populace, although there was great local variance of lucky-versus-unlucky days for various tasks. In general, the earlier in the week, the better it was to start new tasks, leave on journeys, enter into business deals, and so on. Midweek was the best time to plant vegetables and flowers, while it was decidedly bad luck to start new projects on Fridays. Many people ordered their lives according to the ideal time to perform even small tasks as mundane as cutting nails: cutting nails on Sundays would lead to fights within the household; in contrast, it was good luck to cut them on Mondays or Fridays.

The origins of honoring Tuesdays are hazy at best, but they seem to be heavily influenced by Slavic beliefs and customs. Especially in the eastern and southeastern parts of the country, the day was associated with a figure known as the *kedd asszonya* ("Tuesday's woman") or the *kedd boszorkánya* ("Tuesday's witch"). Others said the day was sacred to the *Boldogasszony*, Saint Anna, Saint Lucy, or the Virgin Mary. In communities where this entity had more positive associations, Tuesday was a good day to start new ventures because she blessed efforts started on her day. She was also the patron of pregnant women, and fasting on Tuesday would aid a woman in conceiving a child. "Since [the *kedd asszonya*] was the goddess of new life and new beginnings, we should start work on her day...[but] it is not good to end things on her day...as this would offend [her]."[94]

In communities where the *kedd asszonya* had a darker image, Tuesday was considered an unlucky day. In these areas, it was not unheard of for people to shut themselves into their homes after dusk, with some even refusing to work inside their homes for fear of being reprimanded by the spirit.

94. Kálmány, *Boldogasszony*, 9.

Even in less-stringent communities, the *kedd asszonya* was the patroness of spinning and working with fiber. Her sacred work associations included sewing, embroidery, knitting, weaving, spinning, and washing—and none of these tasks were allowed to be done on her day. It was said that if a young woman attended the *fonó* on a Tuesday evening, the devil would force her to dance until she died from exhaustion. If a woman did work with fiber on a Tuesday, the fearsome *kedd asszonya* would slap her face, slam her doors open in the middle of the night, or break her spinning wheels. The woman might also scald herself, become mute or deaf, or have various body parts paralyzed.

Washing clothes on Tuesdays was the equivalent of placing the *Boldogasszony*'s hands in scalding water. Some avoided washing or combing their hair. Even bathing a baby was forbidden—the result would be a child with frequent headaches, so it was better if the child was wiped with a damp cloth instead. It was also forbidden to wash clothes on Fridays; throughout the country, legends were told about a community that was stricken by repeated lightning strikes until one person confessed to wearing clothes that had been washed on a Friday. Once they took off the clothes, the lightning strikes stopped.

Friday had positive associations with spellcasting; both healing spells and love spells were often specified as needing to be performed on Fridays. Pregnant women in some communities fasted on Fridays, and babies who had various birthmarks or were late in talking or walking could undergo various healing rites on Fridays as well.

Saturday was a day of preparation for Sunday. The family baked their *kalács* for the Sunday meal and also cleaned the home. People had to purify not only their homes but themselves as well. It was said that those who donned fresh, clean underclothes on Saturday while making the sign of the cross would have the Virgin Mary herself beg her son to forgive the wearer's sins; others said that they would be free from disease if they wore fresh underclothes. The sun would be sure to shine on Saturday, if only for a little while; the explanation given was that the Virgin Mary could wash and dry the infant Jesus's diapers. As this was a day of purification and preparation, it was unlucky to do other kinds of work such as picking grapes or spinning. (In the latter case, the household chickens would develop leg deformities.)

Sunday was considered the final day of the week, and traditional practices centered around religion and community. People attended church services first thing in the morning, then returned home to have a leisurely, multi-course lunch. The afternoon and evening were spent visiting friends and family in the village. (According to a survey, the results of which were published in 2022, only 7 to 9 percent of Hungarians attend weekly church services;[95] the concept of "Sunday lunch" is so ingrained in the culture that many families still get together for a leisurely, multicourse meal with relatives.)

On Sundays, as on major holidays, it was prohibited to do any nonessential work whatsoever. Animals were not taken out to pasture, barns were not mucked out, no one worked in the fields or gardens, and no regular household chores such as cooking, baking, washing dishes, or sweeping were done. People could not exchange money, borrow, or lend. It was forbidden to disturb the sanctity of the day in any way. The day itself could be personified as a spirit; if someone did work on Sunday, another person might angrily correct them, saying, "*Verjen meg a Vasárnap!*" ("May Sunday strike you [if you do not cease your work]!")[96]

Consequences for working on prohibited days could be minor (like bread not rising properly) or severe (the entire year's harvest failing). Other severe consequences included a person being turned to stone, lightning hitting a home, being bitten by a snake, or a calamity striking the person or their belongings. Many illnesses and conditions were explained by saying that the victim had done some prohibited action on a certain festival or day of the week (e.g., a woman who ate sausages at her wedding feast would get swollen legs).

95. Máté-Tóth and Rosta, "Vallási riport, 1991–2022."
96. Róheim, "Kedd asszonya," 91.

Chapter 17

WINTER

While modern Hungarians follow the familiar four-season calendar of the temperate Northern Hemisphere, many traditional accounts only refer to two seasons: winter and summer. St. George's Day in late April and St. Michael's Day in late September are most often cited as the days the seasons switched from one to the other. Summer days were long and busy, and many people spent entire days out-of-doors in various agricultural pursuits; in contrast, the winters of the Carpathian Basin were dark and frigid, and they stretched on for many months. The people filled their days making tools and handicrafts and spent time with one another amidst festive music, dancing, and storytelling.

In the old days, some people considered the winter solstice the start of the new year, and others considered springtime as the mark of the occasion. Since the sixteenth century, however, the first day of January has been the official start of the Hungarian New Year, so this is where we begin our study of the Hungarian year as well.

The festivities began the night before, on *Szilveszter* ("Sylvester's Day"). One or more villagers could dress up as a chimney sweep and sweep good luck into the village. Throughout the afternoon and evening hours, villagers went from house to house, singing short rhyming verses that wished the householders good luck in the coming year. Verses invoked *bort, búzát, békességet* ("wine, wheat, and peace"); other popular blessings included wishes for health and wealth for all. These themes were repeated in many songs and rhymes and continue to be a traditional New Year's greeting today.

As the sun was setting, a young man dressed up as an old man to personify the "old year." He put on tattered clothing, a torn hat, and a fake white beard. The other villagers shouted, made noise, and chased him out of the village. Outside of town, the youth cast off his tattered clothing and threw it into a blazing bonfire. After a few toasts, the young man returned to the village to be greeted joyfully by the others. In another variation on this custom, the "old year" was chased down the main street by a child or youth who struck him with branches or a broomstick, demonstrating how the new year was chasing away the old.

During the course of the night, it was vital to frighten away evil spirits who might bring ill fortune to the new year. As on many other special days of the Hungarian calendar, ritual noisemaking, usually performed by older boys and young men, was a part of the New Year's festivities. This was known by different names including *csattogtatás* ("cracking of the whips") or *kongózás* ("clanging"). Methods included cracking whips specially woven for the occasion, hanging bells around the neck, ringing cowbells, or banging together pots, pans, or other pieces of metal. For added protection, church bells were also rung at midnight. The tradition of making noise at midnight to ring in the new year is celebrated in many regions of the world to this day.

The *aranyvíz* ("the golden water") was the first water of the year to be drawn from a well or river. It was rumored to have magical properties, and washing one's face with it ensured freshness and health throughout the coming months. The first person in the household to wake up had to silently fetch the water. Upon returning to the house, they were greeted by the others, who ritually asked what they had brought home. The person said, "I brought strength and health, blessings, peace, and luck!"[97] The householders could drink from the water to absorb the luck. The remaining water was splashed toward the house in hopes that wealth would also flow into the house by the bucketful.

If the first visitor to a household in the new year was male, good fortune would soon arrive; the opposite was the case if the first visitor was female.

97. Paládi-Kovács, *Magyar néprajz nyolc kötetben*, vol. 7, 110.

(In the latter case, all the household dishes would soon shatter.) Early in the morning, the men and boys of the community went from house to house, hoping to bring luck to their neighbors. They scattered wheat or sunflower seeds, corn kernels, or rye while shouting blessings upon the household. The *gazda* gifted the men wine or coins in return for their efforts. After their visitors left, the *gazdasszony* gathered the seeds and feed them to her chickens to make them healthy and lay well.

The way a person acted on the first day of the year determined their fate for the rest of the year. Wishes spoken aloud would manifest, so people greeted one another with positive words to attract good luck into the community. Whatever happened to a person that day, good or bad, would repeat through the year. People avoided fighting with one another lest they have a violent year ahead of them. If someone was hurt by another, they faced a year full of abuse. People were advised not to lie down during the day lest they lie in bed, sick, in the coming months; even the bedridden were encouraged to get up and move around so that they would rise in health during the year.

It was vital to not chase good luck away from the home on the first day of the new year. Nothing could be removed from the house, not even trash—nor should anything be lent to a neighbor. Money should not leave the house either. It was also frowned upon to borrow anything from another person, as that would mean being beholden to others for the rest of the year. Even dust that was swept had to remain in the house, and manure could not be shoveled out of barns. Of course, no one wanted to go into the new year with a dirty, messy home, which would attract bad luck, so everything had to be put in order, mended, cleaned, and decluttered in the weeks prior to the holiday.

If the first day of the new year was sunny, this was a good omen; a stormy day was an ominous one. A red dawn foretold windy days ahead, and visible stars predicted a short winter. Forecasting the weather by using an onion was common, and many variations existed. In one version, on New Year's Eve, the *gazda* took an onion and peeled one layer for each month, lining the pieces up on the windowsill. On each layer, he sprinkled some salt. The next morning, the amount of liquid in each peel predicted the precipitation in each of the coming months: if the salt melted into a puddle, the month would have much rain or snow, but if the salt remained crystallized, dry weather would dominate.

It was important to eat special, auspicious foods on the first day of the year in an effort to bring good luck. Foods reminiscent of coins (such as lentils, rice, or barley) would increase the household's wealth. An entire loaf of bread was placed upon the table so the family would never want for food in the coming year. Pork was eaten in the belief that the spirit of the pig would root out treasure. The women of the household prepared a pastry called a *rétes*; if the dough stretched well without breaking, the family would have good luck in the coming year.

Some foods needed to be avoided, such as sauerkraut, which would sour a family's fortune in the new year. If one ate poppyseeds, they would get fleas. My grandfather loved fish, but would never eat it on the New Year lest the family's wealth swim away; similarly, eating poultry would cause wealth to be scratched away.

Although not all the traditional customs are followed today (few people are silently rushing to the river to fetch purifying water at dawn!), New Year's is still a day for festivities, celebration, and looking forward to the future. People eat lucky foods, set off fireworks, dance, blow noisemakers, and, in some areas, symbolically burn figures to represent the passing of the old year.

Farsang

The season of *farsang* started after the twelve days of Christmas were over and lasted until Lent. The name of this season comes from the German word *Fasching*, which refers to a festive drinking toast. True to the name, *farsang* was a festive time full of parties and gatherings, feasting, dances, games of skill and chance, and a special fried treat similar to a donut called a *farsangi fánk*. At get-togethers that involved dancing, guests were encouraged to jump as high as they could during the celebrations so that in the coming seasons, the crops would grow as tall as they jumped. Many young people made good use of all the community get-togethers to find a marriage partner.

One of the most important components of *farsang* was storytelling. While today many people assume that fairy tales are merely for children, traditionally people of all ages listened to them. On long, winter evenings, families would gather around fires and spend the night listening to stories, legends, and myths. Instead of being seen as childish, magical feats and mythical beings were natural additions to these tales, something people of all ages came to expect.

Storytelling was also a method of passing down social teachings in an indirect way. Besides describing the world of spirits and magic, the traditional tales reinforced social values important to the people, such as wit, persistence, and bravery. Different stories were told to people of different genders, ages, professions, and social statuses. Stories for young adults often had lewd elements, and many were interactive, needing audience participation. Popular stock characters for stories of all ages included witches, giants, elves, midwives, fairies, peasants, kings, judges, and magical animals. Newer stories highlighted dualistic characters, with Christian characters substituted for earlier pre-Christian entities. Thus, a wise character named Jesus was set up in opposition to a less-noble character named *Szent Péter*, and sometimes God himself was said to be facing off with the devil. These characters would argue and enter competitions, which often ended in humorous results.

Formulaic beginnings indicated that the listener was about to hear a fairy tale and was not expected to interpret the story with ordinary human logic. The typical beginning of a made-up story was *"Egyszer volt, hol nem volt,"* meaning "Once there was, where there was not." That was usually followed up by a description of the fantasy world where the story was set. Typically, this was deemed to be "past the Óperencia Sea." As the Óperencia was itself mythical, this beginning hinted that the story took place in the spirit world, which was governed by different rules than our world was.

In contrast, many legends—thought to be true accounts, even if they included magical elements—were prefaced with "This really happened." The same phrase was also used later to indicate that the legend had ended, reiterating the fact that the storyteller truly believed the tale to be true; these were known as "living belief stories." Other legends ended with the speaker stating "But this is just a story," indicating that either the story was purposely made-up or that it was once believed to be true, but not any longer.

Gyertyaszentelő Boldogasszony

Many cultures celebrate the lengthening days of late winter with a festival of light. The cross-quarter day halfway between the winter solstice and the spring equinox is known by many as the holiday of Imbolc. In Hungary, this festival is known as *Gyertyaszentelő Boldogasszony* ("Candle-Blessing *Boldogasszony*"). True to the festival's name, candles were traditionally blessed on this day for ritual use throughout the year. Blessed candles were a versatile object; they could be lit on holidays, at the bedsides of the sick and dying, to clear the air after arguments in the household, or during terrible storms, especially ones where lightning or hail threatened. When not in use, blessed candles were traditionally kept in a decorated chest or special drawer. Alternatively, they might be displayed in front of the family's sacred artwork or decorated with ribbons and displayed on the wall in a prominent place.

Gyertyaszentelő Boldogasszony was also a day for weather divination. People said that it was better for a wolf to howl from the cold on this day than for the sun to shine. And while Americans check if the groundhog sees its shadow, the Magyar people watched for an emerging bear or badger; if the animal saw its shadow, it retreated into its den because the winter was not yet over.

Bálint-nap

Szent Bálint—the same figure Americans know as Saint Valentine—is associated with love, but in traditional Hungary, the most significant aspect of *Bálint-nap* was its association with birds. This was a lucky day for the family hens to incubate their eggs, and it was also the day when sparrows were believed to choose their matches. If a young woman saw a sparrow on *Bálint-nap*, she would marry a poor man but be happy; if she saw a finch instead, she would marry a wealthier man but would be less happy. In some communities, birds were fed seeds and dried fruits on *Bálint-nap*, while in others, it was a day to practice deterrent magic to keep birds away from the vineyards; pruning a grapevine at each of the vineyard's four corners was believed to be protective.

Busójárás

Of all the *farsang* festivities, perhaps one of the most widely known today is the *Busójárás* ("Procession of the *Busó*")—so well-known, in fact, that in 2009 the event was added to the UNESCO World Heritage List. The festival, celebrated in the city of Mohács in southern Hungary, features men dressed up in shaggy costumes with frightening carved masks of various devils. According to legend, the local populace frightened away the invading Turkish armies wearing such outfits, while in other accounts the tradition was linked to frightening away the spirit of winter itself. For this reason, an alternate name for the festivities was *téltemetés* ("the burial of winter"). The *Busójárás* festival now lasts nearly a week, and up to ten thousand visitors come from far and wide to join in the processions. Pictures of the frightening *busó* are widely circulated on social media.

The End of *Farsang*

The last three days of *farsang* were known as *farsangfarka* ("the tail of *farsang*"). This was an especially raucous time, comparable to Carnival in other nations. Costumed revelers paraded through the streets, playing tricks on the other festival-goers or stealing food from various village pantries. Young men dressed up as roosters and jumped onto maidens, imitating roosters jumping on hens; since roosters were a symbol of virility, this act was believed to make the young women fertile. The young women rewarded them with eggs, which the men gathered into baskets.

Each community had to hold at least one wedding during *farsang*. If this did not happen, a mock wedding feast was arranged during *farsangfarka* to avert bad luck. In this type of mock wedding, a man stood in for the bride and a woman stood in for the groom. Instead of a chest containing a marriage dowry, a broken chest was placed on a wagon normally used to haul manure. This wagon was rolled through the streets, accompanied by parodies of wedding or funeral songs. When it arrived outside the town limits, it was set on fire or set afloat in the river.

On the last day of *farsang*, the community staged a mock beheading. Someone dressed up as a prisoner, and the villagers accused him of all the crimes that had taken place in the community within the last year: thefts, fights, vandalism, and so on. At the conclusion of the accusations, the prisoner was symbolically beheaded. In certain villages, the "body" of the prisoner was carried inside the tavern, sat at the head of the table, and symbolically toasted by the other guests, as if he was the guest of honor at a funerary feast.

At the end of the day's celebrations, a young man put on fancy clothes and padded out the clothing, dressing up as a fat king to represent *farsang*. Another youth dressed up in rags to represent a scrawny servant, a nod to the coming season of Lent. After a dramatic mock sword fight, the servant slayed (or chased away) the king and emerged victorious. The time for joy, merriment, and feasting had come to an end. Now, it was time to fast.

Chapter 18
EASTERTIDE

Food was in short supply in late winter and early spring. The Catholic Church reinforced this scarcity by designating the forty days before Easter as a time of the Lenten fast, known in Hungary as *Nagyböjt* ("the Great Fast"). Today, fasting is not universal, and it is mostly performed in a religious context, but back in the day, *Nagyböjt* was celebrated by the entire populace. True to its name, the most defining aspect of *Nagyböjt* had to do with dietary restrictions. In the old days, people ate one meal a day, which consisted of salted bread and plain vegetables. Over time, these rules became more relaxed. On some days, neither food nor drink could be consumed, whereas on other days, people could eat small, infrequent meals as long as they refrained from consuming meat. Some communities (as well as more pious individuals) took a harsher attitude toward fasting, such as refraining from eating dairy products or eggs, or eating from special dishes only used during Lent. A bran-based, sour soup named *kiszi* or *cibere* was widely eaten during this season.

In the weeks before *Nagyböjt*, people tried to eat all the food in their pantries so that they would not consume it during the fasting season. On the day before the fast started, known as *Húshagyókedd*, "Meat-Leaving Tuesday" (known as Fat Tuesday in many English-speaking regions), the people ate as much food as they could and expressed hopes that as they grew fat, their pigs would grow fat as well. In some communities, the custom was to eat seven (or even nine) times that day. Due to the festival's name, this was also a good day to protect livestock (specifically baby chicks) from predators via various magical means. One spell involved looking at chicks through the eyes of a pig's skull and ordering birds of prey to be blind to them. Another involved throwing the innards and feathers of a chicken killed on this day in a distant bush so that potential predators would look elsewhere.

The following day, *Hamvazószerda* ("Ash Wednesday"), was the official first day of Lent. The faithful went to church in the morning to receive a smear of blessed ashes on their foreheads, as many do today; in the old days, this was thought to prevent headaches. (If a community did not have a priest to bless ashes for them, the villagers could make their own by burning the pussywillows blessed on the previous Easter.) Older generations did not light a fire on this day, and the women spread the blessed ashes from church around their home to keep sin and sorrow away. In some communities, women even marked their dishes and utensils with ashes.

During *Nagyböjt*, people could not get married or attend public celebrations such as dances. Some said that if a person danced during Lent, their fruit trees would bear little fruit for the rest of the year—or worse. According to one legend, the young people of a village held a dance the evening before Lent started. At midnight, all the couples stopped dancing, except for one couple who refused to do so despite their peers begging them to stop. In the morning, both the dancers and the building they had gathered in had sunk into the ground as punishment for their blasphemy. In strict communities, people could not even sing or whistle to themselves, and young women who normally dressed in bright colors would dress in simple, darker-colored garments.

However, for all but the most pious individuals, the Lenten weeks were not an altogether quiet and solemn time. Villagers set up special temporary playgrounds, and both boys and girls played ball games and team sports with one another. One popular game was called *mancsozás* ("the paw game"). This involved balls being thrown into the air, which the players hit with bats. Whoever was unable to hit the ball on its way down was out of the round. Girls made the balls for the game out of rags covered with cowhide, while boys carved the bats and gifted them to the girls they liked. Boys also used sticks to throw wooden hoops into the air or rolled or threw them to one another. Older boys lit the hoops on fire for an extra challenge. Sometimes they sent the hoops flying in the air while shouting aloud the name of a girl they wished to magically ensnare within it.

In many communities, instrumental music and dancing were forbidden during *Nagyböjt*. In less strict communities, people could still dance as long as it was only amongst their same gender, and people were permitted to sing as long as there was no instrumental accompaniment. Young men performed dances with various acrobatic skills, and both genders danced while imitating various animals. Circle dances—a category of traditional folk dances performed by girls and women—were another popular option; many told stories and had symbolic movements. In some regions, girls and young women danced by riversides, springs, or meadows as they sang songs inviting spring into the community.

Nagyhét

The festivities of the *Húsvét* ("Easter") season celebrate the martyrdom and subsequent resurrection of Jesus. The week before *Húsvét* is known as Holy Week to English speakers and *Nagyhét* ("Great Week") in Hungary. During this last week of Lent, people were more strict about fasting. It was important to purify not only the spirit during this time, but also physical surroundings. The house was aired out and deep cleaned. (As usual, there were exceptions to this rule. Near the village of Zenta, for example, people were warned not to clean anything during this week, otherwise the house would become ridden with fleas.) After purifying their physical bodies, people confessed their sins to a priest, thereby cleansing their souls as well.

The Sunday before *Húsvét*—what English speakers know as Palm Sunday—was known in Hungary as *Virágvasárnap* ("Flower Sunday"). The *gazdasszony* traditionally planted flowers the week prior so that they would bloom beautifully all spring. Pussywillows were brought to the church to be blessed and handed out to the parishioners. The branches, known as *barka* (or, less commonly, the *pimpó*), had many magical uses, mostly protective and healing in nature. Branches were taken into cemeteries after the church service so that the dead could rest peacefully; others were stuck in fields and gardens so neither hail nor pests would damage the crops. In some places, a priest would bless a bucket of water into which the villagers would dip their *pimpó*, then return home to sprinkle the water onto their homes.

Blessed *barka*

Some believed that the blessed *barka* should never be brought into the main parts of the house because flies would follow it. In other areas, the exact opposite was recommended: families placed their *barka* next to the home's altar, hung it from rafters, or fastened it to gateposts. This protected a home against physical threats such as lightning, illness, and hail, and it also served as protection from the supernatural: witches' curses, evil spirits, and the evil eye could all be warded off by the smoke of the burning branches. A compromise between the two opposing beliefs was to take the branches into the attic or cellar. To this day, my relatives have a branch or two visible in their homes at all times, sometimes stuck in quite incongruous places—my grandmother preferred to keep hers stuck in an old lemon juice bottle on the shelf next to her television.

The *barka* had countless uses. Some of these included:

- If someone had a sore throat, they could swallow one of the buds for relief.
- During storms, the buds or branches could be burned for protection against lightning or hail.
- Making a cross with the branches and hanging it over the barn doors would protect the cows' milk from being stolen magically; striking the cows with the branches would ensure their milk did not turn bloody.
- Placing the branches in front of beehives would make the bees give plenty of honey.
- Throwing buds into a well would make its water stay clear and clean.
- A child who was affected by the evil eye could be hung upside down over burning *barka*; the smoke would cure the child from their curse.

The eggs laid during *Nagyhét* were saved to be decorated for *Húsvét*. Women competed to see who could design the most intricate *hímes tojás*.[98] They dyed the eggs with onion skins, vegetable peels, tree bark, and other natural materials, then painted various geometric designs with sacred meanings. The most popular color to dye eggs was red; in fact, in some regions the Easter egg was simply known as the *pirostojás* ("red egg"). These could be used in various spells and were also given as a romantic gift, and placing one of these eggs into one's washing water would ensure ruddy cheeks through the year. If someone ate one of these eggs before Easter Sunday, it was said their breath would be bad for a whole year.

The Thursday of *Nagyhét* was *Zöldcsütörtök* ("Green Thursday") and was traditionally celebrated as a day to ensure health for the coming year. True to its name, green food was consumed by both people and animals, most often taking the form of spinach and nettles to keep those consuming the leaves fresh and strong. Garlic was also eaten as protection from snakebites. After sunset, the *gazdasszony* could sweep around the house so that it would be free of irksome frogs for the year.

Nagypéntek, known in English as Good Friday, is the anniversary of the day when Jesus was martyred. In some communities, no fires were to be lit on

---

98. The term *húsvéti tojás* also refers to Easter eggs, but *hímes tojás* refer specifically to the decorated ones.

Nagypéntek as a sign of mourning. In others, the opposite custom was practiced, and villagers lit ceremonial bonfires with various explanations, such as the original disciples waiting by firelight near the tomb of Jesus. In the morning, an anthill was dug up and thrown into the pigpen so there would be as many piglets born as there were ants in the pen. *Nagypéntek* was one of several days in the Hungarian calendar when people ritually washed themselves and the animals in their care. It was said that if a person immersed in water three times before the sun rose, no infectious diseases would be able to get a hold of them in the coming year. Afterward, girls and women would comb their hair under willow trees so their hair would grow long. Although many communities prohibited routine work, an exception was made to allow women to bake a loaf of bread; this loaf was stored in the attic to prevent the home from burning down that year.

A type of whip woven for Easter festivities

Men and boys publicly scourged themselves on *Nagypéntek*. Flagellation with a special braided whip known as a *korbács* or the *siba* was one form of springtime purification. Men and boys struck themselves (or one another) while chanting instructions to the body to maintain good health in the coming year. Verses commanded various body parts to behave in certain ways (e.g., the hands should be deft, the head should not hurt, the feet should run swiftly). As each body part was mentioned, the scourge was struck on the corresponding body part.

At dawn the next morning, on *Nagyszombat* ("Holy Saturday"), the villagers lit a sacred fire in front of the church called the *újtűz* ("new fire"). Not only were the candles for the holiday service lit from this fire, but each household also took a lit candle home to their oven so that they could cook the Easter feast on its flames. As usual, the barnyard animals were not forgotten; a few embers from the bonfire were placed in each creature's watering trough. The ashes from the sacred fire were scattered throughout the house or garden, or they were saved for future use; during a lightning storm, a handful of the ash could be thrown into the oven so lightning would not hit the home.

Easter Sunday

On Sunday morning, the family headed to church. Children and young adults received new boots, usually red or yellow. Even young brides expected their new husbands to buy them a lucky pair of boots. It was not unheard of for the women to go barefoot through the streets to avoid getting mud on their new footwear, only pulling their boots on once they arrived at the church doors. Women also brought baskets full of food, known collectively as the *kókonya*, to church so that the priest could bless their holiday meals. The festive dishes included ham, *kalács* (sometimes with eggs braided into the loaf), hard-boiled eggs, horseradish, wine, and fresh spring greens.

After the lengthy church service, the family returned home. Sometimes the members of the household ran home instead of walking; whichever family reached their house first would have the most successful harvest that year. The blessed foods were consumed on a table spruced up with springtime branches and decorated eggs. But eggs were not only used for decoration and sustenance at the Easter table—when one egg was split between two people, the two would grow closer, and if separated, they would always remember one another. After the meal, the blessed food remnants were strategically placed around the homestead. The other leftovers were saved to crumble and sprinkle onto the fields in the shape of a cross to keep birds away or buried near the house to keep troubles away. Ham bones were especially useful: they were hung from fruit trees so they would produce well. During storms, a ham bone could be thrown into the fireplace so that lightning wouldn't strike the house.

The afternoon was spent visiting friends and family, and children played games with the eggs they received throughout the day. After the sun had set, a decidedly less heartwarming custom took place: the young men of the village got together and brought satirical gifts to those villagers who had broken the norms of conduct in the previous year. If a woman gave birth out of wedlock, she was gifted with a cradle. Thieves were gifted chains, drunks were gifted a bottle of alcohol, and so on. This ritualized shaming was known as the *didergés*, "the shivering."

While in the United States Easter is thought of as a single-day holiday, this was not the case in Hungary, where it was a holiday lasting two (and sometimes three) days. *Húsvéthétfő*, "Easter Monday," was an essential part of the holiday festivities, on which the young men of the village "watered" the girls and women at dawn in a practice known as *locsolás*. The men asked a young woman for permission to water her with a verse. Some of these verses were humorous, others vaguely threatening, and some described the magical rewards of being watered, such as having one's hair grow long like the tail of a colt. Many times, the verse was just a formality; whether or not she gave her permission, the young woman was carried off (sometimes willingly, sometimes forcibly) and thrown into a river or trough, or she had a bucket of cold water poured onto her. The young women got revenge on the culprits the following day, *Húsvétkedd* ("Easter Tuesday"). The girls gathered in groups and lay in wait for the young men to walk by, then threw buckets of water on them or beat them with sticks. The guilty parties often snuck through the backs of yards to avoid their fate.

Today, most people have forgotten about the traditions of Easter Tuesday. Sunday and Monday remain the focus of family visits, decorated eggs, chocolate brought by the Easter Bunny, *pálinka*, and of course, *locsolás*! Nowadays, *locsolás* is not nearly as violent but retains some of the same imagery:

men and boys spritz scented water or perfume on female family members, friends, or romantic partners while saying verses. In a modern twist, some young men turn to social media to exchange their favorite rhymes, ranging from sentimental to lewd to humorous. The tradition lives on!

Chapter 19
SPRING

When winter was nearing its end, the community celebrated a ritual known as the *kiszehajtás* ("driving away of the *kisze*"). The young women of the village made a straw figure and dressed it up as a bride or old woman. They named this figure the *kisze* or the *banya* ("hag") and paraded it through the main streets of the village, singing songs with lyrics talking about taking the *kisze* out and bringing in various things in its place (birdsong, green branches, warmth, etc.). Villagers watched the figure carefully to see which way the *kisze* turned in the wind; if its face looked backward, toward the village, winter would soon return.

After walking through the main streets of the town, the girls went to the river. They gathered fistfuls of straw, then threw the *kisze* into the river to be washed away. As it disappeared, the girls shouted at it, ordering it to take the winter away. Then they tossed the clumps of straw into the water to see which one floated downstream the fastest, as that indicated which girl would marry the soonest. Wiping one's face with the clump of straw before throwing it in the water would send any freckles or spots away with it. If there was no river available, the *kisze* could be burned in a bonfire instead, and the girls danced around it.

One example of a *kisze* figure

The men of the village had their own form of welcoming springtime. This was known as "walking the borders," or *határjárás*. They gathered at dawn (or dusk, depending on the community). By the light of torches, they walked the outer limits of their village territory, making noise by chanting, whistling, shouting, drumming, and shooting guns. They performed practical activities, such as replacing missing border markers, clearing out streams, and examining bridges and roads. They also performed a magical activity whereby they woke up protective spirits from their winter rest and reminded them of their duties. A young person who was walking the borders for the first time was buried up to his waist or given several lashes with a stick at each border marking to help them remember the landmark.

Another popular springtime custom was known as *zöldágazás* ("green-branching") or *zöldágjárás* ("walking the green branch"). Although the tradition's specifics varied from community to community, the basic premise was taking budding branches from living trees in the wilderness, carrying them into the villages, and tying them onto fences, gateposts, and homes. In some places, schoolchildren decorated the towns. In others, men tied branches to homes in which their female acquaintances of any age lived; since most homes had at least one woman living in them, nearly the entire town would be decorated in such a way. Still another variety of green-branching, known as *villőzés*, involved young women carrying branches from house to house, then making archways out of them through which a *gazdasszony* could drive her hens and chicks so they would be healthy. In return, the *gazdasszony* struck the young women with the branches while wishing they would find a husband soon.

A popular children's game played around this time of year is called *Bújj, bújj, zöld ág*, meaning, "Go through, go through, green branch." In the game, children line up in two columns and join hands to create a tunnel through which other children must pass. It is believed that this game, along with similar games, is a remnant of older rites that used to be performed in pre-Christian times, the movements of which faded into child's play over time.

On certain days—usually on *Szent György napja*, the first of May, or the holiday of *Pünkösd*—women got up before dawn to gather dew by dragging a piece of cloth (such as a sheet, tablecloth, skirt, or apron) on the grass, then wrung the wet cloth into a bowl or pitcher. While collecting dew, it was important to chant *Hagyok is, viszek is* ("I take some, I leave some") or some variation on that verse. Many stories warn of the dangers that might happen if this verse was omitted.

Magical dew had many uses. It could be added to bread dough to make the loaves rise better, given to cows so they would give richer milk, and used in beauty and healing magic. Watering plants in the garden with blessed dew helped them grow. A sheet used to collect dew could be laid on the wheat field while it was still damp so the remaining magic would seep into the wheat stalks.

Gyümölcsoltó Boldogasszony

The festival of *Gyümölcsoltó Boldogasszony* was celebrated on March 25. It alludes to the process of grafting trees, an agricultural technique by which two trees were joined together in hopes that they bore more fruit than they would have individually. Trees grafted on this day would survive and produce much fruit, but if the tree was cut down, it would bleed as a human would. The guilty party who harmed the tree would go blind and be further punished in the *Túlvilág*.

The priests could not eradicate the deeply ingrained customs of this springtime festival, and they permitted the populace to celebrate it by explaining that it was the day that God had created the world. It is notable that the date falls nine months before Christmas. Although we have different ways of measuring pregnancy in modern times, in traditional wisdom, this was considered the day that Jesus would have been conceived per the Christian calendar (and roughly when light would have been conceived, if one was celebrating the rebirth of the sun at the winter solstice). Because of these symbolic conceptions, it was considered an especially productive day to conceive a child.

Szent György napja

April 24 was *Szent György napja* ("St. George's Day"). Countless magical traditions were associated with the festival and the evening preceding it. In certain regions, these same celebrations were held on the first of May or even later in the season. However, *Szent György napja* was widely considered the most popular day for witches, second only in popularity to *Luca napja* in

December, so for simplicity's sake, I have encompassed these customs with April 24.

On the eve of the festival, witches were purported to meet on mountain-tops for diabolical revelries. Households guarded their properties by burning incense, washing their milk pitchers out with blessed herbs, or decorating their gateposts with wild rose branches or garlic to keep the witches at bay as they traveled through the countryside. If the witches managed to carve an unguarded gatepost, they could steal all the milk from the household.

In many communities, it was on *Szent György napja* that livestock was herded out to the pastures after spending the winter in the safety of the barn. The occasion was cause for celebration, with music, dancing, and feasting, echoing the ancient Roman rites of Palilia (or Parilia), the holiday of the shepherds. Animals, shepherds, and any young female attendees were all doused with buckets of water for good health and fertility. Then, the herds-men drove their animals over various magically protective items such as axes, chains, ploughs, or the apron of the household's *gazdasszony*; these were all thought to protect the livestock from witches, illness, and wandering off. Shepherds also used switches on the animals in hopes that they would give lots of milk.

Szent György was, according to legend, a slayer of dragons. Thus, reptiles—especially snakes and lizards—were caught on his day and used in various healing spells, especially for sore throats. One spell involved catching a lizard and rubbing it against one's throat while intoning, "May my throat hurt only when this little lizard's does." [99]

This was also a potent day for thieving magic; if thieves were able to steal something on the eve of *Szent György napja*, they would more successfully steal for the rest of the year.

Május elseje

Hungary celebrated *Május elseje*, the first day of May, with decorated *májusfák* ("May trees"). Priests justified the practice by emphasizing a legend in which a young woman joined two missionaries on their journey as they walked from town to town, preaching God's word. A group of people saw her

99. Pócs, *Magyar ráolvasások I*, 102.

walk out of the city with the missionaries and assumed that she was being unchaste, fraternizing with males. They pursued the trio, hoping to bring her back into town and make an example of her to other women. When she realized what was happening, the young woman struck her walking stick into the ground, knelt down beside it, and started praying. The walking stick sprouted leaves and became the first *májusfa*. When her pursuers saw this miracle unfolding, they realized God had blessed her endeavors and left her unharmed.

There were two main types of *májusfák*: a romantic gift and a community tree. The ideal tree used as a romantic gift varied from region to region; popular varieties included birch and willow. Some were entire trees, whereas others were just the trunks stripped of bark, and still others were green branches attached to beams or poles. The branches could have already sprouted green leaves or still be in blossom, but either way, they needed to be young and fresh.

A young man took special care to choose the perfect tree and relocate it in front of his sweetheart's front door in the night, sometimes carrying a tree for several kilometers. (Stealing a tree from public property was technically illegal, but the custom persisted throughout the centuries.) Once the tree was planted, the young man decorated it with flowers, ribbons, fruit, bottles of drink, paper chains, candy and chocolate, kerchiefs, mirrors, glass ornaments, combs, or strings of beads. Some stood guard overnight to make sure a rival did not steal the tree and erect his own instead. A popular girl might find several trees had been erected at her house overnight. If a young woman approved of the gift, she offered wine to the responsible party or lit a match in appreciation.

In a dark twist, this festival was also an opportunity to publicly shame young women who were considered to have loose morals and those who refused to marry. Such a maiden might wake in the morning to find a dead tree or a thorny bush erected in her front yard, decorated with rags. Other "gifts" could include the skull of a horse, stuck on a pole, or chains made of broken eggshells. Finding such items in one's yard would bring great shame to the young woman's entire household.

A second form of a *májusfa* was erected in public spheres, such as in village squares or at important crossroads. These were also decorated with ribbons and paper chains, and anyone could hang (or remove) food, drink, sweets, and small gifts from the *májusfa*. Hired musicians often provided background music in the vicinity of a public *májusfa*, and villagers gathered to sing, dance, celebrate, eat, drink, and play games around the tree. Young men competed with one another by climbing to the top of the *májusfa*, a feat made even more difficult due to the tree being stripped of its bark. The winner could usually count on a victory drink from a jug tied to the top, full of alcohol, but he needed to be careful—a popular prank was to replace the alcohol with water mixed with powdered red pepper.

Whether romantic or platonic in nature, *májusfák* stayed up for several weeks. Those who erected the *májusfa* were in charge of taking it down and ceremonially burning it amidst singing and dancing.

A *májusfa*

Május elseje is still celebrated today, but instead of erecting a *májusfa*, people may gift bouquets or baskets of flowers called the *májuskosár* ("May basket") to one another, either in person or sent via the post.

Florian's Day

Szent Flórián was a patron saint of fire. Households who had his picture on their wall were thought to be safe from house fires. On his feast day, May 4, there were many different traditions having to do with fire. In some places, only men were allowed to start the fires, sometimes with additional safeguards such as ritually washing their hands and sprinkling water around the house to prevent the flames from leaping out of the oven. In other places, a fire had to be started late in the day or not at all. Some communities instructed the *gazda* to start the flames the old-fashioned way, by rubbing a string back and forth against dry wood. Family members might all be encouraged to dip their hands in water so they would not accidentally start a fire over the course of the year. In certain villages, one sacred fire was lit on behalf of the whole community, and all the households carried a flame from the sacred fire home to light their own fires.

Pünkösd

In the late springtime, the Hungarian people celebrated a variety of traditions having to do with fertility, beauty, and nature. The church holiday celebrated in late spring is Pentecost (known as *Pünkösd* in Hungarian), the Christian celebration of God's blessing on the early church. Those who are familiar with the Celtic festival of Beltane will recognize many similarities between these celebrations.

Despite the festival being one of the holiest days for Christians, *Pünkösd* had a reputation for getting rather rowdy; many seem to be throwbacks to older springtime fertility rituals. The official flower of the season was the peony, the *pünkösdi rózsa* ("Pentecost rose"); some said that its petals resembled the "tongues of flame" described in the biblical story in which fire miraculously appeared over the faithful. The flowers were also symbols of romance and were given as love gifts; many of the customs of this festival revolved around romance and courtship. One could place the blooms into the morning washing basin to promote health.

The Hungarian equivalent of the May King and May Queen were the *pünkösdi király* and *pünkösdi királynő* ("Pentecost King" and "Pentecost Queen"). Young men vied to be the *pünkösdi király* by competing in races on foot and horseback, wrestling, throwing heavy objects, shooting at targets, and various other feats of strength. The winner of the contests was awarded a wreath woven from flowers as well as a scepter fashioned from a green branch. The other young men in the competition swore their fealty to the winner as his horse was strung with bells.

While his reign lasted, the *pünkösdi király* was allowed special privileges in the community, such as drinking for free at the local tavern or having his peers do odd jobs for him; he would also be invited to all the community dances and celebrations. Even law officials might look the other way if he committed petty crimes. In most communities, the king was allowed to hold his title until the following spring, when the next king was chosen. In other communities, the honor lasted only a day. Thus, if something did not last very long, it was said to be "short-lived, like the reign of the *pünkösdi király*."

People tried to make the May Queen laugh. If she remained stoic, she was praised, but if she laughed, the festival-goers jeered. The *pünkösdi királynő* and her handmaidens wore white dresses and floral decorations. The handmaidens held a canopy over the queen's head as she walked, holding a bouquet of flowers. Her face was covered by a veil, and the handmaidens sang and scattered petals for her to step on as she walked. The royal entourage went from house to house, then performed a song and dance at each household. At the end of each song, the handmaidens lifted the queen into the air while announcing that the crops should grow just as high.[100] After the rite, the group received gifts of food and money from the household. If someone at the house was rude to the group, the queen squatted down so the person's wheat wouldn't grow at all.

---

100. In some communities, the May Queen was a little girl (or even a doll) whom the handmaidens threw into the air.

Chapter 20
SUMMER

I n an agricultural society, summer was without a doubt the busiest time of the year. In some cases, people worked from before sunrise until the end of the day in the fields, gardens, and barnyards. Luckily, various magical aids could be utilized to enhance their efforts, and festivals provided days of respite from the exhausting daily grind.

Úrnapja

Úrnapja ("Lord's Day") is known to English speakers by its Latin name, *Corpus Christi*. The Hungarian celebration was focused around asking for God's blessing on the blossoming vegetation. Villages were decked out with flowers, and there were altars outside private homes as well as in public places, such as outside the village borders at each of the four cardinal directions. Altars were often enclosed in tents or under canopies and decorated with branches, flowers, and herbs; thyme was traditionally included on many altars. Intricate designs were crafted from flower petals on the streets and in yards. Villagers carried religious statues around town in a procession led by the priest, who blessed each altar that he visited with holy water and incense. Young girls clad in white joined the procession and scattered flower petals along the way. Royalty might even join the commoners during these processions.

Once the holiday was over, the plants blessed during the course of the festival were carefully saved. They had numerous magical uses: Placed around the home or barn, they protected the household from all sorts of dangers, both physical and spiritual. Stuck in garden soil, the blessed plants protected the harvests from pests and disease. The blessed flowers could be tossed into fires during storms to protect against lightning strikes or placed into a sick person's bathwater to aid in their healing. The flowers could also be placed under the head of someone struggling from insomnia so they could rest peacefully. The thyme could be fed to cows so they would give more milk or placed in front of beehives so the honey would be plentiful.

There were a slew of work prohibitions linked to this festival. Clothes washed on this day would never dry, snakes would crawl on someone working in the fields, and bread cooked on this day was said to turn to stone.

The Summer Solstice

The summer solstice is known in Hungary as *nyári napforduló* (literally, "summer sun-turning") but is more commonly referred to as *Szent Iván napja* ("St. Ivan's Day"), and the night preceding it is *Szent Iván éjjele* or *Szent Iván éjszakája* ("St. Ivan's Night"). The saint was named the patron of this important holiday because in the New Testament, he is quoted as saying that Jesus "must increase, but I must decrease." [101] The saying alluded to the fact that the days started getting shorter from then on, until the *téli napforduló* ("winter solstice"), when the birth of Jesus was celebrated during the holiday of Christmas.

Fire and water played important roles in the *Szent Iván napja* celebrations; both were used for purification of individuals as well as the community as a whole. This was also an important day for magic and divination. Blessed incense was brought to the wells and springs in and around the village so no snakes, toads, or dragons could poison the water. Although collecting dew was often associated with May Day or *Szent György napja*, some communities believed that dew collected before sunrise on the solstice had magical qualities as well.

The highlight of the *Szent Iván* celebrations was the evening bonfire. At dusk, the entire community came together to make the sacred bonfire known as the *örömtűz*: the "joyfire." It was unthinkable to skip this ceremony. If the fire was not lit for any reason, the community would be beset by harmful

---

101. John 3:30 (King James Version).

mists, pestilence, or hail. The exact methods to light the fire varied greatly from community to community. In some areas, it was young women who lit the fire, whereas in others it was the task of young men. Some communities required each household to contribute kindling; others used old harvest and wreaths; some even lit bonfires from garbage. In one record, an older boy had to run around the unlit bonfire three times with a torch before setting it ablaze. Although the bonfire was often square in shape, another type of fire involved taking an entire pine tree, standing it up in a clearing, then decorating it with straw and flower wreaths before lighting it on fire.

The flames from the ceremonial fire had many uses. People threw fruit into the flames in the belief that they would reach the *Túlvilág*. Mothers who had lost infants or small children would send cherries, strawberries, or apples to the spirits of their babies. Others tossed apples into the sky three times so the angels could gather whichever ones they wanted for the souls of the babies. After fruit was given to the dead, living children also received their share, then the adults. Fruits baked in the bonfires were believed to ensure health to all that ate them, especially from tooth and stomach pains. Baked apples were sometimes called "golden apples," which appeared in many traditional myths and legends to impart wisdom, strength, and special powers to those who consumed them.

Herbs were waved through the bonfire smoke to make them effective healing agents. Young women braided wreaths by the fireside, which would then be tossed onto the roofs of their homes for protection against house fires. If a young woman was single, she went to a mulberry tree and tossed the wreath up into its branches; if the wreath stayed in the branches, she would soon marry, but if it fell back to the ground, she would stay single.

Everyone in the community—young and old—had to jump over the flames (or be helped across by family and friends) to ensure good luck and health. This was known as *tűzugrás*, "fire-jumping." There were many chants and verses to shout while jumping, such as "May there be no abscesses on my body [nor] sores on my feet!"[102] Girls and boys challenged one another to see if they could jump over the flames, often while singing or saying chants. One taunt

---

102. Bellosics, "Magyarországi adatok a nyári napforduló ünnepéhez (Harmadik közlemény)," 118.

was "*Ne félj, pajtás, ugord át, nem süti meg a pofád!*" (Loosely translated: "Don't worry, buddy, give a good jump; surely the flames won't roast your hump!")[103]

A frequent theme of fire-jumping was to couple up. In one version of this custom, courting pairs and newlyweds lined up and jumped together in pairs. Other times, young women who wanted to marry would jump over the flames alone. If they succeeded, they would soon marry; if they stopped short, they wouldn't marry at all; and if they landed in the flames without going over completely, they would soon lose their virtue to a young man who would not marry them. Fire spinners and dancers twirled around the flames, and long songs were sung throughout the night. The songs were usually so long that when someone was rambling, they were said to be preparing a song for *Szent Iván éjjele* (the night of the summer solstice).

This was a good night for hunting magical treasure as well as for fertility and love magic.

Péter napja

June 29 was a holiday for fishermen, who walked through the villages selling fish from long poles they slung over their backs. In the evening, they cooked a feast of fish stew for the community. *Szent Péter* was the patron of fishermen and of locksmiths because he was often depicted with keys in his hands. He was able to "lock" or "unlock" a young person's fate to marry. If a young man or woman heard the church bells ring early in the morning, their fate was "unlocked," and they would find someone to marry by the end of the year.

Péter was also the spirit in charge of unlocking the harvest: before his feast day, no one was allowed to harvest anything from the fields.

The Harvest

The wheat harvest, known as *aratás*, was among the busiest times of the year, and many workers migrated to the most fertile parts of the country, where the work would be most plentiful. It was crucial to time the harvest properly; it would make for a poor harvest if the work was started on a Tuesday, Friday, new moon, or when there was an unburied dead person in the village. The tools used for harvesting were blessed the night before they were used, and

---

103. Paládi-Kovács, *Magyar néprajz nyolc kötetben*, vol. 7, 187.

participants prayed before starting their tasks. Before entering the fields, the men lifted their hats. Then they all rose their hats as a gesture of gratitude to *Isten* and the spirits who had protected their crops. The *gazda* made the first symbolic swipes with his scythe and then the rest of the workers could begin. The first sheaf of wheat contained very powerful magic. Workers tied it to their waists so the labor wouldn't hurt their backs. Wreaths made from its stalks were placed on statues, on altars, on the walls of a home, or in gardens to protect the harvest.

While the work of harvesting was serious, the atmosphere was quite festive. The workers sang and played music; many songs were composed specifically for the harvest. The workers also played pranks on one another. A young man working at his first harvest was likely to be hazed by his elders by being slammed into the ground unexpectedly or being chased by young women. If the young women caught him, they tied him up to resemble a sheaf of wheat and piled on top of him so that he could feel what the wheat felt. Workers also pranked a *gazda* who visited the fields; he too was tied up with straw, and the workers only let him loose if he agreed to pay them with money or wine or promised to buy new kerchiefs for the women.

The workers always let a corner of the field remain unharvested so that anyone who was hungry—whether human or animal—could freely eat from it. Some said that this unharvested grain was for the birds of the sky while others said that it was food for the horses of Saint Peter. If the workers did not leave this corner untouched, rains would destroy the crops the following year.

The last sheaf of the harvest, like the first, was special. All of the workers took home a few tufts of it, and the women wove the bulk of the sheaf into a harvest wreath called an *aratókoszorú*. These wreaths could be shaped in many different ways; some were regular circles, whereas others were shaped like crowns, spirals, bells, or another creative design. Often, they were decorated with flowers and ribbons.

When all the work was completed and the wreath was finished, the workers formed a procession to the *gazda*'s house. They sang and danced on the way, sometimes carrying upon their shoulders straw figures dressed like a harvester. As the procession made their way to the *gazda*'s house, onlookers threw buckets of water on the people chosen to carry the wreath in hopes that the harvests would continue to be plentiful in the future and the wheat fields would not lack rainfall the following year. The harvesters presented the owner of the field with the harvest wreath, who then hung the wreath from the central beam of his house. The workers also took some wheat home and place it on their household altars. All the workers were invited to feast and celebrate through the night.

An *aratókoszorú*

Of course, these celebrations only took place if the harvest had been successful. If it had been a poor year for the crops, the procession was much more somber, without cheerful singing or dancing, and there was no evening celebration.

István napja

As mentioned in chapter 2, *István király* ("King Stephen") was the first king of the modern state of Hungary, and August 20 was his feast day. Thus, August 20 is the celebration of Hungary's nationhood. Although today it is celebrated with fireworks and displays of national pride, there were once more humble customs associated with István's festival, such as being considered the best day of the year to pick raspberries.

It was said that this was the day of the year when the King of Mosquitos was defeated in battle—from this day forward, there would be fewer of the pests flying around.

Chapter 21

AUTUMN

The Hungarian autumn was a time for harvesting fruit and nuts, preserving food, making handicrafts, and generally preparing for the winter. People spent many evenings working together as they processed the fruits of the harvest. Markets, known as *vásárok*, were also popular this time of year. These were festive events, attracting visitors from neighboring villages and providing opportunities for socializing and trade outside the strict boundaries of the village. Heralds announced the start of the gatherings with drums, music, and banners; merchants displayed their wares of crafts, toys, and clothes in the town squares; and musicians and comedians entertained the visitors so attendees would make merry and dance late into the night. Employers could find servants to help them in their households, and those who wished to marry frequently found matches at the markets, as the events brought together young people from many villages. And, of course, there were plenty of *jeles napok* to celebrate as well.

Kisasszony napja (Maiden's Day)

The Catholic celebration of the Feast of the Nativity of the Blessed Virgin Mary (i.e., Mary's birthday) coincides with *Kisasszony napja*. The *Kisasszony* was one of the seven aspects (or daughters) of the *Boldogasszony*. Around her festival, celebrated on September 8, swallows started migrating south to winter in warmer locations, so one of the titles for the *Kisasszony* was *Fecskehajtó Kisasszony*, "The Maiden Who Chases the Swallows Away." (As usual, the opposite belief also existed, with those saying that it was such a holy day that even the swallows did not start their journeys on it.) The seeds for the next year's crops were placed outside on the eve of the holiday so that they would be touched by the dew, but they were brought indoors again before the first rays of the sun shone on them.

Several traditions of this festival had to do with women. The women of the community climbed the nearest hillsides as the sun rose in hopes of seeing an image of the *Boldogasszony* surrounded by a shower of roses; others expected to see a cradle next to the goddess. It was sometimes said that on this day the sun was expected to rise in an unusual "dancing" manner[104] or was excessively playful—it too was joyful about the holiday. Women were forbidden to work on this day; spinning and sewing were especially taboo. Instead, they bathed in natural waters (i.e., lakes or rivers) on *Kisasszony napja*.

Szent Mihály napja

Mihály napja ("St. Michael's Day") came at the end of September, on the twenty-ninth day of the month. In Catholic tradition, the archangel Michael's duties included accompanying the soul of the dead to the afterlife, and he was also tasked with doing spiritual battle with Satan. He was sometimes described like common representations of the Grim Reaper: "He walks with a scythe… and reaps [both] the young and the old. He just has bones, he has no skin on him…he gives a bitter cup to a person, tells them to drink it, and then cuts their neck."[105] Fittingly, Hungarians considered him to be a patron of cemeteries from medieval times, and the device used for carrying coffins to the cemetery was known as the *Szent Mihály lova*, or "Saint Michael's horse." An old name for the Milky Way was *Szent Mihály útja*, or "The Road of Saint Michael," as the dead were poetically described as traveling to the world of the spirits by that route. Mihály's role as an angel who guided people through trials made him the ideal patron saint to usher in the season of cold and darkness ahead.

Szent Mihály napja was regarded by many as the day when the warm half of the year gave way to the cold. The livestock, which had been herded out to the fields on the first day of summer, were herded back to their winter lodg-

104. Benedek and Kürtössy, "Szeptember 8. Kisasszony napja."
105. Bosnyák, "A moldvai magyarok hitvilága," 220.

ings, and shepherds who had spent the warm season living away from the communities finally returned to the villages. Some villages celebrated a festival named the *farkasünnep* ("holiday of the wolves") to protect the livestock from predator attacks.

At this point of the year, the harvesting was more or less finished, and attention was focused on preserving the crops. On the festival itself, women were forbidden to do any washing lest their hands get wounds on them. Ironing would make thunderclouds gather over their house for the next year.

A number of weather *babonák* were linked to this day, such as:

- If Saint Michael's horse was white (i.e., if it was cloudy), winter would soon arrive.
- If the swallows did not leave for their winter migration by this day, autumn would be long.
- If the sheep or pigs lay together that night, winter would be cold.

Sowing the Seeds

One of the most important autumn tasks to be done in an agrarian society was sowing the seeds for the following year. Figuring out when to sow the seeds for the next year's harvest was no easy task. Not only did the farmers have to consider the climate, but they also had to consider the spiritual timing as well—and opinions differed about what the ideal timing was. Sowing, like harvesting, had to be aligned with the correct moon phase. If one could sow on the full moon, this was fortuitous, because the wheat would grow round like the moon. If both the moon and the sun were visible in the sky at once, it was forbidden to sow. If seeds were sown on *Mihály napja* ("St. Michael's Day"), the crop would grow unruly, as the spirit himself was unruly.

Once the *gazda* did, indeed, determine that the ideal time for the sowing arrived, he prepared for the ritual itself. The *gazda* ate as many eggs as possible the week before the sowing so that the wheat would grow golden, but it was inadvisable to eat toasted bread during the sowing season or the wheat would grow mildew. The night before sowing, the *gazda* had to sleep apart from his wife. In the morning, he washed his feet and put on a fresh pair of underwear. He put a clove of garlic into his pocket so that witches would stay far away from the fields and not curse any seeds in secret. Then, he mixed breastmilk or fingernail clippings into the seeds; the breastmilk would increase the fertility of the seeds, and the clippings would keep harm away in his stead. When he loaded the sacks onto his wagon or cart, the *gazda* had to ensure that the sacks' mouths faced backward so that the harvest would return toward his property.

Before entering the fields, the *gazda* paused and kneeled to pray. He would stay silent until his work was done for the day. To remind him of this, he placed three seeds under his tongue. If a *gazda* was particularly short, he might hire a tall man to do the work for him so that the wheat would also grow tall. Sometimes women stood at the edge of the field and sang, clapped, and laughed so that the wheat would grow happy. No one passing by the fields was allowed to smoke, lest they insult the watching spirits.

The *gazda* could use the tablecloth from the Christmas table to spread the seeds from. When he was done with his work, he threw the empty seed sacks high into the air to show the wheat how high to grow, then stuck a birch branch in the middle of the field to protect the crop against harm from evil spirits. When the *gazda* returned home, he threw the sowing cloth onto the roof of his house so that hail wouldn't harm the crop.

If seeds were saved to be sown in the springtime, they were treated with extra care throughout the winter and could be placed under the *karácsonyi asztal* ("Christmas table," used as an altar) for blessing. On the last day before Lent, housewives made long noodles to show the grain how long it should grow.

Vendel napja

October 20 is *Vendel napja* ("St. Wendel's Day"). The legend of Vendel stated that he was a prince who left royal life and chose to live a humble life as a swineherd, and after his death, he became the patron saint of animal husbandry. His feast day was a holiday for livestock, exempting them from working in fields and pulling carts. Many villages had a statue dedicated in the saint's honor, usually depicted with a lamb or a sheepdog next to him.

In one village, the shepherd crook was broken off the local Vendel statue. The villagers explained that when a disease swept through the area and killed many cows, an enraged *gazda* broke the crook from the statue's hands while berating the saint: "What do you need this for, if you don't even protect our animals!" [106]

Halottak napja

Halottak napja ("Day of the Dead") was—and remains—one of the most important holidays in the Hungarian calendar year. It was said that on this day, "everyone is allowed to go home, whether they are in hell or whether they are in heaven." [107] In the first days of November, people traveled great distances to visit, clean, and decorate family gravesites and tombs; some even adopted abandoned graves. These days, votive candles and flowers are the most popular decorations, and toys are sometimes left on children's graves. In the past, the entire week leading up to *Halottak napja* was considered part of the holiday and included various work prohibitions. For instance, people did not work the fields lest they fall ill. It was also taboo to leave out standing water the week before *Halottak napja*, and people could not do any washing lest the visiting dead became trapped in the water. A light was left on throughout the night so any visiting ghosts could see inside the house clearly; this way, they could be kept up-to-date about any changes their loved ones had made inside the home.

Feeding the dead is not as common today, but it was a very popular custom in the past. While some people brought gifts of food directly to the gravesites, others threw the food into the flames of the oven, left food on the table overnight in case any ghosts visiting the household were hungry, or simply set an empty place at their dinner table so their loved one could join them. (Sometimes, the food offering was the decedent's favorite food, or it was symbolic food or drink such as *pogácsa*, salt, milk, or wine.) In still another variation of feeding the dead, when mourning families saw beggars gathered at the cemetery entrances, they gave them *kalács*; as the beggars ate, the spirits of the dead would also be sated.

According to some legends, the dead attended church services on this night. This was known as the *halottak miséje* ("Mass of the Dead"). In one telling, a woman went to bed early and was awakened by the sound of church

106. *Magyar Katolikus Lexikon (MKL)*, "Vendel."
107. Bosnyák, "A moldvai magyarok hitvilága," 125.

bells. She hurried to church, which was lit with an unusual light. All the women inside had white kerchiefs on their heads. When she took a closer look at those gathered, she recognized her own *koma-asszony*, who had passed away. The woman's *koma-asszony* spoke to her and said to not be afraid, but to leave or else she would join them in death.

In other legends, the dead gathered for services in graveyards or churches, covered in their white burial shrouds. If someone managed to catch a glimpse of a face under the sheets, they would join the ranks the following year.

Márton napja

Saint Martin (written *Márton* in Hungarian) was a Roman soldier. According to legend, he was traveling home from war when he saw a beggar in the street. Márton offered his own red cloak to the shivering man to keep him from freezing. To commemorate this act of generosity, on the sunset of November 11, a young man dressed up as the saint and rode through the village streets on horseback, leading a procession of singing children who carried lanterns suspended on rods. They gathered in the village square and performed a skit about the saint as a bonfire was lit. The revelers consumed hot beverages and then returned to their homes to eat the traditional dish of roasted goose.

The more a family celebrated and feasted on this night, the more *Szent Márton* would bless the household with provisions so they would be able to eat and drink well for the rest of the year. The more a family drank on this day, the more strength and vitality they drank into them. A famous saying was "Whoever doesn't eat goose on *Márton napja* will go hungry the rest of the year." After the meal, the bones of the goose were used for divination. If the bones were long and white, then there would be a long, snowy winter. If they were short and brown, the winter would be short and muddy. According to weather divination, if *Szent Márton* rode in on a white horse (i.e., if it was snowy), then the winter would be mild. If he rode in on a brown horse (i.e., if it was a mild day), the winter would be harsh.

On this day, shepherds gifted their masters with a branch from a hazelnut or silver birch tree, known as the *mártonág*, "Martin's branch." An ideal *mártonág* had many small twigs on it, for the *gazda*'s pigs would have as many piglets as the branch had twigs. The branch was stuck on top of the pigsty for good luck or saved for the spring; if, come spring, the pigs were herded out to the meadows for the first time with this branch, they would become healthy and lively. In return for their magic branch, the shepherds were rewarded with sausage, bacon, or baked goods.

Chapter 22

ADVENT

In the Christian calendar, the four weeks preceding Christmas are called Advent. Since this was a time of fasting, no raucous gatherings or weddings were permitted during these weeks. It was, instead, a time for self-reflection, personal meditation—and even divination.

One such method was divination by sprouting. At the start of Advent, young single women would place a branch from a fruit tree (commonly a cherry tree) in water. If it sprouted before Christmas, they would marry within a year's time. Today, the custom of this branch is all but forgotten, and the most common sign of the season is the Advent wreath, a circle of evergreen branches with four candles. On the first week, one candle is lit, on the second, two candles, and so on until all the candles are lit on Christmas itself. Today, even completely secular families have an Advent wreath in their homes as they await the winter holidays.

András napja

St. Andrew's Day falls on November 30 and is linked with the start of Advent, which starts on the Sunday closest to it. *András napja* was one of the most common days of the year for the youth (especially young women) to perform love divination to see whom their future spouse would be. They fasted during the day and then performed one of many methods to uncover their love match; revisit chapter 14 to read about love divination techniques in greater detail.

Borbála napja

December 4 is *Borbála napja* ("St. Barbara's Day"). It was forbidden for women to work with fabric on this day. If they ignored the prohibition, Borbála would get angry and ruin their project. Furthermore, she caused bad luck for the family by sewing the hens' bottoms shut so they could not lay eggs or tying up the cow's legs with yarn to make them lame.

On the other hand, Borbála approved of women working with down feathers. Many communities held work parties to process the feathers needed for pillows and comforters. The young people of the community sang, danced, told stories, ate, and drank together. At the end of the evening, boys gathered the discarded feathers and threw them in front of the houses of the girl they liked. If the girl cleaned up the feathers, she clearly had an industrious spirit and was good marriage material—Borbála would be pleased with her and bless her household.

Luca napja

The thirteenth of December, *Luca napja* ("St. Lucy's Day"), was the most powerful night of the year for witches. In the pre-Gregorian calendar, December 13 fell on the winter solstice, which could explain why this, of all days, was considered such a spiritually powerful holiday.

On the eve of this holiday, a malevolent spirit named the *Luca* roamed the countryside. Sometimes she appeared as a pig or as a woman clad in white who had the head of a pig. This aspect was called the *lucadisznó*, or the "Lucy swine." Parents warned their misbehaving children that the spirit would take them with her.

Also on the night before the holiday, the young men of the village played tricks on the village folk, whether in revenge for slights or to impress potential romantic partners. One popular prank was to take apart a person's wagon, carry it up to the roof piece by piece, and reassemble it. Other tricks included taking gates off their hinges or throwing wagons into wells. Many times, the youth got away with their antics because even if the *gazda* heard a commotion, he could not be sure if it was a rowdy band of young men or a witch who was trying to lure him out of his home to place a curse on his family.

As witches were deemed to be extra powerful on this night, people did what they could to hunker down and guard their homes from curses. Before sunset, the *gazda* rubbed garlic on the doors of his home as well as his barns. He might also anoint each of his animals with a paste made of garlic. The *gazdasszony* added copious amounts of garlic to dinner—failing that, each member of the household would eat a clove of garlic before retiring for the night. It was taboo to lend anyone anything lest a witch use these items to curse the household. People spread ashes around their houses or on their doorstep in the evening and checked the dust in the morning to see if any witches had tried to enter the house during the course of the night, perhaps in the shape-shifted guise of a cat.

On *Luca napja*, young women would dress up as the Luca, placing a sieve in front of their faces and covering themselves with white sheets. Carrying a chain, rolling pin, or wooden spoon, the personified Luca would quiz the girls and young women in various topics, such as knowing their prayers or if they knew how to do their handiwork. Wheat kernels were placed into a bowl in hopes that they would sprout into the *lucabúza*, "Lucy wheat," by Christmas Eve. Some watered this wheat in special ways, such as from their mouths or with holy water. This was placed on the *karácsonyi asztal* ("Christmas table," also known as the Christmas altar), then fed to the livestock or brought to the cemetery and placed on gravestones. If the family's seeds failed to sprout, it was considered terrible luck—it was a premonition that the family's fields would not grow in the following year.

Men who wished to craft a *lucaszék*, or "Lucy chair," started the project on this day. A *lucaszék* was a round stool made from nine special woods—hawthorn, juniper, maple, pear, elderberry, cypress, acacia, ash, and rosewood—and built in such a way that it did not use any metal nails or fasteners, yet it needed to be strong enough to support a grown man's weight. It was so difficult to make these chairs that all challenging work was described as "as difficult to complete as a *lucaszék*." If one managed to complete the project, it could be brought to Midnight Mass on Christmas Eve. A person standing upon it would be able to see the true form of any witches hidden within the congregation because their invisible horns, antlers, or feathers would become visible. As it was linked to the evil spirits it was able to uncover, the *lucaszék* had to be burned as soon as possible after use.

A *lucaszék*

Men also started braiding special whips so they would be ready for noise-making rituals on Christmas Eve and New Year's Eve. Unlike *lucaszékek*, these whips did not have to be destroyed after the rites but could be used for more practical purposes. For example, horses and cattle driven with these whips were said to be easier to control.

Mikulás

Mikulás (Saint Nicholas) is the Hungarian version of Santa Claus, and his festival continues to be a popular holiday today. On the evening of December 6, children shone their shoes and placed them in their windows in hopes that *Mikulás* would fill the shoes with treats. That night, the white-bearded *Mikulás* was said to travel throughout the land wearing a red cape, furry hat, and boots while carrying a sack of gifts. Good children received candy, apples, or nuts, while naughty children received red onions, potatoes, and switches. If a child received a switch, it was placed in a prominent position in the house to remind the child to behave better in the coming year. Children learned many verses, songs, and poems in preparation for this day.

The debt-collector, *Krampusz*, is said to roam the world freely on this night, following in the footsteps of *Mikulás*.[108] *Krampusz* is a dark, devilish figure with hooves and horns, accompanied by demonic helpers who spirit away naughty children who are not safely hidden in their homes. In the olden days, young men smeared soot on their faces and stuffed straw in their shirts, and they carried metal cans with burning embers to create smoke around them. They went from house to house, rattling chains and swinging broomsticks to frighten children and young women. In order to protect the people living there from harm and illness, the young men struck the ground with sticks that had rattles attached to them. Sometimes they struck one another to show that evil always got its comeuppance, even from other evildoers. The band went to the *fonó* to visit young women and cause all sorts of mayhem there as well. Over the centuries, the antics got so out of hand that royal edicts were issued to prohibit tomfoolery on this night.

During the Soviet occupation, authorities changed the religious name of *Mikulás* to that of *Télapó*, meaning "Father Winter." The name was still apt; the first snowfall of the year, which often took place around this time, was attributed to *Télapó* shaking his white beard.

Tamás napja

Tamás napja ("Thomas Day") falls on December 21, which coincides with the winter solstice. Traditionally, this was the day of the pig slaughter, known as the *disznótor*, or "funerary feast of the pigs." There were many ritual elements to the pig slaughter. While it is interesting to learn about this in a historical context, if you are sensitive to animal cruelty, you might want to skip the rest of this section altogether! Consider yourself warned, because it does get a little gruesome.

If one did not kill a pig on (or around) his festival, *Szent Tamás* was said to take the life of a person or animal himself to make up for the lack of a sacrifice. If the solstice fell on the new moon, a Friday, or a Sunday, the slaughter had to be done in the days leading up to it lest the meat become "wormy"

---

108. In other regions of Hungary, the debt collector was known as *Láncos Miklós*, "Nicholas with a Chain."

and unusable. Yet, the *disznótor* could not be performed too early; it wasn't until the Orion constellation was readily visible in the night sky that it was time for the slaughter—otherwise, the pigs would likely not have fattened sufficiently to provide a good amount of lard for the year.

First, a pig had to be chased before being slaughtered. Then, it was stabbed and had its throat cut as the blood was caught in buckets. It was forbidden to feel sorry for the animal while it was being slaughtered lest it have a difficult time dying. When it was being butchered, anyone in the vicinity had to laugh loudly so that there would be a good supply of bacon. However, while the meat was being salted, the people had to be silent. They also had to remain wordless while the sausage was being cooked, otherwise the casings would burst. Participants took turns drinking shots of *pálinka* from the pig's *köröm* (literally "nail," but meaning the hollowed-out pig's foot) for good luck; this custom is still followed today at some pig slaughters.

All of the pig's parts were used in some way. Most were cooked or preserved; some were used for magic or healing. Nipples and sex organs were thrown back into the pigpens to increase the household's fertility. A pregnant woman was forbidden to walk near the slaughter lest her child be born hairy; she was also forbidden to eat from the marrow lest her child have a runny nose. Women were not allowed to eat the snout; if they did, all of the dishes in the household would shatter. The fat from a sacrificial pig was known as the "Thomas lard"; it was blessed and used throughout the year as a salve for healing. The salted blood was also preserved and used in a similar fashion for healing magic. Portions of the slaughtered pig were gifted to friends, neighbors, and the poor, and the liver was studied, as it foretold what the coming year's weather would be like.

Later in the evening, the older boys of the village banged old pots and pans together as they walked through the streets. They carried a staff called a *kutyaverőbot* (the "dog-striking stick") and struck it onto the dirt floors of the houses to bring good luck. If they were able to make a hole in the floor, that was considered extra lucky. If they were refused entry to a house, they yelled rude insults. In other communities, the older boys had less confrontational traditions. They wrote obscene words, verses, or drawings on paper slips, stuck them on branches, and went from house to house, sticking the branch through each home's window. It was vital that they concealed their identities while doing this, but they had to attract attention to the stick by making some sort of noise. The people inside the house would stick *pogácsa*, bacon, or sausage on the branches. Sometimes, however, the homeowners pranked the boys and gave them sausages filled with sawdust.

In rural communities, the pig slaughter is still known as the *disznótor*, although it is not a requirement for it to correlate with the solstice, and few ritual movements have survived through the generations.

Chapter 23

CHRISTMAS

For many of us, it is difficult to imagine a Christmas celebration without a Christmas tree. This was also true for many Hungarians through the centuries; in some Germanic areas, the trees were decorated as early as the 1600s. A folktale explains why the evergreen was chosen as the tree of this holiday: Jesus was hiding from his enemies, and he asked one tree after another to hide him within their leafy branches. All the trees refused, fearing that they would be destroyed by the people pursuing Jesus. Only the pine tree agreed to shelter him, and for this, Jesus blessed the tree with never losing its leaves.

Despite the sentimental legend, the tradition took centuries to spread to all parts of Hungary—even into the 1960s, many private homes did not erect their own Christmas trees. Some communities preferred the tradition of the *termőág*, or "branch of creation." These were thorny branches (or branches into which nails had been driven) onto which decorations such as apples, nuts, rosemary sprigs, and onion and flower bulbs could easily be attached. A red ribbon was wound around the *termőág*, and candles were either hung from it or placed at its base. Priests tolerated the practice by saying that the decoration represented the biblical Tree of Paradise, and the ribbon was the snake winding around it. Most communities displayed these decorations at wedding feasts, but others associated them with Christmas.

For a long time, gifting was not the focus of the seasonal festivities. When gifts were given, children were—and still are—told they were receiving gifts from the *Jézuska* (the baby Jesus) or an angel. In some places, a young woman dressed up as an angel and knocked on doors, carrying gifts that she handed over to children after a blessing and a prayer. (I remember my grandmother arranged for some of the older neighborhood girls to dress up as angels for Christmas Eve once or twice!)

The main holiday celebration centered around the feast. Some communities ate as early as mid-afternoon, while others waited for sunset or even later. Regardless of the meal's timing, there were many magical movements that had to be completed before sitting down to eat. Each household member had to take a ritual bath or wash their face. Red apples and coins were thrown into the water to make the person wealthy and healthy in the coming year. The *karácsonyi asztal* ("Christmas table") served the function of an altar; ritual objects were placed upon it, under it, and around it to ensure blessings and spiritual protection. The table also had to be prepared. Because it was such a sacred and powerful location, the *karácsonyi asztal* would attract harmful spirits that could show up and harm the family or ruin the food if the proper precautions weren't taken. Before the table was set, blessed water might be sprinkled on it, or a blessed candle might be placed upon it. Various objects (such as axes, chains, or even musical instruments) might be placed under the table to deter or distract any mischievous spirits who were attracted to the holiday festivities.

Straw or hay, reminiscent of the straw in the baby Jesus's manger, was a frequent addition on or under the table; this straw would be saved to feed to the household animals to make them healthy or used to cense fruit trees to ensure a bountiful harvest. Household tools and seeds were thought to be more productive in the coming months if they were placed under the table. Objects that had spent time on or under the *karácsonyi asztal* might develop magical qualities. Pieces of clothing (most often, hats) could be placed on the table; subsequently, they would be able to heal livestock when tapped or rubbed on the animals.

Special attention was paid to the *karácsonyi abrosz*, the Christmas tablecloth, which was usually pure white but was sometimes trimmed in red designs. When placing the cloth on the table, the *gazda* and *gazdasszony* would arrange it together. While doing so, the *gazda* would ask his wife, "What are you pulling?" and the wife would repeat thrice, "*Üszögöt, konkolyt, Boldogasszony tízparancsolatját,*" meaning, "I'm pulling blight, and weeds, and the ten commandments of the *Boldogasszony*." [109] This was believed to protect the fields against weeds in the following growing season.

Before the meal started, the *gazdasszony* tied a fiber cord around each leg of the table. With each knot she made, her husband ritually asked, "What are you doing?" She responded, "I am binding the hands and feet of the evil people, so that the evil will stay far from our house." She repeated this three more times, tying a cord to each of the table's legs. [110] The *gazda* said a blessing of thanks for the family's blessings and asked for continued divine help for the coming year, and then the meal could officially begin. It was important that the *gazdasszony* remain sitting throughout the meal. If she stood up, the hens would likewise get up from their nests and would not be good layers. An entire loaf of bread was placed upon the table so the family would be healthy in the coming year, and a slice of it could be dried and hung around the homestead to prevent house fires.

During the Christmas meal, different foods with special symbolic meanings were eaten, often in a set order, and everyone had to eat some of each dish. (In one community, twenty-one separate foods were placed on the table, each with a different meaning!) In many parts of Hungary, the meal started with a ceremonial walnut. One was distributed to each member of the family; if the cracked shell revealed an unspoiled nut inside, the person would have a healthy year, but a spoiled nut meant that they would be sickly. Another popular custom was that of slicing a red apple into as many pieces as there were family members. These were distributed by the *gazda* and eaten at the same time. A common saying proclaimed that people who ate their *karácsonyi alma* ("Christmas apple") together would stay a loving family for the rest of the year. Shortly before Christmas Eve, colorful wafers were stamped with various designs, then blessed and distributed to each village household; in exchange, the households made donations of money and food to the church. These wafers, called *ostya*, were believed to have magical qualities and were a necessary addition to the holiday table. Other ceremonial foods varied from community to community but commonly included nuts,

---

109. Pócs, "A karácsonyi vacsora és a karácsonyi asztal hiedelemköre," 76.
110. Paládi-Kovács, *Magyar néprajz nyolc kötetben*, vol. 7, 244–45.

cabbage, poppyseed rolls, black pepper, garlic, wine, baked pumpkin, beans, grapes, honey, fish, black pepper, cottage cheese pastries, and blessed wafers.

The leftovers of the meal, called *karácsonyi morzsa* (literally, "Christmas crumbs"), were dried and ground into a powder. Some leftovers were fed to the livestock so they could gain the benefits of the blessed meal, while other portions were saved for various magical purposes. If someone was ill, a portion of the *morzsa* was burned next to their bedside to release some of the sacred magic within. Sick animals were given a few bites to eat, and if someone died, a portion might be placed in their coffin as they were taken for burial. If the *morzsa* was buried, a flower with magical healing properties would grow from the spot seven years later.

After the meal, the tablecloth was saved for magical purposes—and it had numerous uses. A sick person or animal could be wrapped up in the cloth or covered with it. It could be used to carry the seeds for sowing in the springtime or as a baking aid that ensured dough would always rise and bread would never burn. If a family member fell ill, they were wrapped in the cloth in hopes they would be healed. The *abrosz* might even be draped upon a coffin as it was being carried to the cemetery. The tablecloth had so many uses, in fact, that it wasn't uncommon to set multiple cloths upon the table, sometimes with objects hidden between the layers (such as bread or the spoon used to stir the sourdough starter).

The cloths might be left there for several days, perhaps even the full twelve days of Christmas. Even if the cloth was stained during the meal, it could not be washed lest it lose its magical potency. Some households locked the *karácsonyi abrosz* in a chest or cabinet, believing that with it, they were locking up their family's good fortune so that it couldn't leave the house.

Christmas Eve was the one night a year when church services were held after the sun had set. In fact, they were held at midnight—the darkest part of the night during the darkest part of the year. Young women who wished to marry dressed by the light of a candle that had already served as a light during a wedding feast. The *gazdasszony* placed *kalács* and water on the table, on the windowsill, or by the oven, with the explanation that "if the baby Jesus visited, he would be able to eat something." [111] If the family failed to do so, there would be no harvest the next summer. (This custom was, in all probability, a leftover tradition from the time when food was offered to the ancestors on the night of the winter solstice.)

The *gazda* led the way to church, lighting the family's way with torches made from birch branches. Shepherds lined the streets and cracked their whips or shot pistols into the air to frighten away evil spirits who would otherwise harm those who walked outside after dark. The shepherds continued to circle the church during Mass to keep the ghosts and witches at bay. Some people skipped Mass altogether to eavesdrop at barn doors, believing that this was the one night of the year when animals talked to one another in human language to gossip about their masters.

When they arrived at church, young women threw corn kernels, pumpkin seeds, or millet seeds into the blessed water font in hopes that they would have as many suitors, and that the suitors would arrive with the same haste as the seeds had been tossed into the water.

The *lucaszékek* ("Lucy chairs") crafted several weeks prior were brought to the congregation to uncover any potential witches. It was a good idea to have a pocket full of poppyseeds for protection. If someone uncovered a witch's identity using the *lucaszékek*, she would grow angry at having her secret exposed and start chasing the person, but if the individual tossed a handful of poppyseeds onto the road behind them, the witch would be drawn to the poppyseeds and be compelled to pick them up, one by one. She would be so distracted that she would forget all about her intended victim.

The young people of the community decorated a centrally located well with evergreens and wreaths for the *Jézuska* to bathe in during Mass, endowing the water with magical properties. In all likelihood, this was a pre-Christian custom that was given a very surface-level Christian explanation. This water, known as the *életvíz*, or "life water," not only had healing powers but was also an important component of love magic. Young women who wished to marry raced to the well after the church service. The first to draw water from the well would be the first to marry. On their way home from Mass—or at the very least, on the following morning—everyone in the village tried to take a drink

111. Paládi-Kovács, *Magyar néprajz nyolc kötetben*, vol. 7, 246.

from the well so they would have a long and healthy life. If the stars shone brightly, the household hens would lay many eggs in the coming year or the corn harvest would be good.

The Twelve Days of Christmas

While most of the Hungarian Christmas traditions were linked to Christmas Eve, the festivities did not end there. The twelve days after Christmas were considered part of the holiday season, and they were to be spent visiting family and friends as well as resting from hard work. The weather was also carefully watched, for those twelve days were supposed to foretell what the weather would be like in each of the following twelve months. The day of the week Christmas fell on was said to foretell the weather and fortune in the coming months; if it fell on a Tuesday, for instance, there would be a lengthy winter and a year full of fruit and wine, but many people would die.

On December 26, the adult males of the community performed *regölés*. They went from house to house, chanting and singing while accompanied by drums, flutes, and other noisemakers. They sang about the various blessings each household should receive, such as abundant livestock, good harvests, health, spouses for the unmarried, and so on. The song lyrics hinted that if the master of the house gifted the minstrels, they would be blessed, but if they were stingy with their rewards, a curse would be put upon their house. The chants also included recitations of mystical stories from Magyar legends, such as the myth of the *Csodaszarvas*. These verses were accompanied by a nonsensical refrain of *Haj regö rejtem*, which was chanted repeatedly throughout the song. Although the meaning has been lost to time, it is believed that this was a chant used by the shamans of pre-Christian religion during their mystical trances. *Regö* is likely related to the word *rege*, or "epic legend," and *rejtem* means that the speaker is hiding something and likely alludes to mysteries of the spirit.

The festivities continued on December 28 with the festival of *Aprószentek* ("Tiny Saints"). This festival commemorated the biblical story in which King Herod ordered the execution of all male children under the age of two. On this day, the young boys of the village were sent to a neighbor's house to borrow a mustard seed, which alluded to a biblical verse about having faith the size of a mustard seed. There, the boys were set upon by their neighbors, who struck them with switches cut from a fruit tree that was known to produce much fruit. Children visited one house after another, eager for their scourging, as they believed it would bring them good luck. They recited verses that told the *gazda* of his consequences if he did or did not do his part: "I stand on the other side of the door, waiting for my mustard seed. If you don't give me any, I will leave, but in that case, may your oven break!"[112] Usually, the *gazda* wielding the switch performed the task gladly, believing the fruit trees the branches were cut from would produce even better the following summer.

In other villages, the tradition was reversed, and it was the children who did the scourging. At each house they visited, they asked the *gazda* permission to strike each member of his household with their switches. They struck young women to make them more fertile, and young men were told to find spouses. The *gazdasszony* was ordered to not let her family go hungry, and even the animals were told to work hard for their masters. As with other scourging rites, various body parts were struck to keep them healthy in the coming year.

Whether they were the giver or recipient of the lashings, the boys were gifted with various edible treats as a reward.

Vízkereszt

On January 6, thirteen days after Christmas, the Catholic Church celebrates a festival known as Epiphany. In Hungary, this festival was known as the celebration of *Vízkereszt*, which can be roughly translated as "water-christening." On *Vízkereszt*, priests blessed incense and water to be used throughout the year. This holy water was then sprinkled in front of a house's main entrance, and a little would be poured into the well to purify the water. Priests also went from house to house, blessing each home by sprinkling water and salt on its walls.

These days, the festival is known mostly for the fact that it is the day Christmas trees are taken down. *Vízkereszt* is the official end of the Christmas festivities and the start of the season of *farsang*, completing the cycle of the Magyar year.

---

112. Paládi-Kovács, *Magyar néprajz nyolc kötetben*, vol. 7, 258–60.

Part V

RITES
OF PASSAGE

Birth, coming of age, marriage, and death are all universal experiences, very often marked by various rites of passage. These occasions were not just an excuse for a good party (although there was definitely some of that going on) or even a chance to reflect on the greater meaning of the life stage. Rites of passage were also a chance for both the individual and their community to take part in various magical techniques to ensure good fortune in the celebrant's future endeavors. In this section, we will examine some of these ceremonies and rites of passage.

Chapter 24
COMING OF AGE

Many folk stories and fairy tales focused on a character who was coming of age. In these stories, the young hero or heroine started off on a journey, either to try their fortune or to fulfill some sort of quest. To aid them on their journey, they were usually gifted a satchel known as a *tarisznya*, filled with wine and *pogácsa* ("biscuits"). This was magical, strength-giving food, sometimes baked with the mother's breastmilk, symbolically endowing the young person with vital energy. During the course of the story, the hero or heroine was often asked to share their *pogácsa* with a beggar or hungry animal; if the character was generous and good-hearted, they usually won supernatural help to aid them on their journey.

Children prepared for their young adulthood by listening to and internalizing the messages from these stories. As in fairy tales, many young people did indeed journey away from their families of origin to try their luck. The community marked their new status in rites both formal and informal, such as the Christian rite of confirmation. Young adults were tested by church leaders about religious teachings, songs, prayers, etc. Many times, the dedicants prepared (or purchased) a gift for the church, such as embroidering an altar cloth or carving a statue. After vowing to live a moral life, they were admitted as full members of the church. Many communities incorporated elements of pre-Christian rites, such as decorating the church with flowers and green branches.

To prove that they were ready for the rights of adulthood, both men and women had to prove that they could handle adult responsibilities. Usually this involved joining the workers at the harvest or other communal work events. If the young man or woman did a full day's work without complaint, the others accepted them as an adult.

In some communities, those who wished to be seen as an adult might be subjected to various trials. Girls most often tested each other in the spinning houses, where their work ethic was readily evident to all. Although young men also worked together, they tended to subject boys to elaborate trials (many of which would be considered hazing today), such as having to harvest a field alone, wrestle a fully grown man, carry a heavy stone from one edge of a field to the other, lift a millstone, tolerate pain without flinching, climb a mountain, go out of the village alone at night, or steal something. After completing the trial to the judges' satisfaction, the youth was ceremonially "baptized" with wine, water, or alcohol alongside some mock-formal words of wisdom. The other members of the group made a parody of a knighting ceremony by slapping the youth or striking him with a stick. In some particularly rough areas, the older boys joined together to give the candidate a beating. After the ceremony, the rest of the villagers accepted him as a man.

Once a young person was accepted as an adult, they had entered a new phase of their life. They were able to wear the clothing of adults, and they were addressed with honorifics instead of the more informal *tegeződés* way of speaking to children or those of lesser social status. They took their place among the men or women of their households and were expected to work alongside the others in full capacity. In some communities, young, unmarried men tended to reside together, sleeping outside in the summer and in kitchens or barns in the colder months.

Adults were able to attend balls, dances, and gatherings; they could go drinking, if male, or to the *fonó*, if female. They were able to seek employment, date, and potentially marry. Boys could smoke and drink, and girls were allowed to wear different outfits and hair coverings at community celebrations, something that will be looked at in more detail later in this chapter.

Young womanhood was a special phase in one's life. *Kislányok* ("little girls") were often formally initiated into *nagylányok* ("big girls") when they were invited to take part in the various springtime dances, such as the Lenten circle dances. Others were invited to the *fonó* and asked to work alongside their peers. From this time, they would receive invitations to social events and could be courted by young men. The *nagylányok* of a community were also tasked with performing certain spells or rituals, such as summoning rain during a drought.

Part of becoming a *nagylány* was getting one's first menstrual period. The blood from one's first cycle was thought to be extra magical; a young woman could wipe it on her face to prevent freckles or blemishes. Once a woman started getting her period, she entered into a certain stage of her life where she was restricted from performing certain actions depending on what part of her cycle she was in, such as not being able to perform certain household chores during certain times of the month. It wasn't until a woman reached menopause that she returned to a state of permanent ritual purity; in some communities, women could not be a community healer until their cycles had ceased.

While physical virginity was valued by the church, the state of being a maiden depended more on being unmarried and without child. Newly married couples were still welcomed at dances and other celebrations where young people gathered, as they were believed to serve as role models for their younger peers. Once a couple had children, they tended to stay home from these community gatherings and only join in on celebrations where people of all ages were welcome.

Komálás

One very important activity to be done during young adulthood was *komálás*, a process of formally declaring a lifelong friendship with a member of the same gender. Once they had declared themselves *komák* (or, in the case of females, *koma-asszonyok*, "*koma*-women," or *mátkák*), the friends would have a special place in each other's lives for the rest of their days. *Komák* rarely moved far away from one another, because it was their role to support each other through the trials of life.

Although both genders created *komaság* bonds, the process was especially ceremonial and elaborate for females. The rite typically took place on the first Sunday after Easter, known as *Fehérvasárnap* ("White Sunday"). To signal that a girl wanted to become a *koma* with another, she sent a *komatál*, a friendship platter, to the other girl. These platters consisted of baked goods, fruit, and wine. The platter was carried over to the intended's house by younger girls of eight or ten years of age, who handed them over with a verse. If the platter was accepted, the host mixed her own wine with the gifted wine, and the two young women drank it together. Some young women were especially popular and had several platters sent to them, from which they had to choose their favorite. After their friendships were so declared, the two would be *koma-asszonyok* to one another. *Koma-asszonyok* were especially important when it came time to bear children; the friends often became godmothers to each other's children and helped each other recover after giving birth.

Young men also declared their good friends their *koma* or *komámuram* ("my *koma* sir"), although there was no ceremonial friendship platter. Some young men chose to cement their bonds with a blood oath; after exchanging blood through the prick of a finger, they considered one another brothers. This echoes historical accounts of *vérszerződések* ("blood oaths") in which parties bound their agreements by mixing their own blood in a cup of blood or water and then taking turns drinking from it to become unified in their purpose.[113]

Interestingly, *komák* typically used formal registers when speaking to one another instead of the more informal register used between friends or peers. The formal register designated the high honor with which they treated one another. As time went on, the term of *komaság* lost its formality, and the term *koma* became something akin to saying "pal" or "buddy."

Clothing and Head Covers

Although the most dramatic shifts in status were when a person came of age in their teens and twenties, there were more subtle changes in people's roles throughout their lifespans. Many of these were indicated mainly through the clothing and accessories individuals wore.

Well-off women might have thirty or more ceremonial outfits for various special occasions throughout the year, like holidays, weddings, or going to church; others wore a single ceremonial outfit for all holidays and special events. Mourning clothes were a separate category of clothing worn when loved ones died. As women typically made their own clothes, the more outfits a woman had, the greater her prestige was. It indicated that she was *szorgalmas*— that is, a hard worker. Men had fewer outfits; besides being practical, male

113. Vörös, "Kutyaáldozatok és kutyatemetkezések a középkori Magyarországon I," 179.

clothing choices (as well as the style of facial hair) generally reflected the wearer's profession, age, and social standing.

When a woman's oldest daughter married, the mother had to start wearing the clothing of an elder woman. Sometimes this could be as early as the mid-to-late thirties. By the age of forty, women were considered middle-aged and could no longer wear bright colors, and by the time a woman had reached her sixties, she wore black as a sign of old age.

One of the most visible signs of a woman's life stage was her head-covering, or lack thereof. Specific customs and styles of these head-coverings varied greatly from community to community, and many women had special styles for holidays and festivals and others for everyday wear. Single women usually went bareheaded; girls and young women wore their hair in various braids (as many as twenty to twenty-five) or rolled hairstyles, the styling of which oftentimes visually indicated whether they were of an age to marry or not.

A *párta*

A visible symbol of maidenhood was the *párta*, an embroidered, crescent-shaped headband worn like a crown during community get-togethers. Some *párta* even included pearls and gems woven into them. Prior to a marriage, churches would announce the upcoming union. The bride-to-be had to attend at least one church service wearing her *párta*; if she didn't, her future children could be born deaf. Although it was a great privilege to wear this type of head-covering for a time, wearing it for too long could become problematic as well; women who failed to marry in a timely fashion were mocked as being *pártában maradt*, i.e., having "stayed in their *párta* too long." In some communities, a young married woman was able to continue wearing this head-covering until she was visibly with child (or when she had reached a certain age and was no longer considered young by the community's standards).

Once she married, a woman covered her hair with a kerchief, often called a *főkötő* or *fejkendő*. There were countless variations of head-covering, which could be made out of lace, leather, straw, cotton, and many other materials. The shape and amount of hair the *főkötő* covered varied. Although women in certain communities covered all of their hair, leaving no strands visible, this was rare—it was generally understood that the point of head-covering was not to hide one's beauty, but rather to denote one's status as a married woman. The *főkötő* was such an important designation of womanhood that if a husband tore it off his wife during an argument—especially publicly—it was considered the highest form of insult possible.

The *főkötő* was also an important visible sign of one's age and social standing. The style of *főkötő* a woman wore might change as many as ten times in her life as she grew older and moved through various life stages. Younger women tended to wear bright, floral kerchiefs, but as they got older, the colors they wore got darker, and the patterns became more subdued as well.

A woman who had given birth out of wedlock was not honored with a formal head-covering ceremony; it was the midwife who tied the kerchief on her head after she gave birth. She was never truly admitted into the ranks of the other women; at community events she had to stand aside, and even at religious services she was relegated to standing at the back of the church. If the woman did manage the unlikely feat of marrying afterward, she was not allowed to wear a wedding wreath upon her head, nor was she allowed the privilege of wearing the *párta*.

Although much emphasis is put on women's covering practices, men also paid special attention to their head covers. The ribbons, feathers, or flowers decorating one's hat indicated whether the wearer was a child, young man, a grown man who was courting, or even a man engaged to be married. If a man wore a hat without a decoration, this meant he had settled into old age.

Chapter 25
LOVE AND MARRIAGE

Finding a suitable marriage partner was one of the keys to a successful and happy life. Making a match was often a community affair, sometimes with direct matchmaking by parents or older relatives. Dedicated matchmakers could help parents sort out which eligible mates might be a good fit; these matchmakers vetted prospective mates with loose morals. Even when a couple decided on a marriage themselves, the parents and community had to approve of the match, and even a disreputable parent or relative could rule a potential match out.

Being late to marry—or, even worse, not getting married at all—was judged harshly by society. The prospect of not finding a suitable partner caused a great deal of anxiety among young people. Many magical techniques existed to assist a young person in securing a match. The most powerful form of love magic was deemed to be the love potion. People believed in these potions well into the twentieth century, and they are not unheard of today.

The most basic form of a love potion was to use an ingredient from the caster's own body and mix it into a food or drink that was to be consumed by the victim. The ingredient could be a small piece of an intimate item of clothing (such as a stocking), hair (either from the head or other parts of the body, like the armpit or pubic area), spit, blood (including menstrual blood), breastmilk, semen, or urine. Other times, a recipe's ingredient was put in close contact with the body in some way, such as straining wine through one's armpit hair, holding sugar under the armpit for a time, or letting an egg yolk run down one's back before adding it to the food. Couples who wanted to be together forever could intentionally feed one another pieces of their hair.

It also didn't hurt to make oneself as beautiful as possible to catch the eye of a potential match. For much of Hungarian history, the ideal woman was plump and rosy-cheeked. Apples were a perfect symbol of beauty, as they were both round and red; placing them into one's washing basin would help the woman grow equally plump and ruddy. Springtime snows were a symbol of freshness; washing one's face in the melted snow meant they would be healthy and fresh. "Washing" with honey could attract men. Freckles could be "sent away" with the first swallow seen in the springtime.

Long hair was also desirable. Standing bareheaded in a springtime shower would ensure one's hair would grow long. Males in some communities were advised to cut their hair on the full moon and females on the new moon, although the reasoning was lost over time. One could not cut their hair during the waning moon, lest their hair fall out. On certain days of the year, such as the summer solstice, girls could wash their hair in dew gathered before daybreak, then run through the village while calling out, "May my hair be as long as the tail of a colt, or maybe even longer. May it be as long as the world, or maybe even longer, as long as the Danube River!"[114]

While spells of various kinds were techniques for attracting a partner, an individual might also turn to magic in order to bring love to an end, to get revenge on an unfaithful lover, or to force a partner to return to the person they had left. A spell to make an unfaithful partner return involved throwing three handfuls of dirt taken from the grave of an unbaptized child; this dirt had to be thrown backward over one's head while the church bells tolled. The inverse of a love potion could also be used to break someone up. Someone who desired a breakup might burn a piece of their lover's hair, blood, or spit to "burn away" their passion, or they could feed their spouse a food with a disgusting ingredient, such as a louse, baked into it. A jealous third party could also try to break up a happy couple by giving one or both of them such a food item, by placing the woman's hair into a bird's nest, or by sticking a pin into a lit candle while visualizing the couple.

---

114. Paládi-Kovács, *Magyar néprajz nyolc kötetben*, vol. 7, 192.

Courtship

While many matches inevitably failed—with or without the aid of magic—many couples chose to commit to one another more fully. The next step for most relationships involved a courtship, whereby they spent time with one another under the supervision of chaperones. While the couple might also see each other at festivals, community dances, or work parties, a young man who was seriously interested in courting a woman was invited to her family's house; in some areas, he was even allowed to spend the night before the wedding.

Sometimes young men put their sweethearts to the test to see if they would make good marriage material. One such test was called a *kulcspróba* ("Trial of the Keys"). A key was placed into finished yarn, and if the work was high quality, the key would pass through smoothly. But if the yarn was of poor quality, the key got tangled up instead.

As a couple's relationship got more serious, the two exchanged love gifts. This had a longstanding tradition: early Hungarian couples exchanged a graven image of a house deity, engraved in silver, as a symbol of their marriage, which each of them wore for the rest of their lives. After graven images were outlawed by Christianity, love gifts changed in nature and tended to be practical items that people needed for daily living, but these items were decorated with romantic symbols such as hearts, birds, or flowers. Over the centuries, the gifts became less practical and more decorative, such as painted wooden spoons or *mézeskalács*, a moldable dough made from flour, honey, and sugar syrup. *Mézeskalács* was baked into various shapes and decorated with icing, ribbons, and mirrors and sold at markets or in specialty shops in cities; the ones shaped like hearts were especially popular as love gifts.

A formal engagement party, called *eljegyzés*, indicated that the marriage was agreeable to both the couple and their families. This was when the heads of the family formally met and relatives were present to witness bargaining about what property each party would bring to the union. The decorated dowry chest contained bedding, towels, tablecloths, pillows, wall coverings, and so on, which the bride had been preparing from the time she was in her early teens. The dowry was ceremonially taken to the couple's new house on the day of the wedding, and the contents were displayed at the wedding feast; the couple's social status partially depended on the amount and quality of the bride's work.

The groom brought furniture and tools to the marriage, as well as livestock. The groom also had to assure the parents and relatives of his bride that he had enough money to support her, and that if he died, his widow would be able to support herself and any children they had together. A handshake between all parties indicated that the conditions of the marriage were acceptable, and a formal contract was drawn up.

The *eljegyzés* was also a time to exchange further gifts, many of which were symbolic in nature. The groom's mother gave the bride a silk cloth knotted in such a way that a few coins were bundled into it, while the bride gifted her parents-in-law and sisters-in-law white linen cloths with apples and nuts tied into them. She gave her groom a red cloth, which he pinned to his coat pocket on formal occasions as a signal that he was engaged. The groom gave the bride a ring and perhaps money or a pocket knife, and she gave him an outfit to get married in. Her ring had to stay on her finger for at least nine days, otherwise the marriage would not be successful. Sometimes before a real present was given, the giver presented a tattered cloth wrapped in a soiled kerchief; this had to be refused before the real present was given.

To avoid the hassle and expense of having a formal courtship and engagement, a young man might kidnap a young woman with the help of his friends. They kept her captive for several days, at which point her parents usually consented to the marriage, knowing that their family's honor would have been compromised already. Whether the couple had had premarital relations was largely irrelevant—the community would assume that they had. In communities that valued virginity in their brides, the young woman would lose the chance of landing a respectable groom in the future, so she might as well marry the man who took her. It was rare that the law wanted to get involved in these matters, so many grooms succeeded in kidnapping their brides in this manner.

While these kidnappings are horrifying, some brides were willing partners and helped arrange their own kidnappings in hopes of forcing their parents to agree to a marriage. However, there was always the risk of the woman's relatives attacking the men or involving the law. Other times, kidnapping was performed with the full consent and blessing of the bride's parents, especially if the girl was poor and her family could not afford a dowry, if the parents wanted to avoid the cost of a full wedding, or if the girl wanted to marry someone outside of the village. In these cases, the kidnapping was largely symbolic.

The archaic custom of marital kidnappings is sometimes dramatically reenacted at weddings for the amusement of the guests. When I was in my teens, before I had ever witnessed or even heard of this wedding custom, I was working in a hotel that hosted occasional weddings. Imagine my surprise when during one bridal dinner, a group of horsemen galloped into the courtyard and kidnapped the bride! I thought a real crime was being committed, and in my shock it took me a minute to understand why many of the guests were laughing in approval!

A *vadházasság*, or a "wild marriage," was like a common-law marriage, mostly entered into by those for whom a large wedding did not make sense: widows and widowers, those of low status, those with few living relations, or those who already had children out of wedlock. It was enough for the couple to move into a house together and declare themselves married; the community generally accepted their marriage and held them to the same standards as other couples. Other terms for common-law marriages hearkened back to pre-Christian traditions, such as:

- Married by moonlight
- Exchanged vows under the willow trees
- Made an oath over a horse's skull
- Tied the twine together
- Married by a stone wall

Some people had an even more informal view on marriage, and that was a trial marriage (a *próbaházasság*). A couple entered into a temporary marriage, usually lasting a specified amount of time, such as a month or even a year. Sometimes the pair did not even live in the same household during their trial marriage and would only visit one another at night. If they had a child during that time, they would likely make the marriage permanent. If not, they might still get married, but otherwise they were permitted to part amicably.

The Wedding Feast

As we have seen, while not all marriages were preceded by a traditional wedding celebration, most did start with a formal ceremony. Although new marriages were blessed by the church, the complex rites of the *lakodalom* were passed down from pre-Christian days. A *lakodalom* (or, colloquially, a *lagzi*) was a traditional Hungarian wedding feast. Wealthier families could organize a party lasting several days, but most feasts lasted only one day and one night, especially by the early twentieth century.

Among the most important roles in the wedding was the master of ceremonies, called the *vőfély*. He was in charge of entertaining the guests and directing the complex rituals of the wedding feast. The *vőfély* carried a staff called a *vőfélybot*, which was carved with various symbols. The groom and his friends gathered prior to the *lakodalom* to decorate this staff, using materials such as ribbons, kerchiefs, herbs (especially rosemary), fruit (especially apples), walnuts, and feathers. Over the centuries, the staff became less ornate, sometimes to the point of being an ordinary branch with some ribbons tied around it.

After the staff was decorated, the groom and his companions walked to the bride's home and gathered outside the gate. The groom's *násznagy*, another important member of the wedding party, ceremonially asked the bride's parents and relatives for permission to take her with them to wed the groom. Traditionally, the real *menyasszony* ("bride") was hidden inside the house, and her parents first brought forth an *álmenyasszony* ("fake bride")—such as an old woman, a child, or simply the wrong woman—either covered by a veil or simply dressed up in bridal clothes. The *vőlegény* ("groom") had to recognize and turn down the fake bride before the real bride was presented to him. The bride's parents then gave their final blessings to her, and she put on a pair of boots with a piece of garlic inside for good fortune and protection against evil spirits.

The bridal party loaded up a wagon with the dowry while the bride's parents and relatives sang mourning songs, as they would at a funeral. The bride, in turn, sang a song or said verses to thank her parents for taking care of her as she grew up. After the final goodbyes, the wedding party took their leave, heading to the couple's new residence. Villagers lined the streets to witness how many wares the bride was able to take to her new home. The procession took a winding route through town so many people could see it; the dowry was prominently displayed at the *lakodalom* as well, which aided the couple in establishing their new household's status. The townspeople might ritually bar the couple's way by putting various obstacles in their path; the groom and his assistants had to pay a fee or give the villagers wine to let them pass.

If it hadn't already been done, the wedding party could stop at the church to have their marriage blessed by the priest. Finally, they proceeded to their new home, where the wedding feast was celebrated. (The home would have been decorated ahead of time with green branches, ribbons, and banners.) Families sometimes saved up for years to be able to feed the entire guest list in a lavish manner. The more elaborate the meal, the higher the couple's social standing would be. If the groom's parents contributed to the meal, it showed the community that they approved of their son's match.

Uninvited guests stood outside the gates. Sometimes they wore costumes or masks or played pranks on the invited guests; sometimes they were invited for a round of drinks. Upon their entrance, the new couple would be showered with grain so they would be fertile and offered sweet treats so they would have a sweet life together, and a loaf of bread would be held over their heads so they would always have sustenance. The bride also made a few symbolic sweeps with a broom to show she would be an industrious housekeeper. (This action might have had a symbolic purifying intention as well, as blessings were swept into the house or negative energy was swept out.)

If the weather was good, the feast might be held outside. During the course of the meal, the groom and bride had to eat from one plate or one cup to show their fates were now intertwined. Throughout the meal, the guests carefully watched for signs that would show the couple's future. For instance, if someone upset a glass of water, whomever the water spilled toward would soon celebrate a baptism. Guests toasted the new couple to wish them luck in their marriage. Sadly, in some communities, the bride was not allowed to take part in the festivities herself, but instead had to sit quietly while her guests celebrated so she would be considered respectable.

Since starting a family was on the mind of many young couples, there were certain rituals they could participate in to ensure their future fertility. If a bride stepped over a child lying on the threshold of her new home, she would not be without child. A young boy was often placed in the bride's lap while she ate so that she would soon have a son as well. If a woman wanted her future children to be plump, she was told to sit on a pillow during the course of the night, and if she wanted a child with dark eyes, she could look into the soot-filled insides of the home's chimney. To ensure that a new bride would have an easy time birthing children, her female companions could smash a raw egg on the ground by her feet. The groom could consume rooster to absorb its vitality.

Throughout the evening, the *vőfély* entertained the guests by reciting various rhyming love poems and serenading the couple with ballads—many of which were irreverent and even lewd. When he wanted attention during the feast, he used his staff to knock on the ceiling. He led playful games to entertain the guests, gave the guests practical instructions, and generally directed the party, including the dances. Some dances could get rather rowdy, like the pillow dance. In this dance, the unmarried guests stood in a circle. A man entered the ring and tossed a pillow in front of a young woman he liked. They both kneeled on the pillow and kissed one another. Then the man tossed the pillow to another man, and the process repeated.

The bridal dance was the last opportunity for a bride to dance before she assumed the status of a married woman. While she danced, guests gifted her with money, either placed in envelopes or thrown into a communal pot. The *vőfély* made sure that the guests were not offended by having a lower-ranked male dance with the bride before all the higher-ranked males had a chance to do so. All of the groom's relatives had to dance with the bride to show the community they accepted her into their family. Even old people who were too frail to dance "danced" by holding the bride's hands while they were sitting down. The last to dance with the bride was the groom, who either gave her a high-status gift to show his esteem for her or a purposely inexpensive gift, such as an apple or a bread roll. The latter was especially common if the marriage was based on love as opposed to more practical motivations.

The final dance of the evening was the *gyertyás tánc*, "the candle dance." Although there were different variations of this dance, a typical version involved the *vőfély* and the bride dancing within a circle of candles lit for this portion of the evening. As they danced, the *vőfély* extinguished the candles one by one. When all the flames were out, the guests cheered and shouted wishes for fertility for the new couple. Then the bride was led off to the bedroom as the guests threw the now-unlit candles in her direction. Young children were encouraged to roll around on the marital bed before the couple went into the chamber so that the bride would soon conceive children. It was also traditional to prank the couple by hiding items in the sheets that would make noise when disturbed, much to the amusement of the guests waiting outside. The newly married couple was locked in the bedding chamber for a time, possibly several hours or even overnight, while the guests continued to celebrate.

In the bedding chamber, the bride would perform a symbolic act to show that she accepted her subservient role in their marriage, such as by removing the groom's boots for him. If the bride was not content to be subservient in the marriage, she could wait for her new husband to take his hat off; when he put it down, she could quickly toss her own bridal wreath on top of it, magically ensuring that she would be the stronger party in the relationship.

When the couple emerged from the bedding chamber at dawn, the bride was led off to have her hair ceremonially covered for the first time. The *főkötő* kerchief was usually tied on by her godmother; the duo was surrounded by a circle of adult women. The bride might be encouraged to put up a fight and cry out for all the things she was losing from her youth, but the women surrounding her had to convince her of the joys of womanhood instead. While the head-covering ceremony was happening, the groom would have a small ceremony of his own in another part of the house, where he had to offer alcohol that he had made himself to the various village *gazdák* who had been invited to the wedding. If they accepted the drinks, the men were also indicating that they accepted the groom into their ranks.

Before the sun rose, the wedding party gathered outside the home or in a specially designated area of the village known as the *hajnalkert* ("dawn garden"). There, a sacred bonfire was built. The members of the wedding party danced around the bonfire in a circle and helped the bride jump over the flames. With this ceremony, the wedding feast was concluded.

Chapter 26
PREGNANCY AND CHILDBIRTH

O nce married, a bride could not stay without child for too long. Since infant and child mortality were common before the advent of modern medicine, many young couples planned to have several children. A couple's *hetedik gyerek* ("seventh child") was considered especially blessed. A *hetedik gyerek* often had magical powers, such as being able to find treasure buried in the ground. In one account, when a *hetedik gyerek* reached seven years of age, his right thumbnail was anointed with the oil of white poppies; he was able to find buried treasure by gazing at his thumb: the treasure reflected on his nail's surface.[115] The *hetedik gyerek* was said to have a magical touch, only needing to draw their hands across a person's painful body part to heal it. Their powers could be lost, however, if they failed to be gentle or godly, or if they used bad language.

Family Planning and Pregnancy Termination

If a woman was not in a position to have a child, there were a number of magical birth control methods she might use, such as sitting on the edge of an open chest on the way home from her wedding. On the other hand, if a woman wished to conceive, she fasted and prayed. If she did not conceive, she might turn to various magical techniques to help conception along, such as taking ritual baths or drinking herbal potions. A woman who wished to

115. Balásy, "Székely kincsásó babonák," 296–97.

have twins could eat a "paired fruit," such as two cherries that had connected stems.

Despite all the lengths many women went to to get pregnant, not every pregnancy was desirable; there were many reasons why a woman might not want to continue a pregnancy, ranging from financial issues to health-related concerns. Knowledge about how to avoid pregnancy was often scanty and incorrect. The most popular opinion was that a baby received *Isten szikra* ("God's spark," i.e., its soul) about halfway through pregnancy, around the time a mother could feel the baby move independently inside her. A midwife could help a woman terminate a pregnancy before this point though herbal or physical methods. Even magical methods were used, such as having a woman swallow gunpowder, having the woman look inside an empty barrel, or standing her on a scale and then "measuring away" the fetus by subtracting weights. These processes were referred to as *angyalcsinálás* ("angel-making").

Attempting an abortion was risky. If a woman survived the procedure, there was no guarantee that her pregnancy would be successfully terminated. If the infant survived to birth, it might be born physically or mentally damaged. However, even if a woman successfully terminated her pregnancy and lived to tell the tale, she was not in the clear: her own baby's spirit might become a danger to her by nursing from her in the night, making the mother weak and gaunt. In order to be rid of the spirit, the mother had to cover her breasts with garlic, burn blessed incense by her bedside, sprinkle blessed water on the spirit, or keep a baptismal gown within arm's reach to quickly wrap around the child. The latter was the best option; instead of merely vanquishing the spirit, the baby had a chance to go to the *Túlvilág* and join the mother when she was ready to die so that they could make the journey to the spirit world together.

Sometimes the soul of the mother was placed in danger due to a terminated pregnancy. In one account, several shepherds were eating their meal around a campfire in the middle of a field far from town. They noticed a woman—a stranger to them—in their midst. After the shepherds questioned her, the woman finally confessed that she was a ghost who was being tormented in the afterlife because she had aborted seven of her children. She was unable to go on to the next world until she atoned for her sins. The shepherds offered to have a priest say seven holy Masses in her name for her soul's repose. Reassured by their promise, the ghost of the woman disappeared.[116]

Pregnancy

Once she did conceive, a mother-to-be could ensure a healthy pregnancy by drinking special herbal teas and even by being careful about what thoughts she let her mind dwell on in an effort to influence her child's future personality as well as ease childbirth. To ensure an easy labor, a mother-to-be had to eat the first bite out of every family meal during her pregnancy. Pregnant women were advised what to eat and drink in order to have a healthy pregnancy and baby, just as they are today, although the advice was drastically different then. Pregnant women were sometimes advised to drink a lot of wine and *pálinka* so their children would be strong and hearty. She was even allowed to steal food to satisfy her cravings; many community members looked the other way if a pregnant woman stole food.

An expectant mother could perform certain actions to influence the way her future child would look. If she wanted her child to have black eyes, for example, she could look into a sooty chimney. If she ate pumpkin, her baby would be bald, but if she ate corn without all the silk removed from it, her child's hair would constantly need cutting. Besides influencing appearances, the mother might also predict whether she would have a boy or girl child. To do so, she could stick her finger through a spiderweb; if the spider re-spun the missing piece, her child would be a son, but if the hole remained, the child would be a girl.

There were countless taboos pregnant women had to follow. If a mother-to-be wore makeup, her child would have skin problems. If she saw a snake, she had to spit to ward off bad luck lest her child have a difficult time learning to walk; she also had to spit if she saw a hideous person so her baby would not be cursed with repulsive looks. Hiding a pregnancy would cause her child to die early, falsely denying a pregnancy would cause the child to be mute, and lying or using foul language would make her child grow up to have wicked speech. If a mother miscarried, the misfortune was often attributed to something she had done, such as acting in an immoral way, working on a

116. Pócs, *Hiedelemszövegek*, 145.

Sunday, breaking a taboo, becoming overly emotional, becoming too hot or too cold, or not listening to her body's cravings.

Giving Birth

When a woman went into labor, her midwife assisted with the birth, sprinkling the mother-to-be with blessed water during difficult contractions. To prevent the *rosszak* from finding out that she was in labor, the mother was forbidden from loudly crying out. If labor stalled, the midwife made practical suggestions, such as telling the mother to jump up and down or crawl around on her hands and knees. If more drastic measures needed to be taken, her husband (or the midwife) could put the woman in a burlap sack and roll her around the ground, squeeze her torso with towels, or lift the mother up and shake her. If even these measures failed, the midwife turned to magical remedies, such as opening any drawers, knots, and locks in the house, having the laboring woman's husband step over her three times as she lay on the ground, or giving her water to drink from his own mouth. It was considered especially powerful if a birthing mother's own mother prayed for her well-being, especially if the prayer was said under the open sky.

A healthy infant was the hope of all, but birth registrars unfortunately recorded many stillbirths. If a child was born sickly or did not appear strong enough to survive long past birth, the midwife baptized the child. While not all unbaptized children turned into a malevolent *nora*, even in the best-case scenario, the child's spirit would be known as a *kereszteletlen* ("unbaptized [child]") doomed to wander in darkness until the end of the world. (More generous beliefs stated that they would only have to wander for seven years, at which point Saint John the Baptist would find them in the World Beyond and baptize them himself.)

If an infant was skinny, sickly, and had excess body hair (all common presentations of premature babies), the child would be declared an *agos gyerek*, which is an obscure term sometimes translated as having "dog sickness," thought to have been caused by the mother having kicked a dog or another furry animal during her pregnancy. There were several ways an *agos gyerek* could be cured. One such method was for the mother nurse the infant on her doorstep while the church bells rang, all the while imploring the Virgin Mary to remove the fur from her child.

Another type of malformed child was the dreaded *üszöggyerek* ("blighted child"). There were various explanations for how this child originated. Some said it was due to the mother's attempt to abort the child or the mother looking at a corpse while pregnant. Others said it originated when a pregnant woman poured water on the embers of a fire; the resulting steam and smoke entered her stomach and deformed the child into this supernatural creature whose skin was either black or blistered, often covered with fur. Some accounts go well beyond describing unusual appearances, however, noting that the *üszöggyerek* could demonstrate demonic behavior, leaping out of the laboring mother and sprinting around the room. It could run up walls, jump, scurry across the ceiling, and fall back down without dying. A midwife had to be ready to beat such a creature to death with a broomstick lest it run back inside its mother, killing her.

After a healthy baby was born, the midwife severed the umbilical cord, thus starting the baby's independent life. The cord itself could prove to have omens connected with it. Some midwives interpreted the number of knots on the cord as the number of future children a mother might have. If the cord had been wrapped around the infant's neck, this was a bad omen, foretelling that the child would not live long or would leave the world as they entered it: with a cord wrapped around their neck, a result of being hanged for criminal activities.

The midwife examined the infant carefully to see if there were any deformities, birthmarks, or other signs that could predict the child's personality or fate—or even magical inclinations. As discussed in chapter 11, if a child was born with special markings or in the caul, they might grow up to have magical powers. Birthmarks were believed to be caused by the mother's actions during pregnancy, such as an unfulfilled pregnancy craving or injuries she received during pregnancy. A mother might have stared at, received a shock from, or been frightened by an object or person; if she hadn't spit or redirected her gaze to her palm fast enough, the baby might have a birthmark resembling the cause of the fright. (In a similar vein, my mother told me she was convinced that I would have an allergy to shellfish because she was thoroughly disgusted by a seafood platter she saw while she was pregnant with me!) An unsightly birthmark could be cured in different ways, such as spitting on it, praying while sitting on the threshold, or pulling a placenta across the birthmark three times. Another method for curing a birthmark could be done during the new moon, when the chant "What I see should become like new; what I don't see should pass away" was said over the birthmark.[117]

After examining the infant, the midwife poured cold water on the infant so it would not be afraid of cold in life or catch colds frequently, then gave the child a proper bath. This bath was an opportunity to ensure the child's good fortune. The midwife prepared the bathwater by adding various items to it, such as:

- The cleaned foot of a goose, so the baby wouldn't have cold hands or feet
- Water from a goose's water dish, so the baby wouldn't get eczema (the word for eczema was *libabőr*, which, literally translated, means "goose-skin")
- Milk, so the baby's skin would be soft and white
- Apples or roses, so the child would have a blushing countenance
- Salt, so the child would be strong and healthy
- A tool, such as an axe, so the child would grow up to work hard
- Coins, so the child would not be impoverished as they grew

After the bath, the midwife lay the baby on a fur coat or sheepskin to make the child's hair turn lush and curly. When the infant was dressed, their clothes were put on backward in order to deter any malevolent spirits—the spirits would be confused and leave the infant alone. The midwife pressed various objects into the baby's fists, such as a coin so they would grow up to be frugal or a hammer so they would be a hard worker. Prayer books or beads were touched to the child's face or hands so they would be religious. If the child was a girl, the midwife called out many boy names so she would find a husband easily.

When the baby was settled, the midwife cleaned up. Disposing of the bathwater was a task in and of itself. It could only be discarded while the sun was in the sky, in an area where there was no chance of anyone accidentally stepping in it and stealing the child's fortune. Spitting in the water added a layer of protection. Ideally, a boy's bathwater was spilled at the base of a tall,

117. Pócs, *Magyar ráolvasások I*, 77.

straight, strong tree so the child would grow up to have similar qualities. A girl's was spilled at the base of a rose bush, if possible, so she would grow up as lovely as a rose. If it was raining, it was good luck to pour it into the rainfall trickling down from the roof so the child would be as fresh as running water. The bathwater had to be disposed of before nightfall, lest the baby's dreams be spilled away with the water.

A postpartum bed found in a traditional *tisztaszoba*

The midwife also fastened a canopy around the postpartum bed known as the *Boldogasszony ágya* ("bed of the *Boldogasszony*"). The light net canopy was held by a knife stuck into the wall or ceiling. This knife would then be placed under the pillow. Whenever she left her bed, the mother had to stick this knife in the ground in front of her for protection against the *rosszak*. For the same purpose, garlic and bread might be tied into the fabric canopy. Typically, this was the bed used for birthing and dying, located in the *tisztaszoba* of the house, discussed in chapter 8. If a family was less well-off and did not have dedicated space in their home for such activities, the new mother might stay in her own bed, although her husband would likely sleep elsewhere during her postpartum time.

When the mother was ready to settled into her postpartum bed, the midwife ritually asked her, "Where are you going now?" The mother replied, "To the tent of the *Boldogasszony*." [118] In order to prevent illness, the evil eye, or bad spirits from harming the infant or mother, blessed water and candles, prayer beads, images of saints, or protective talismans such as garlic, salt, knives, needles, brooms, axes, or scythes were placed in or under the bed. If the mother stepped out of her bed, she had to wear footwear known as the *Boldogasszony papucsa* ("slippers of the *Boldogasszony*") as a form of protection; these slippers could not be worn at any other time of a woman's life.

The infant slept in this bed for the first few weeks with their mother, after which they were moved to a cradle. It was said that the *Boldogasszony* would personally protect the vulnerable duo, sometimes along with two angels: one to guard the mother and the other to watch the infant.

118. Kálmány, *Boldogasszony*, 19.

Chapter 27

POSTPARTUM AND INFANCY

After a woman gave birth, both she and her infant were considered especially vulnerable, both physically and spiritually, for the first weeks of the child's life. Mother and infant remained in the postpartum bed for several weeks, only leaving for short periods. For the first week, the mother was not allowed to get up out of bed at all except to relieve herself; after a week, she could get up and move about the house.

During the postpartum period, the mother was not allowed to do any work around the house such as baking or cooking; she was not even allowed to draw water from the well, lest the water in it become impure. Instead, the mother had to rely on other women to help. In a large family, this was easily solved; grandmothers, sisters, hired help, and other female friends filled in the gaps for those who lived in smaller households. (Fathers, conveniently enough, were let off the hook. Like in many modern sitcoms, folktales frequently reiterated the idea that if men got involved in domestic chores for whatever reason, disaster would ensue; "women's work" was left to the women in all but the most dire circumstances.) For the first few days, the new mother's *koma-asszony* brought meals to the family; the friend first had to try a few bites with great enthusiasm, then sat with the new mother while she finished the meal.

In the days after a baby's birth, the father took the placenta and afterbirth outside and buried it. If the couple wanted their next child to be a boy, the placenta and afterbirth was buried under a pear tree; if they wanted a girl,

264 • Chapter 27

an apple tree. If they wanted no more children at all, the placenta was buried under a willow. Alternatively, if a couple wanted to divine whether their child would have a long life or not, they could put the placenta on an anthill in the morning. If it was fully carried away by the ants by sunset, the child would live many years.

For the first week after the birth, the midwife visited the mother daily to monitor her and the baby for complications and help establish breastfeeding. The midwife also helped with practical tasks such as doing laundry and supplying the postpartum bed with fresh straw and sheets. Postpartum bleeding was thought to be extremely toxic, able to poison animals that went near it—it could even make trees wither away! Used straw had to be burned or thrown into a moving river, much like the *kisze* (the straw figure representing the spirit of winter) was burned or thrown into a river at the start of spring.

The mother was only allowed to leave the house after she went to church to be blessed, which could be anywhere from a week to up to forty days after birth. She carried a blessed candle on her way to the church for spiritual protection. At the church, she received a blessing, and from then on she could rejoin the world. (If a woman had given birth illegitimately, the church would deny her the necessary blessing. The midwife then accompanied the mother to the church, and the pair circled the building thrice when no one was around to see them.) If a postpartum mother set foot outside her front door before her blessing, hail would destroy her garden; if she so much as looked out her attic window, everything her sight had touched would be destroyed by a strong wind.

Infant Care

Caring for an infant had many prescriptions and prohibitions. A baby could never be bathed after sunset lest their dreams be washed away, resulting in sleeplessness. The same happened if their diapers were left out overnight. Whenever the mother removed the baby from their cradle, she placed a weighted doll in their place. It was bad luck to rock an empty cradle because the child that was supposed to lie within it would sicken or the dreams hovering around the cradle would depart, leaving the child sleepless and inconsolable.

After the umbilical stump dried up and detached from the infant, the mother saved it. She gave the stump to the child when they turned seven and asked them to untie it. If they were able to, it boded well for their future: a boy who had the dexterity to untangle their cord would be good with tools, whereas a girl had a future sewing or embroidering. They would also be successful at solving problems in the course of their life. Many families saved the dried cord in a little pouch.

Cursed Children

Infants were vulnerable to many dangers—both physical and supernatural. One researcher, Moór Elemér, wrote, "The most important concern of parents was to protect their children from curses." [119] An infant was not left alone, shown to strangers, or taken out of the house after sunset lest they fall victim to a curse or the evil eye. Mothers attempted to protect their vulnerable infants from the *rosszak* with countless techniques, such as placing various blessed objects like rosaries, garlic, or metal objects (such as needles, scissors, or knives) in the child's vicinity, dressing them in inside-out clothing, sprinkling holy water on them, or tying a small bell around their arm with a red ribbon.

A healthy infant was taken to the church a few days after birth to be baptized. This ceremony was believed to confer some degree of divine protection upon the infant. Before then, it was tempting fate to compliment a baby, refer to them with any terms of endearment, or even say their given name aloud. In order to trick evil spirits who might wish to harm the innocent baby, people talked about them in insulting, negative ways. If someone accidentally complimented the baby, the rest of the family members had to quickly insult the child instead, or spit.

If a child suddenly died in their sleep, they were thought to be a victim of a curse, but milder versions of curses also existed. If an infant or young child became suddenly ill, very fussy, or restless, they were said to have fallen victim to *szemverés* or *rontás*, and appropriate measures had to be taken to cure it. Ritual baths, especially in water with coal dust in it (known as *szenes víz*, "coal water") could often wash away these curses. A similar method of

119. Moór, "A gyermekneveléssel járó szokások és babonák," 179.

soothing a colicky infant was to bathe them in water heated by nine pieces of coal dropped into a pitcher of cold water; as each hot coal was placed in the water, the healer visualized the troubles falling away from the child with each piece. The healer chanted "Not even nine, not even eight, not even seven…" and counted down until all the coal pieces were in the water.[120] Another cure instructed the healer to take dust from a threshold and apply it to the child's navel, the soles of their feet, and the soft spot on their heads. Other methods of curing a cursed child included washing them with holy water, burning a blessed candle by their bedside, or having them drink from a skull (preferably that of a child).

Changelings

An even worse fate was the baby being turned into a *váltott gyerek* (a "changed child," also known as a changeling). This was when a healthy human child was stolen by a malevolent entity only to be replaced with the supernatural creature's own demonic offspring. The entity responsible for the change varied. Sometimes it was a real-life acquaintance who was accused of the crime. Other times, it was a witch, the devil, fairies, *törpék*, or the *Szépasszony* herself who was able to turn an infant into a changeling by suckling them; in other legends, it was Death's wife who wanted a human baby of her own, as her husband was only able to father mutants.

A mother might suspect that her child was in danger of being changed if she felt uneasy or panicked. Some mothers claimed that they had felt, heard, or seen someone coming through the window or reaching across the bed. Sometimes the mother was able to stop the change from happening, but in other instances, she was too late or not powerful enough to stop the force. In one instance, a mother experienced sleep paralysis but heard the town's pig herder muttering under her window. When she awoke, her child's head had grown to an unnatural size.[121]

If a mother thought her child had been switched, she could ask her midwife (or possibly her *koma-asszony*) to help her confirm her suspicions; they carefully examined the child and performed various tests. Frequently, tests

120. Haynal and H. Orosz, *1998. esztendei kalendárium kalendárium és szakácskönyv magyar háziasszonyok számára*, 21.

121. *Magyar Néprajzi Lexikon (MNL)*, "Váltott gyerek."

involved tricking the child into revealing their true age (which was inevitably much older than would be expected). In one story, the midwife gave a suspected *váltott gyerek* a small jug with some food at the bottom of it and a large spoon that did not fit into the jug's mouth. When the midwife left the room and watched from a doorway, the child exclaimed, "I have lived for such-and-such-number of years, and never have I seen such a thing as this!" "*Kicsi csupor, nagy kanál, nagyobb ördög nálamnál*" was a verse known throughout Hungary as something a changeling might say. This can be translated as "Little pitchers and big spoons are bigger devils than I am."[122] Another way of testing a child was to commit something blasphemous or unusual in the child's presence, such as by spilling milk onto a stove or trying to serve water in an eggshell. The infant cried out in its shock, at which point the midwife had proof that it was not the mother's own infant.

Even if a child was confirmed to be a changeling, all hope was not lost. In some stories, a stranger (such as a traveling vagrant) or a devil advised the mother how to change her child back to their original form, or the midwife might know some techniques. The most popular method was to symbolically cook the infant. The baby was held over a boiling pot of water, placed in a cooking pot on a stove that had not been lit, or placed on a large paddle used to put loaves of bread into an oven. The midwife or mother loudly announced her intention to cook the child, saying something like "*Szépasszony*, give me back mine, or I'll burn yours!" Fearing that her child would be cooked alive, the "real mother" would come and switch the children back. Sometimes it was enough to pretend to start cooking preparations, such as boiling water in a pot on the stovetop, then placing the infant on a cutting board. The midwife or mother then called out her intentions to chop the baby up, and that would be enough for the *Szépasszony* to switch them back.

Dömötör Tekla detailed quite a few ritual specificities in her book *A magyar nép hiedelemvilága*, noting that the fire for the symbolic cooking had to be made from nine corn stalks or from three branches apiece of three different varieties of thorny bushes. Sometimes one woman held the infant as two others circled the cauldron or the house; in some versions, all three women had to share a name, or the child had to be bathed in milk first. Many

---

122. Balassa, *Karcsai mondák*, 29.

rites had symbolic dialogue between the participating women. Pócs Éva, who wrote about this ritual in detail, recorded the following dialogue:

> "What are you cooking my koma friend?"
> "A [changeling]."
> "Then cook it red like a rose, and fatty as lard."[123]

Other methods of curing a changeling included rechristening the child or taking it to a táltos, who might recognize the evil spirit inside it and convince it to leave.

Baptism and Beyond

As the mother was still in the midst of her postpartum confinement when the time came for her infant to be baptized, she was not able to attend the ceremony herself; the child's godmother had to take her place. The midwife might also accompany the family, or she might stay behind with the mother. Family members had to remain silent while carrying the baby to church. Once at church, family members interpreted the child's personality from their behavior during the ceremony, such as declaring that if the baby cried during the ceremony, they would have a short life. On the way home from the baptism, the baby's godmother scattered candy in the street. If the village children grabbed at the candy eagerly, the child in question would be desired by many potential love matches when they grew up.

When the newly baptized child arrived back home, they faced a symbolic welcoming from the household. The newcomers might have to knock three times before the mother would let the baby back in the house. Other times, the procession would circle the house thrice, then pass the baby through the window. In some forms of the ritual, before she was allowed into the home with the child, the godmother had to announce that she had taken a wolf to the baptism but had brought a little, blessed lamb home with her.

Sometimes, the child's father (or the oldest male within the extended household) had to formally accept the child into the family. The godmother placed the baby in front of the doorstep. The father picked the child up and

---

123. Pócs, *Népi vallás és mágia Közép-Kelet-Európában - Válogatott tanulmányok II*, 42.

held them high in the air so they would grow as tall, then set them on a table so they would be as "good as a mouthful of bread." [124]

After the child was accepted into the family, relatives and neighbors gathered to celebrate the new child. In many communities, the midwife would be the guest of honor and played a similar role to the *vőfély* during a wedding feast. She would play various lighthearted tricks, such as replacing the real child with a doll or humorously asking for various donations in return for the services she had rendered.

In the days and weeks after the baby was baptized, the household was able to receive guests other than immediate family, the midwife, or the *koma*. However, menstruating women could not visit lest the mother's own bleeding increase as well. Once they had arrived, visitors were urged to sit down lest they "steal the child's dreams." Before a visitor left the house, they were required to bless the mother with their wishes that she recover her strength and health and produce adequate quantities of milk.

As the child grew, different aspects of their care had to be considered in a spiritual manner as well as a practical one. For instance, a mother had to chew off her child's fingernails due to the belief that if nails were clipped with an instrument before the baby reached a full year of age, they would grow up to be a thief. The first year of a baby's life was precarious; many children died before their first birthday. Even surviving children could have developmental issues that required their parents to find creative solutions. If a child was not meeting their developmental milestones (such as walking, talking, and teething) on time, magical remedies might be employed to get them back on track. For example, if a child was late to walk, the mother needed to stand in a doorframe on three sequential Fridays at noon and, without speaking, swing the baby three times between her legs. If a child was skinny, the parents could fatten them up (known as "cooking meat" onto them) by setting the baby in a pot, then circling the house while holding the pot, all the while asking, "Is there enough meat yet?" [125]

124. Kiss, "A szüléssel, kereszteléssel és felneveléssel járó szokások, babonás hiedelmek Hódmezővásárhelyről," 87.

125. Kiss, "A szüléssel, kereszteléssel és felneveléssel járó szokások, babonás hiedelmek Hódmezővásárhelyről," 90.

When a child turned a year old, the family would place before them several objects, such as a book, money, and wine. Whichever the child reached for first indicated what sort of adult they would grow into. With minor variations, this ritual is still popularly celebrated in many parts of Asia; the practice is known as *Zhuazhou* in China, *Erabitori* in Japan, and *Doljabi* in Korea. [126]

Breastfeeding

Nursing was believed to benefit a child physically and spiritually. Breastmilk was featured in many fairy tales as a magical substance that mothers baked into enchanted *pogácsa* for their children to take on long journeys. In the story *Virág Péter* ("Flower Peter"), a *táltos* tricked three children who had forgotten their identities into consuming their mother's milk, and they instantly realized who they were. In the real world, too, breastmilk was a popular ingredient in all sorts of positive spells, such as those for healing, love magic, or fertility magic.

A mother who did not produce enough breastmilk was first encouraged to consume special foods, drinks, and herbs thought to increase her supply or to wear a satchel filled with "midwife's herbs" (*bábafű*). If these didn't do the trick, another mother might lend her milk through magical means. One method involved the woman with plentiful milk baking *pogácsák* with her breastmilk and feeding it to the woman who needed to lactate more. If a woman's milk dried up suddenly, it was often attributed to magical causes. If a mother's milk dripped or spilled onto the floor, ants and snakes would develop a taste for it and return to drink from the mother, drying up her milk.

Milk might also be taken by another woman. Witches were rumored to know special magical knots that could bind a mother's milk. No objects were taken out of the house for the first three days after an infant was born, and in a child's infancy, nothing was thrown out after sunset lest the mother's milk "leave with it." Milk could also be taken unintentionally. A visiting mother who wanted to prevent accidentally taking the new mother's milk squeezed a few drops of milk onto the postpartum bed, which the mother would then sit on after her visitor left. If the women failed to do this ritual, the visitor could

126. Bora Das, "As Cultures Worldwide Seek to Peek into a Child's Future."

"take the milk with her," increasing her own supply. This unfortunate situation could be remedied if both women squeezed a few drops of milk onto the same broomstick.

Most children were weaned around the ages of two or three, but it was not unheard of to nurse a child up to the age of seven, especially if there were younger children in the home. It was advisable to nurse a child not only for practical reasons, but for spiritual ones as well. Various folk stories and legends talked about the magical abilities children might absorb via nursing. In some, it was clear that the longer the child nursed, the more powerful they would become. For instance, the legendary Fehérlófia developed extraordinary strength from nursing from his mother for seven years, and then went back to nurse for seven years more to obtain his full powers. In contrast, *Virág Péter*, nursed for only a week before he was strong enough to leave his swaddles and wrestle a sour cherry tree. He then nursed for several more weeks to gain his full powers.

The best time to wean a child was thought to be summer, when fruits were ripe. If a woman weaned in autumn, she was liable to lose her teeth early, and she would grow old early—in fact, the term for having gray hair and the word for autumn are one and the same in the Hungarian language: *ősz*. When the mother decided it was time to wean her baby, the child was "frightened" away from the breast via various methods, such as putting garlic, soap, or even animal dung on the nipples, or by brushing a coarse brush against the child's face while they nursed so they developed an aversion. Milk could also be dried up through magical techniques, such as:

- Squirting some breastmilk onto a hot surface (like a hot stone, iron, or stove) so the milk turned into steam
- Having the mother wear her shirt backward until the milk dried up
- Sticking a pin in the mother's shirt so the milk flew backward (i.e., in the direction the pin was pointing)

Chapter 28
DEATH: THE FINAL PASSAGE

Countless Hungarian beliefs dealt with keeping the dead away from the world of the living. Perhaps the best way to prevent a restless spirit from coming back to haunt their family was by making sure one's affairs were in order before they died. Elderly people or those who were gravely ill prepared for their departure by making arrangements for their burial, telling their heirs what they would be bequeathed, and making sure their livestock would be cared for after they died. Many even prepared their coffins and burial outfits ahead of time. When a person was on their deathbed, the individuals who had wronged them would visit to apologize, giving the dying person a chance to forgive them instead of enacting revenge in spirit form. All of these were methods to ensure that there would be nothing holding the dying person back from going to the *Túlvilág*.

Loved ones could help make a person's death easy and peaceful by behaving in a calm and dignified manner around the dying person. Blessed candles were burned at the dying person's bedside or pressed into their hands to hold; if the flame faded or burnt dimly, their spirit was preparing to leave their body. If a person was too comfortable, they would have a difficult time dying, so it was better to remove pillows and comforters from the bed, or to lay the person on the hard floor.

When a person did succumb to death, their spirit was thought to separate from their physical body in stages, and it wasn't until the body was given a proper burial that the soul departed for the *Túlvilág*.[127] After a person's vital functions had ceased, the soul needed assistance to detach from its body. At the moment of death, the house might give off certain signs, such as mirrors falling off the wall, furniture or dishes cracking, or the door opening on its own. Family members would then open the windows, stop the clocks, and turn the mirrors toward the wall (or cover them in a black cloth)—if a mirror was not hidden, the soul could catch a glimpse of itself and thus have a difficult time leaving the house. The soul was also sometimes visible to loved ones, taking the form of a mist or an animal, such as a butterfly or bee.

In the coming hours, the body was prepared for burial in the home. Before the first sunset after a person died, their body was ritually washed "so it would be cleansed of sin."[128] The water used to wash the body was poured somewhere no one would walk—if someone did step in the water, they might sicken. The combs used on the dead were thrown away, but the soap was saved; a sick person could wash away their illness with it. If the deceased's hair or nails were trimmed, the clippings needed to be placed inside the coffin lest the spirit come back to search for them.

Next, it was time to dress the body. It was rare to bury a person in the clothes they had died in. Instead, the deceased was dressed in a ceremonial outfit. If possible, at least the underwear was brand new. Sometimes, clothes were buttoned incorrectly on purpose so that a potentially harmful spirit would be confused by the irregularity. Some communities buried the dead in their matrimonial outfits, which were stored away after their weddings. Young women might want to have additional outfits to wear in the next world, so they were often buried with all of their ceremonial outfits. If the dresses didn't all fit within the coffin itself, they might be buried in a separate chest that was lowered into the grave above the coffin.

The paths leading to the *Túlvilág* were thought to be thorny, so some sort of footwear was recommended, but solid shoes weighed a soul down. As a compromise, the body was buried with special linen footwear, a cross between a slipper and a sock, which was so loose as to fall off a person under normal circumstances. If, for some reason, a person insisted on being bur-

---

127. Sometimes, not even then did it leave. In some communities, the soul was thought to stay near the family for days or weeks, sometimes as long as forty days past death.

128. K. Kovács, *A kolozsvári hóstátiak temetkezése*, 60.

ied in shoes or boots, the metal pieces were removed from the soles so their soul would not be weighed down. There was an exception to the no-footwear rule: a baby who had never worn shoes in their life received a tiny pair of boots when they died so they would know the joy of wearing them. Further aesthetic preparations included tying a strip of white linen around the deceased's chin and placing weights such as coins on the eyes so the lids wouldn't open.

After the body was washed and dressed, it was laid out on a bed or a board suspended on chairs. A large bowl of water was placed under the body, and a heavy metal object (such as a horseshoe, hoe, or scythe) was placed on top of it to weigh the body down should it attempt to rise once more, as spirits were "afraid of iron." The body was also measured with a special ruler to determine what size the coffin should be. This measuring stick was believed to have magical properties and could "measure away" (i.e., chase away) rats. It was vital that the stick only be used to measure a deceased person; if it were used on a living person, it might "measure away" their spirit.

The Wake

A body was never to be left alone, but rather watched over and kept company at all times until it was able to be buried. Men and woman tended to separate themselves at a wake. Women situated themselves in the room with the body and spent the night praying, talking, or singing. The soul was given advice and repeatedly reminded how to reach the *Túlvilág*. If the deceased was a child, the women told fairy tales to amuse and comfort the soul and give it wisdom. The men sat in another room, making the necessary arrangements for the burial and preparing the lyrics to a biographical song that was sung during the burial itself. The song recounted what the person had done and seen in their life. Famous warriors and leaders had elaborate songs composed for them, but even commoners were mourned in this manner.

Bread or *kalács* was served to the guests throughout the night as sustenance, but it was forbidden to cook or light a fire in the house while the body was not yet buried for fear of driving away the spirit prematurely. If someone fell asleep at the wake, the others shook a special stick with a rattle on it because "when a person falls asleep, their spirit flies out of their body, and the wandering spirit of the dead can take over their body." [129] During the wake, garbage was not removed from the house, but piled under the body; nothing was removed or lent out from the home. If the floor had to be swept, even the dust was swept under the body.

Over the course of the wake, the body might change as it went through various natural processes. If a young person looked old in death, an old person would be the next to die; the opposite was also true. In case the spirit was lonely, mourners asked them not to take any of the living with them to the grave. Other times, relatives would actually implore the deceased to take one of the living along with them on their journey, such as a mother taking their infant to the next world alongside them. If it was an infant who died, their mother squeezed some milk onto the child's face so that the child would take the milk into the afterlife.

It was best to bury the person as soon as possible, which typically meant the day after death took place. If relatives had to travel from distant areas, the funeral could be pushed back several days; the wake continued as long as necessary, and guests took shifts so the dead would not be alone. Once all attending relatives were present, the body could be buried.

The Procession of the Dead

In the earliest Magyar burials, bodies were wrapped in a white shroud. Later on, coffins were introduced. Simpler coffins might have been lined with soft materials such as moss, straw, or wood shavings; down feathers were never allowed to be used, as there were various taboos against the dying or dead coming in contact with feathers. As time went on, the coffins became more ornately decorated, and full bedding was added to make a comfortable resting place for the body. Some coffins were painted different colors depending on the age of the deceased; the younger the individual, the lighter the coffin was painted. Floral designs were painted on the coffins of young women and children. If someone had died a violent death, their coffin might be painted red.

Before a body was placed in a coffin, blessed incense was carried around the room three times to ensure there were no harmful spirits present. A mother could not place her own child in the coffin, or she wouldn't be able to

129. Virt, *Elszakasztottad a testemtől én lelkemet*, 9.

have more children. After the body was safely lodged in the coffin, the guests could begin the funerary procession.

The journey of a body from the house to the graveyard had many ritual elements. The coffin was removed by the pallbearers feet first so the spirit was not able to return home. Sometimes the coffin was deliberately touched to the front doorstep to emphasize the transition out of the home, while in other areas this was expressly prohibited. To confuse the spirit, some people avoided doorways altogether and passed the coffin through a window instead. After the coffin was out of the house, guests still inside the home made noise (such as breaking pottery on the floor or slamming the door) so the spirit followed the body instead of lingering. Sugar was burned to clear the air of lingering smells, and pieces of furniture might be turned upside down to further make the environment inhospitable for the spirit.

In the courtyard, the procession might pause to allow the animals of the household to say goodbye to their master. The coffin was then taken to the graveyard in a formal procession including the family and loved ones, the priest and his assistants, family members, and professional mourners. The younger the deceased, the more music and decoration there was during the procession. Cemeteries were typically located on the far side of a river to provide protection from ghosts who returned to haunt the living, and the route to the cemetery was often meandering, winding through the entire village. This gave everyone the ability to say goodbye to the deceased (and, perhaps, vice versa) even if they were not attending the burial itself. If someone had been executed for a crime, they were simply buried without ceremony; if they were carried through the town, it was said that hail would destroy the village crops.

It was believed that if a young adult died before their wedding day, they would become a restless spirit unable to move on to the *Túlvilág*, so the community attempted to make up for the spirit's loss by making the entire burial process as festive as possible, including the preparations, the procession, the burial, and the feast afterward. Attendees dressed in a similar fashion to weddings. The body was dressed as if for a wedding: a bride in white or pink with a veil and a crown of flowers, and a groom with a bouquet of flowers, as if he was bringing them to present to his bride. If the young adult was not already engaged, an eligible single in the community stood in as a partner. If the deceased was female, when the guests arrived, they asked for the body as they asked for a bride, with a pine branch decorated in flowers and ribbons and kerchiefs, singing songs to invite the bride to "a sorrowful wedding feast." After the burial, attendees danced at the graveside, and again at the funeral feast.

The boundaries of a graveyard were always well demarcated with a fence or hedge; those who had died by suicide, those who were executed, and unbaptized, unrepentant sinners were buried outside these limits. Many cemeteries appeared as lush gardens, as mourners planted flowers and fruit trees over their loved ones' graves.

Burial

Before entering the cemetery, the coffin might be ritually struck thrice into the gates of the cemetery or tapped on the ground, cementing the idea that the coffin had arrived in its final resting place. When the procession arrived at the gravesite, there was one last opportunity to say goodbye before the coffin was closed. If they had not already been added to the coffin, funerary gifts could be placed next to the body, but people were careful to not let any part of their own bodies fall into the coffin. For example, if someone with long hair was placing an item next to the body, they could not allow a single strand of hair to fall within it lest a part of their spirit follow the soul to the afterlife. Many funerary gifts were practical, such as food, tools, weapons, and personal care items like combs, handkerchiefs, or razors. Coins were useful so the soul could pay the toll to ferry them across the river to the *Túlvilág*. Drinkers were sometimes given bottles of alcohol, smokers were given tobacco, and infants were given bottles of breastmilk. Spiritual gifts included prayer beads, prayer books, charms, or amulets. Other gifts were sentimental or symbolic. Loved ones placed mementos into the coffin, and wheat seeds and eggs were often given as a sign of rebirth. In some cases, belongings were buried in additional chests so the coffin would not become overcrowded.

Once the gifts were in place, any buttons or fastenings on the deceased's clothing were undone, and the body was covered with a white cloth. The cloth was edged with pastel thread for a child or bright colors for a young adult. It was also frequently embroidered with symbols for the loved ones left behind, particularly if the deceased was a parent of young children. A married couple might plan to use two halves of the same cloth in their burial, or a woman might plan to use a sheet that she had lain on during her post-partum time. The cloth was not tied down; it was just laid over the body so that if the person should happen to return to life, they would not become tangled and tied to the grave. After all coverings were in place, the coffin was closed and nailed shut. Only a few nails held a coffin together. If digging up an old grave, the coffin's nails could be removed to be used as lucky charms (especially for thieves). The nails also had healing powers; one account said that "touching [the nail] to a painful ear is quite useful, as the pain will pass from [the ear]." [130]

Graves were positioned so that the coffin faced east so the deceased could gaze at the rising sun and, thus inspired, also rise in their new life. Directly before the coffin was lowered into the grave, a cantor could sing the biographical song written during the wake. In some communities, this was sung from the dead person's perspective. After telling their life story, they addressed the mourners present by name, at which point the loved ones were given a chance to say goodbye to the departing spirit. In another variation of the custom, the cantor spoke on behalf of the mourners and told the spirit what the mourners wanted them to know.

After the coffin was lowered into the grave, flowers or handfuls of dirt could be tossed in after the coffin while the guests called out wishes such as, "May the earth be light upon you." [131] In some places, it was customary for mourners to walk around the grave three times.

While the mourners were burying their loved one, volunteers cleaned the home where the wake had occurred. This may have included giving the walls a fresh coat of paint, and sometimes even the flooring was replaced.

The Funerary Feast

After the burial, the family organized a traditional funeral feast known as a *tor*. In the olden days, the feast was held in the cemetery. Eventually, the custom of the *tor* transformed into a ceremonial dinner held in the yard of the deceased (or at a neighbor's house). Wealthier families invited the entire community, but

---

130. Kiss, *Hódmezővásárhelyi temetkezési szokások*, 12.

131. *Magyar Néprajzi Lexikon (MNL)*, "Temetés."

many celebrations included only close family members; in some communities, priests were not allowed to attend, as the celebration was seen as too Pagan of a rite, although in other communities they were welcomed.

The assembled guests ritually washed their hands before sitting down to eat. At the start of the meal, the spirit was addressed three times in succession and ritually asked if it was present, and someone had to ritually answer, denying the spirit's presence. Nonetheless, the deceased was given their own place setting at the table, which no one was allowed to touch; their meal would later be donated to the poor. Food had to be donated to the poor so the deceased person's soul would not come back to haunt the family.

Various cultures with strong links to the Hungarian nomads practiced horse sacrifices at funerals, and there are some records that the Magyars had similar customs, but the Christian religion forbade animal sacrifices on behalf of the dead. The funeral feast, therefore, consisted of more typical fare. Wine and salted bread were frequent additions to the table. While some people cooked hot meals, others avoided lighting fires for fear of the flames offending the soul. A compromise was only lighting a fire outdoors, instead of inside the house.

In many communities, the guests at a *tor* tried to create a festive atmosphere to ease the spirit's departure. After eating, the guests sang, talked, told stories, danced, or played games. One popular activity involved having a person lie on the floor, feigning death. Guests sang to them and said goodbye to them as they left on their journey.

As time went on, guests still gathered for a festive meal after the funeral, but they no longer invited the spirit to eat with them. Just to be on the safe side, the living did not want the spirit entering the house. Unless weather prevented it, the *tor* was still held under the open sky, and a place at the table was set for the spirit, lest they showed up uninvited and felt discontent that they were left out.

Mourning

After a death, loved ones entered into mourning for a specified amount of time; the closer a person was to the deceased, the longer they mourned. A mourning person said prayers on behalf of the dead, did not attend public celebrations, and dressed in special clothes. In some communities, men did

not shave or cut their hair, while others did not comb their hair for a specified amount of time. Although initially wearing dirty or otherwise unassum-
ing clothes was the symbol of mourning, over time, clothes in specific colors
(such as white, black, or dark red) became the norm. Middle-aged widows
wore mourning clothes for the rest of their lives, but younger women could
go back to wearing normal clothes after a year had passed.

The dead expected mourning songs called *siratóénekek* (literally "songs to
cry to") to be sung to them in the first year after they died. If a family was not
able to go to the cemetery regularly to sing mourning songs to them, they hired
professional mourners to do the task. These were typically elderly women,
often widows, known as *siratóasszonyok* ("mourning women"). Singing songs
to remind the dead how much they were missed was one way they were able to
sustain themselves financially if they didn't have families to support them. This
tradition has largely died out in mainstream Hungarian culture.

Loved ones had to be careful not to overdo their mourning. If someone
cried too much while mourning, the deceased's soul would have to wade in
the flood of their tears in the afterlife, or the deceased's clothes would get so
wet from their tears that the angels wouldn't take their soul to the heavens.

One of the most important tasks a mourner had to do was to feed the
dead. A spirit might visit home periodically after their death, and they would
expect to be fed during these visits. The most common time for their visits
was the Day of the Dead, but some communities also fed their dead on other
holidays, such as Christmas. A place setting might also be arranged for the
dead at important events in the family's life going forward, such as at their
child's wedding feast, although it was more common to set up a place for
the collective ancestors of the family rather than feed individual spirits. If an
unexpected memory of eating with the dead popped into a person's mind,
it might be the ghost asking for food. If a person dreamed of a dead loved
one, the deceased individual might be hungry in the afterlife. Food (typically
some combination of bread, garlic, and wine) might be put on the grave, set
on the table or windowsill overnight, or placed in or around the oven. Food
could also be served to the poor the following day as an offering.

The *Kopjafa*

In ancient times, a warrior's weapon or a stick was placed in the burial mound. Eventually, this tradition evolved; instead of sticking a weapon into the ground, a monument called a *kopjafa* (*kopja* adapted from a Slavic word for "spear" or "pike," and *fa* meaning "tree") was erected by the burial site. The same structure was also known as a *fejfa*, "head-tree," similar to the English word "headstone." Some scholars, such as Hofer Tamás, cast doubt on whether *kopjafák* were continuously used throughout the centuries as grave markers, but where they did exist, they were an artful and expressive way of showing respect to the dead of the community.[132]

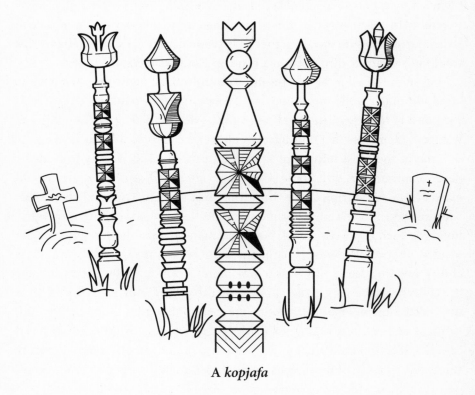

A *kopjafa*

The carvings on a *kopjafa* indicated the person's age at death, as well as their social standing, their occupation, their military rank, information

132. "A sírjeltől a nemzeti szimbólumig."

about their descendants, their family ties, and any significant deeds they had accomplished in their life. They could even indicate whether the individual had a happy or sad fate. Important individuals commissioned large, sturdy posts with intricate designs, whereas people in more humble circumstances had simpler posts they might have carved themselves in preparation for their deaths. Women's *kopjafák* were frequently topped with tulips, a symbol of the sacred feminine; young women who had died before marriage featured blossoms or buds instead. The colors a *fejfa* was painted were also significant, although these varied from community to community. Older individuals had black or dark posts (painted with egg yolk and coal dust), whereas young adults had bright paints. Children's *kopjafák*, half as tall as those of adults, were often painted a light blue, which was a color meant to protect their more-vulnerable spirits from harm on their visits back from the spirit world. Over the centuries, *kopjafa* designs grew more intricate, and as time went on, they became increasingly complex, including paint, poetry, and eaves to protect the inscriptions from inclement weather.

Today, only a handful of *kopjafák* are found in graveyards; most cemeteries are instead filled with modern gravestones. Nowadays, the carved monuments are most commonly considered a national heritage symbol, especially in the eastern parts of the country as well as in the Hungarian communities of Romania.

CONCLUSION

So, there you have it. From the cradle to the grave, generations upon generations of Hungarians lived a truly magical life. Difficult, yes, but interwoven with magic. Life today is infinitely more expansive. Most people are no longer confined to a small village for their entire lives but rather enjoy considerably more freedom of movement. And yet, even as society gained scientific knowledge and made leaps in medical and technological advances, I cannot help but wonder what we, as a people, lost.

My children are growing up in a home far removed from the world of their ancestors, both in time and space. We live in a new land, in a new era. Yet, on the Day of the Dead, we honor the memories of our forebears. Even though we are no longer living in an agricultural society, we still honor the turning of the seasons, and a carved bird (a nod to the traditional *babuka*) is frozen in flight over our dining room table. I may have a few too many embroidered tablecloths and pillowcases featuring the floral motifs sacred to the *Boldogasszony*. I start my mornings at a family altar, make fried donuts during *farsang*, and light candles nightly during Advent. Alongside typical kindergarten crafts, my kids also learned how to twist cords to make *sodort madzagok*. Their bedtime stories included nursery rhymes and fairy tales, but also the legend of the *Csodaszarvas* and tales of three-headed dragons, golden apples, and a magical tree that reached the heavens.

Unlike our forebears, people of our era have much more freedom to pick and choose which traditions to incorporate in our own family homes. Some customs mentioned in this book should without a doubt be left to rest; their time has come and gone. Others are waiting patiently to be revived—or reinvented for a new generation. My acquiring editor, Elysia, was inspired by the ceremonial livestock washing common in the springtime and has deemed *Nagypéntek* her official "cat-washing" day. That's one creative way to update a tradition!

If it turns out that your academic curiosity has been satisfied through reading this book, I thank you for coming along for the ride through the history and culture of the Hungarian people. I hope you enjoyed the journey! And if it turns out that you are not quite ready to leave this magical world yet, fear not; there is much more to explore beyond the scope of this book. I would suggest starting by looking into the ever-increasing number of fairy tales and legends being translated into English. These open up the world of Magyar myth and magic to a new audience. And if that's not enough, you can dive into the various pathways of folklore-related social media; various accounts explore fresh ways in which modern Hungarians are incorporating ancient traditions into their twenty-first-century lives. The rich tapestry of Hungarian folklore and tradition is vast and ever-evolving, offering endless opportunities for discovery and wonder.

Áldás on your journey!

Appendix A
PRONUNCIATION GUIDE

The Hungarian alphabet has the following letters:

A Á B C Cs D Dz Dzs E É F G Gy H I Í J K L Ly M N Ny O Ó Ö Ő
P R S Sz T Ty U Ú Ü Ű V Y Z Zs

(You'll notice that Q, W, and X are not mentioned—they're only used in foreign words.)

Consonants

B, D, F, H, K, L, M, N, P, T, V, and Z are all pronounced exactly the same as they are in English. The rest of the consonants are relatively straightforward as well, but need some clarification:

C: *ts* as in the end of *cats*

Cs: *ch* as in *chore*

Dz: *ds* as in *buds*

Dzs: *dge* as in *edge*

G: Hard G as in *good*

Gy: Don't be fooled—there is no G sound in there at all; *gy* is pronounced *dy*, as if you were saying "mud yard" quickly and letting the words flow into one another

J: *y* as in *yes*

Ly: Also a *y* sound as in *yes*; the L is silent

Ny: This is like the Spanish Ñ, like *señora*

R: Typically rolled a little bit, instead of being as rounded as they are in English

S: *sh* as in *marsh*

Sz: *s* as in *sun*

Ssz: *ss* as in *hiss*; not an official letter of the alphabet

Ty: Pronounced as it is written, with the T and Y in close succession

Y: Usually only found in double consonants (ny, ly, ty, gy, etc.) but might also be pronounced like *ee* in certain words borrowed from other languages, or names

Zs: *zh* or *g* as in *mirage*

Vowels

At first glance, there appear to be a lot of vowels in the Hungarian alphabet—until you remember that the language is phonetic. Unlike in English, where E can be pronounced a number of ways (or even be silent in some cases), each Hungarian vowel can only have one sound.

A, Á, E, É, I, O, Ö, U, and Ü are the main vowels. (Í, Ó, Ő, and Ű are the same as I, O, Ö, and Ü, just held for a longer beat.)

A: Like the A in *what* or the U in *bubble*

Á: Similar to the A in *spa* or *jaw*

E: Short E, as in *bet*

É: *ay*, without the Y sound; try saying "may" but cut off the word before you get to the Y sound

I: *ee* as in *see*, held for a shorter beat

Í: *ee* as in *see*, held for a longer beat

O: Short O as in *soldier*

Ó: Long O as in *Rome*, held for a longer beat

Ö: Like the E in *mermaid*

Ő: Like the E in *mermaid*, held for a longer beat

U: *oo* as in moon

Ú: *oo* as in moon, held for a longer beat

Ü: If you are familiar with the song "Für Elise," that contains the same sound; some say it is helpful to hold your mouth as though you're pronouncing the letter E but trying to say the vowel U instead

Ű: As above, but held for a longer beat

One final thing—the emphasis of a word is *always* on the first syllable. Like, always.

So, there you have it! Now you can read any Hungarian word! Well, maybe not immediately, but with a little practice, you'll be reading even unfamiliar words confidently. A handy way to quiz yourself on your new-found abilities is to head to Google Translate, type in a word, and have the site read it aloud to you. It's not foolproof, but it works most of the time. (At the time of this writing, anyway!)

Appendix B
TRADITIONAL MONTH NAMES
✤

In many cases, month names varied from community to community. For example, many communities described the months seasonally by calling the winter months *Télelő* ("the first part of winter"), *Tél* ("winter"), and *Télutó* ("the latter part of winter"). If you do your own research on traditional Hungarian month names, you may very well come across additional ones to these listed here.

Month Name (English)	Month Name (Hungarian)	Hungarian Translation
January	*Boldogasszony Hava*	Month of the *Boldogasszony*
February	*Jégbontó Hava*	Month of the Icebreaker
March	*Kikelet Hava*	Month of Emergence
April	*Szelek Hava*	Month of the Winds
May	*Ígéret Hava*	Month of Promise
June	*Napisten Hava*	Month of the Sun God
July	*Áldás Hava*	Month of Blessings
August	*Kisasszony Hava*	Month of the Maiden
September	*Földanya Hava*	Month of the Earth Mother

Month Name (English)	Month Name (Hungarian)	Hungarian Translation
October	*Magvető Hava*	Month of Sowing Seeds
November	*Enyészet Hava*	Month of Decay
December	*Álmok Hava*	Month of Dreams

Appendix C
SELECT FESTIVALS AND HOLIDAYS
❧

January
    1: *Újév* (New Year's Day)
    6: *Vízkereszt* (Epiphany)

February
    2: *Gyertyaszentelő Boldogasszony* ("Candle-blessing *Boldogasszony*")
    14: *Bálint-nap* (Valentine's Day)

March
    25: *Gyümölcsoltó Boldogasszony* ("Fruit-grafting *Boldogasszony*")

April
    24: *Szent György napja* (St. George's Day)

May
    1: *Május elseje* (The first of May)
    25: *Orbán napja* (St. Orbán's Day)

June

10: *Szent Margit napja* (St. Margaret's Day)

23–24: *Szent Iván éjszakája* (St. Ivan's Eve, i.e., celebration of the summer solstice)

29: *Szent Péter napja* (St. Peter's Day)

July

2: *Sarlós Boldogasszony* ("*Boldogasszony* with a Scythe")

August

20: *Szent István napja* (St. Stephen's Day, the day when Hungarians celebrate their nationhood)

September

8: *Kisasszony napja* (Maiden's Day)

29: *Mihály napja* (St. Michael's Day)

October

20: *Vendel napja* (St. Wendel's Day)

November

2: *Halottak napja* (Day of the Dead)

11: *Márton napja* (St. Martin's Day)

30: *András napja* (St. Andrew's Day)

December

13: *Luca napja* (Lucy Day)

21: *Szent Tamás napja* (St. Thomas's Day)

25: *Karácsony* (Christmas—the festivities start the night before the holiday and last for twelve days, including Christmas itself)

27: *Szent János napja* (St. John's Day)

28: *Aprószentek* (The festival of "Tiny Saints")

31: *Szilvester* (St. Sylvester's Day, i.e., New Year's Eve)

Moving Holidays

Húshagyókedd: Fat Tuesday. The day prior to Ash Wednesday.

Hamvazószerda: Ash Wednesday. Forty days before Easter Sunday.

Virágvasárnap: Palm Sunday. Last Sunday before Easter.

Zöldcsütörtök: Green Thursday. Last Thursday before Easter Sunday.

Nagypéntek: Good Friday. Last Friday before Easter Sunday.

Nagyszombat: Holy Saturday. Day before Easter Sunday.

Húsvét: Easter. Traditionally a three-day celebration starting on the first Sunday after the first full moon after the spring equinox. (Today it is celebrated for two days.)

Fehérvasárnap: White Sunday. The first Sunday after Easter Sunday.

Pünkösd: Pentecost. The seventh Sunday after Easter Sunday and the following Monday.

Úrnapja: Lord's Day. Sixty days after Easter Sunday.

GLOSSARY

áldás: A blessing.

áldomás: An ancient ritual, often including a libation to the gods. Most information about its original form has been lost to time.

áldozat: A sacrifice.

Alvilág: The Lower World. Able to be entered through caves or holes in the ground. A mystical (sometimes shadowy) realm where magical items and beings can be found. Similar to the concept of *pokol*.

aranyvíz: Literally, "golden water." The first water of the year, drawn from a river or a well. Another word for *életvíz*.

aratás: The harvest, typically of wheat.

aratókoszorú: A harvest wreath.

bába: A midwife. Traditionally believed to have much overlap with the concept of witches.

Babba Mária: A name certain ethnic groups use for the *Boldogasszony*.

babona: Magic or superstition. Can be used as a derogatory term to discredit a nonscientific belief or practice, but can also be used in a neutral or even positive manner, depending on the speaker's attitude toward the subject of magic.

babuka: Also called a *szentlélek madár*. A figure of a bird suspended over a traditional dining table.

barka: Pussywillow branches blessed during the Easter festivities, used for magical intentions.

Boldogasszony: The name of the goddess of the Hungarians. This figure was conflated with the Virgin Mary during Christianization. Sometimes has seven aspects or daughters.

Boldogasszony papucsa: A special pair of slippers a woman wore during her postpartum time.

boszorkány: A witch; sometimes refers to actual people and sometimes to a nebulous concept of a malevolent spirit.

Busójárás: A festival held at the end of winter, with masked and costumed revelers.

csattogtatás: A ritual using special whips to make a loud noise in order to frighten away evil spirits.

Csodaszarvas: The wonderstag. In legend, this magical creature led the Hungarians to their eventual homeland, where they settled from their nomadic life.

délibaba: An aspect of the *Szépasszony*. An evil female spirit that appears at midday and, most often, harms or kills people she encounters.

disznótor: The annual pig slaughter. Involves many ritual elements that seem to be remnants of a pre-Christian ceremony held on or around the winter solstice.

Égigérő fa: The Tree That Reaches the Sky. See *Világfa*.

Életfa: The Tree of Life. See *Világfa*.

életvíz: Literally, "life water." Water used for ritual washing, often drawn at sunrise or midnight.

eljegyzés: The engagement ceremony.

Emese: A legendary ancestress of the Hungarian people who conceived her children from a magical bird called the *turul*.

Etelköz: The land where the ancestors of the Magyars were believed to live prior to traveling west and settling in the current land of Hungary. This place is frequently referred to in origin myths.

farsang: The time between Christmas and Lent. A time of festivities, storytelling, and merry-making.

fejkendő: Literally, "head kerchief."

főkötő: A head-covering kerchief a woman wore once married.

fonó: The spinnery. A place where young women gathered to work with fabric and socialize. They often told stories, entertained young men, and performed magic together.

fürösztés: Ritual washing for protection or healing. Often included various objects in the water, or bathing at certain times or places. Can also be called *fürdetés*.

füstölés: Ritual censing.

garabonciás: A wizard, usually having to do with controlling dragons and/or weather.

gazda: The head of the household, typically the oldest male. Was responsible for his family members and home. Had to perform many ritual duties along with physical ones.

gazdasszony: The highest-ranking woman of the household.

gyermekijesztő: "Child frightener." A category of spirits that specifically targeted children, usually misbehaving ones.

halottak miséje: Mass of the Dead. A gathering of departed souls.

Halottak napja: The Day of the Dead.

halottlátó: "One who sees the dead." A seer or clairvoyant who could be consulted to ask questions of spirits, typically deceased family members.

Hunor: One of the legendary brothers who followed the *Csodaszarvas* westward.

Húsvét: Easter.

ijedtség: Fright. Being frightened by a person or thing could result in spiritual or physical sickness. Often occurred in children.

Isten: The Hungarian word for God; predates Christianity's arrival.

jeles nap: A "beacon day" or "signpost day"—special days throughout the year that were associated with certain customs, traditions, weather divination, and so on. Most of them were named after a saint.

jóslás: The act of telling the future through various means of divination.

kakasütés: "Rooster striking." The ceremonial killing of a rooster at various festivities.

kalács: A ceremonial loaf of bread made with milk. Consumed at many religious holidays. Often braided or otherwise shaped into elaborate forms, frequently having sweet or savory additions.

kalandozások: "The adventures." The time in Hungarian history where the warriors traveled through Europe and central Asia, fighting with and attempting to conquer other people.

Karácsony: Christmas.

karácsonyi abrosz: The tablecloth placed on the Christmas table. Becomes a magical object during the course of the holiday season.

karácsonyi asztal: The Christmas table. The meal was consumed on it, and other items were placed under and on top of it for magical purposes.

kereszteletlen: An infant who had died without a proper baptism.

Kisasszony: The maiden. An aspect or daughter of the *Boldogasszony*.

kísértet: A category of ghost, usually one with bad intentions. Similar to a ghoul.

kisze: A figure made of straw that is ritually destroyed at the end of winter.

koma; *koma-asszony*: A formally declared friendship between members of the same gender, whereby the two parties make a commitment to help one another out throughout their lives.

kongózás: Making noise to frighten away evil spirits, typically on festivals or holidays.

kopjafa: A carved pole marking a grave, the symbols on which indicate certain things about the life of the deceased.

kötés: Binding through use of knots, locks, etc.

kulcsforgatás: Key-spinning, a method of divination.

küldött farkas: Literally, "a sent wolf." Can be used to refer to a shape-shifted werewolf.

lélek: A soul or spirit. The word is not a clear translation of either term, but can refer to either one, according to context.

lidérc: A category of evil spirits that could take several forms, including a chicken, a spirit lover, and an invisible malevolent entity.

lucadisznó: A spirit with the body of a woman and the head of a pig. She roams the countryside on *Luca napja* and performs evil deeds.

Magor: One of the legendary brothers who followed the *Csodaszarvas* westward.

manó: A creature similar to an elf or gnome. Usually lives in the wilderness, but some can be invited to live in a family home.

Másvilág: Literally, "the Other World." A word used to describe the spirit world or the afterlife.

megcsodál: To wonder at. Being very surprised by some person or phenomenon can result in magical consequences.

mennykő: "Stone of heaven." Smooth rocks believed to have originated when lightning struck the ground. Used in magic, especially healing rituals.

monda: A legend. Some *mondák* are based on local events (such as the histories of castles or battles), but others focus on legends common to the Hungarian people, such as the accounts from their nomadic days.

morzsa: The leftovers from a holiday meal. Could be dried and used for magical purposes.

Nagyböjt: Literally, "the Great Fast," known to English speakers as Lent. A period of fasting before the celebration of Easter.

Nagyhét: The week preceding Easter Sunday.

névnap: Name day. Each day of the year is associated with one or more names, traditionally names of saints. The holidays are still celebrated today.

olvasó: A set of prayer beads.

öntés: Literally, "pouring." Pouring wax, molten lead, eggs, etc., into water for divination or magical purposes.

ördög: A devil. Although the word is now linked to Satan and other demons, the word predates Christianity; originally the *ördög* was a trickster spirit.

óriás: A giant. Often linked to legends about mountains or boulders.

palackba zárt szellem: Literally, "trapped-in-a-bottle spirit." A spirit who is linked to a physical object such as a bottle, box, or rag. Able to fulfill wishes for its master, but the wishes come at a cost.

párta: A special, decorated, ceremonial head-covering young women wore.

pimpó: See *barka*.

pingálás: Decorating one's home or belongings with designs, usually spiritual in nature. Also called *cifrázás*.

pogácsa: A type of biscuit often used for divination, feeding the dead, or coming-of-age rituals. Still a popular baked good today. Featured in many fairy tales where the hero was given a *pogácsa* (often a magical one) at the start of their journey.

pokol: In modern usage, the word means hell. Similar in meaning to the *Alvilág*.

ráolvasás: "To read something onto something else." A spell. Does not literally have to be read. Today, *olvasás* refers to reading, but there were other usages previously. Prayer beads were also archaically known as *olvasók* ("readers").

rontás: Cursing.

rosszak: Means "the evil ones." Any number of bad spirits.

rostaforgatás: Sieve-turning, a method of divination.

sárkány: A dragon. Could be formed from snakes. Fairy-tale dragons were humanoid creatures with reptilian heads. In the real world, dragons were linked with weather, caves, and lakes.

sarok: Literally, "corner." The original Hungarian home was divided into quadrants, and different activities (physical and magical) were allowed to take place in them.

sodort madzag: A traditional craft of twisting cord, used in various spells.

szellem: A spirit, soul, or ghost.

szemverés: Literally, "beating with the eye." The evil eye.

szenes víz: Water with coal in it. Used for various healing rituals.

szent: A saint. Many were conflated with earlier, pre-Christian spirits.

szentsarok: The area of the home in which the family's religious items and artwork were kept.

Szépasszony: A malevolent entity, the counterpart to the *Boldogasszony*. The name means "the Beautiful Woman."

szüret: The grape harvest and its associated festivities.

táltos: A shamanic figure who is able to go into trances and travel to various realms for healing and divination.

Tengrism: A largely monotheistic nature religion practiced in central Asia. Magyar ancestors are believed to have followed a form of this prior to their arrival in Europe.

Tetejetlen fa: The Tree Without a Top. See *Világfa*.

tilalom: A religious, spiritual, or social taboo.

tisztaszoba: "The clean room" or "the room of purity." In a traditional farmhouse, this was a room reserved for guests as well as sacred activities like giving birth and dying. Contained the family heirlooms and altar.

tisztítótűz: Purgatory. Literally, "cleansing fire."

tor: A funeral feast.

törpe: A creature similar to a dwarf or gnome. Usually lives underground and is known to guard treasure or magical knowledge or objects.

tudós: Literally, "someone who knows." Someone who was able to do magic or knew about the world of spirits. Many were believed to have special spiritual helpers. Many were linked to specific professions, such as that of a hunter, miner, musician, etc.

Túlvilág: "The World Beyond." Can refer to various forms of the afterlife, including traditional concepts as well as more modern notions of heaven.

tündér: A fairy. Usually found in nature and sparkling silver or gold.

turul: A magical bird who, according to legend, was one of several ancestors of the Hungarian people.

tűzugrás: Fire-jumping over ceremonial bonfires. Some authors hyphenate it *tűz-ugrás*.

újtűz: Literally, "new fire." A ceremonial fire-setting ceremony used to unite a community. Some authors separate the term into two words, *új tűz*.

üszöggyerek: A blighted child. A newborn who has been possessed by an evil spirit.

váltott gyerek: An infant who was swapped at birth (or shortly thereafter) with a sickly or deformed child. The change could have been made by a witch, a malevolent person, or even a spirit.

Világfa: The World Tree. The roots reach down into the World Below, and the branches stretch up into the World Above. Shamans and fairy-tale heroes can travel up and down the tree to visit the other realms. Located at the center of the world.

Virágvasárnap: The Sunday before Easter.

vőfély: The master of ceremonies at a wedding, in charge of entertaining the guests and enforcing social etiquette.

SOURCES CONSULTED

Note: *MNL* refers to the *Magyar Néprajzi Lexikon*, and *MKL* refers to the *Magyar Katolikus Lexikon*.

Chapter 1: The World of Spirits

MKL **Articles:** Égbekiáltó bűnök

Benedek and Kürtössy, "Szeptember 8. Kisasszony napja."

Béni, "Genetic Study Proves that Hungarians Are the Descent of the Huns."

Berze Nagy, *Égigérő fa*, 46, 63.

Bosnyák, "Napkorona, aranyalma, pásztorbot, suba."

Daczó, "A Gyimesi Babba Mária."

Dénes, "Boldogasszony papucsa."

Dienes, *A honfoglaló magyarok*, 49–52.

Diószegi, *A pogány magyarok hitvilága*.

Domokos, "Hajnal, hajnalnóta, hajnalozás," 249.

Kálmány, *Boldogasszony*, 4.

Kandra Kabos, *Magyar mythologia*, 91.

"Kihirdették, melyik lett Magyarország Tortája 2019-ben."

Lang'at, "What Is Tengrism?"

Pócs, "Az asztal és a tűzhely, avagy hol van a szentsarok?" 382.

Pócs, "Zagyvarékas néphite," 12.

Post et al., "Y-Chromosomal Connection Between Hungarians and Geographically Distant Populations of the Ural Mountain Region and West Siberia."

Szakács, "Boldogasszony, Anyánk!"

Szojka, *A természet a néphitben*, 10.

Takács, *Babba Mária*.

Wass, *Selected Hungarian Legends*, 9–14.

Váczy, "Csodakövek a Bükkben."

Zimonyi, *A magyarság korai történetének sarokpontjai*, 55.

Chapter 2: Religious Practice

MNL Articles: Áldozat; Kísértet; Szivárvány; Tilalom

Bellosics, "Magyarországi adatok a nyári napforduló ünnepéhez (Harmadik közlemény)," 119.

Bosnyák, "Visszasírás."

Csonka-Takács, "A születési rítusok és hiedelmek szerepe a közösség kapcsolatrendszerében Gyimesközéplokon."

Dám, "A kővé vált kenyér."

Dienes, *A honfoglaló magyarok*, 47–56.

Diószegi, *A sámánhit emlékei a magyar népi műveltségben*, 276.

Dömötör, *A magyar nép hiedelemvilága*, 13, 22, 40, 42–43.

Fehér, *Középkori magyar inkvizíció*, 206.

Felföldi, "Rituális táncok a magyar néphagyományban," 219.

Gyallay, "A fehér ló szerepe a székely hagyományban," 390.

Kiss, *Hódmezővásárhelyi temetkezési szokások*, 9.

Kolumbán, "Babonás hiedelmek a dévai csángóknál," 42.

Lakatos, *Vadászhit*, 20.

Nyáry, "A halottlátó," 94.

Pócs, "A magyar ősvallás," 454–55.

Róheim, *Magyar néphit és népszokások*, 183.

Szendrey, "A magyar lélekhit," 35.

Szendrey, "Szatmár megye néphagyományai," 34.

Szendrey, "Tiltások és tiltott cselekvések," 249.

Tomán, "A kegytárgyak élete," 686.

Vajkai, *Népi orvoslás a Borsavölgyében*, 31.

Vikár, "A szentiváni ének," 403.

Vörös, "Kutyaáldozatok és kutyatemetkezések a középkori Magyarországon I."

Zágorhidi Czigány, *Oszkó*.

Chapter 3: Spirits of the Skies

MNL Articles: Égitestek fogyatkozása; Eső; Esővarázslás; Holdfoltok; Mennydörgés; Mennykő; Villám

Balassa, "Hagyományos időjóslás, időmágia Magyarországon a 18-20. században." 570, 574, 579.

Bálint, *Karácsony, húsvét, pünkösd*, 72.

Bellosits, "Délvidéki magyar babonák," 305, 394.

Benkóczy, "Egervidéki babonák," 99.

Bosnyák, "A moldvai magyarok hitvilága," 56.

Bosnyák, "Napkorona, aranyalma, pásztorbot, suba," 7.

Diószegi, *Az ősi magyar hitvilág*, 59, 201–2.

Dömötör, *A magyar nép hiedelemvilága*, 104, 114–18.

Elek, "Gömörmegyei népmondák," 380.

Holló, "A garabonciás diák alakja a magyar néphagyományban," 21.

"Illés próféta ünnepe."

Jankó, "Kalotaszegi babonák," 274.

Kandra Kabos, *Magyar mythologia*, 86–88.

Kiss, *Hódmezővásárhelyi temetkezési szokások*, 15.

Madarassy, "A palóc mennykő."

Paládi-Kovács, *Magyar néprajz nyolc kötetben*, vol. 7, 193.

Pávay, "Oláhlapádi babonák és népies gyógymódok s földrajzi elterjedésük," 294.

Pócs, "Élők, holtak és a víz mitológiája," 155–58.

Pócs, *Népi vallás és mágia Közép-Kelet-Európában - Válogatott tanulmányok II*, 352.

Róheim, *Magyar néphit és népszokások*, 43–47, 134–39.

Sebestyén, "A magyar néphagyomány emlékeinek országos gyűjtéséről," 212.

Szendrey, "A néphit mennykője."

Szendrey, "A varázslatok eszközei," 400.

Szojka, *A természet a néphitben*, 6, 9–11.

Zágorhidi Czigány, *Oszkó*.

Zsigmond, "Népi kozmogónia és égitestmagyarázás a mezőségi Magyarszováton," 544–45, 551.

Chapter 4: Fairies and Nature Spirits

MNL Articles: Bányaszellem; Erdei lények; Kút; Vízilények

Balassa, "Hagyományos időjóslás, időmágia Magyarországon a 18-20. században," 582.

Bálint, *Népünk ünnepei*, 40.

Diószegi, *Az ősi magyar hitvilág*, 197.

Dömötör, *A magyar nép hiedelemvilága*, 41, 93–97, 209–11.

Dömötör, *A népszokások költészete*, 53.

Kandra Kabos, *Magyar mythologia*, 115–22, 173, 184.

Központi Statisztikai Hivatal, "Tudom, hol nyaraltál tavaly nyáron."

Kunkovács, *Táltoserő*, 18–20.

Manga, "Szlovák kapcsolatok a palóc karácsonyi szokásokban," 100.

Paládi-Kovács, *Magyar néprajz nyolc kötetben*, vol. 7, 185.

Pócs, *Hiedelemszövegek*, 100, 113.

Pócs, "Zagyvarékas néphite," 182.

Róheim, *Magyar néphit és népszokások*, 110–12.

Seres, "Erdők, vizek csodás lényei Háromszéken és a környező vidékeken," 194.

Stöckert, "Miért hétszünyű a kapanyánimonyók?"

Szendrey, "A nép élő hitvilága," 266.

Szojka, *A természet a néphitben*, 6, 22–23, 25–27.

Versényi, *Bányák, bányászok, hagyományok*, 64–75.

Vinci Balázsné Bálint, "Klára, Dála, Ramocsa."

Wlislockiné, "Kakas, tyúk, és tojás a magyar néphitben," 207.

Zágorhidi Czigány, *Oszkó.*

Chapter 5: The *Rosszak*

MNL Articles: Betegségdémonok; Fene; Íz; Guta; Kísértet; Lidérc; Lidércfény; Nyavalya; Szellem; Szépasszony; Torokgyík

"A Korondi Likaskő."

Balassa and Ortutay, *Magyar néprajz*, 641.

Bathó, "Gyermekijesztők a Jászságban."

Bellosits, "Délvidéki magyar babonák," 313.

Dömötör, *A magyar nép hiedelemvilága*, 54–55, 73, 77–82, 84–88, 102–4.

Ilyefalvi, "'Ebszar, kutyaszar, semminek tartom, meggyógyítom...' Egy gyógyító ráolvasástípus a magyarországi boszorkányperekben," 413.

Kálmány, "Gyermek-ijesztők és rablók nyelvhagyományainkban," 229–34.

Kandra Kabos, *Magyar mythologia*, 191, 206, 216, 499.

Kiss G., *Ormányság*, 290.

Kiss L., *Hódmezővásárhelyi temetkezési szokások*, 13–14.

Kolumbán, "Babonás hiedelmek a dévai csángóknál," 38.

Muraközi, "A lidérc a nyírségi néphitben," 186–87.

Oravecz and Zalai-Gaál, "Burial Rites of the Neolithic," 111.

Paládi-Kovács, *Magyar néprajz nyolc kötetben*, vol. 7, 548–49.

Peisner, "Die Volkskunde," 77–78.

Pócs, "Az asztal és a tűzhely, avagy hol van a szentsarok?" 379.

Pócs, *Fairies and Witches at the Boundary of South-Eastern and Central Europe*, 9.

Pócs, *Hiedelemszövegek*, 164–65.

Róheim, *Magyar néphit és népszokások*, 88.

Schwarz, "A nagyfalvai bolygó vadászról szóló monda," 91–94.

Scott-Macnab, "The Many Faces of the Noonday Demon."

Szendrey Á., "A füstölés a magyar néphitben," 43.

Szendrey Zs., "A nép élő hitvilága," 271.

Vajkai, *Népi orvoslás a Borsavölgyben*, 19, 26–27, 44–45.

Zentai, "Alsómocsoládi hiedelemmondák," 85.

Chapter 6: Sacred Animals

MKL Articles: Kakas-ütés

MNL Articles: Béka; Kakasütés; Kígyó; Kígyókő; Kutya; Madár; Méhészet; Sárkány

Bellosits, "Délvidéki magyar babonák," 309.

Berze Nagy, *Égigérő fa*, 102.

Bosnyák, "A moldvai magyarok hitvilága," 45.

Diószegi, *Az ősi magyar hitvilág*, 205.

Dömötör, *A magyar nép hiedelemvilága*, 107–9, 175.

Fáy, "Harry Potter magyar sárkánya."

Fehér, "Bíbájosok, boszorkányok Recskén és környékén," 221.

Halász, "Hagyományos méhészet a moldvai magyaroknál," 29, 86–88.

Jankó, "Kalotaszegi babonák," 278.

Kandra Kabos, *Magyar mythologia*, 53, 141, 159.

K. Kovács, *A kolozsvári hóstátiak temetkezése*, 17–18.

Kovács S., "Az Méhekrül való hasznos beszéd," 19–20.

Kunkovács, *Táltoserő*, 30, 32.

Lakatos, *Vadászhit*, 69–70.

"Medve."

Nickel, "Reám vicsoritotta az fogait."

Ortutay, *Kis magyar néprajz*, 107.

Pócs, "A boszorkányszombat és ördögszövetség népi alapjai Közép-Délkelet-Európában," 38–40.

Pócs, *Hiedelemszövegek*, 82–91, 401–21.

Róheim, "A halálmadár."

Róheim, *Magyar néphit és népszokások*, 16, 93.

Singer, "Dunántúli babonák," 234.

Szendrey Á., "A magyar lélekhit," 36.

Szendrey Zs., "A növény, állat, és ásványvilág a varázslatokban," 160.

Szendrey Zs., "Szalontai jeles napok," 76, 81, 83.

Szendrey Zs., "Tiltások és tiltott cselekvések," 249.

Szendrey Zs., "Vadász babonák," 28.

Takács, "Nagy Szent Mária egy nagy asztalt terített...A hegyen végzett lóáldozat és a betegségdémonok megvendégelése egy különös ráolvasócsoportban," 53, 71–72.

Versényi, *Bányák, bányászok, hagyományok*, 103.

Vörös, "Kutyaáldozatok és kutyatemetkezések a középkori Magyarországon I," 139.

Chapter 7: The Village

MNL **Articles:** Akasztott ember; Archaikus népi imádság; Betyármondák; Harangmonda; Harangozás; Közvélemény-büntetés; Kukoricafosztás; Nagycsalád; Tolvajlás; Templom

"A kezdetek...(Legendák és a feltételezett valóság)."

Balassa, "Hagyományos időjóslás, időmágia Magyarországon a 18-20. században," 577.

Bálint, *Boldogasszony vendégségében*, 18.

Bálint, *Népünk ünnepei*, 32.

Berze Nagy, *Égigérő fa*, 38.

Bosnyák, "Napkorona, aranyalma, pásztorbot, suba," 7–8.

Lajos, *Este a fonóban*, 136.

Patay, *Zempléni harangok*, 141.

Réső, *Magyarországi népszokások*.

Szendrey Á. and Szendrey Zs., "Részletek a készülő magyar babonaszótárból," 196, 198.

Szendrey Zs., "A növény, állat, és ásványvilág a varázslatokban,"160.

Chapter 8: The Homestead

MKL Articles: Tűztisztelet

MNL Articles: Ágybeli portéka; Építőáldozat; Féregűzés; Ház középoszlopa; Homokrózsa; Húsételek; Kása; Munkasarok; Pingálás; Szentsarok; Szobaberendezés; Takarítás; Tilalom; Tűzvész; Vízkereszt; Vízvirág

Abkarovits, "A Székelykapu."

Bálint, *Karácsony, húsvét, pünkösd*, 83–84, 209.

Bálint, *Népünk ünnepei*, 32.

Berki, "Babonák a tűzről – Mivel csillapítsuk a tűz éhét?"

Berze Nagy, *Égigérő fa*, 48–55.

Bosnyák, "A moldvai magyarok hitvilága," 56.

Dömötör, *A népszokások költészete*, 102–6.

Fehér, "Bíbájosok, boszorkányok Recskén és környékén," 223.

Haynal and H. Orosz, *1998. esztendei kalendárium*, 21.

Ipolyi, *Mythológia*, 111.

Istvánffy, "A borsodi matyó nép élete," 367.

Kiss, *Hódmezővásárhelyi temetkezési szokások*, 14.

Kovács, *Szeged és népe*, 345.

Manga, "Szlovák kapcsolatok a palóc karácsonyi szokásokban," 98.

Nemes, "Pásztor-babonák," 169.

Paládi-Kovács, *Magyar néprajz nyolc kötetben*, vol. 7, 65, 114, 174, 210–11.

Pócs, "A karácsonyi vacsora és a karácsonyi asztal hiedelemköre," 21.

Pócs, "Az asztal és a tűzhely, avagy hol van a szentsarok?" 379.

Pócs, *Hiedelemszövegek*, 153.

Pócs, *Népi vallás és mágia Közép-Kelet-Európában - Válogatott tanulmányok II*, 121, 153–54.

Radóczné Bálint, *Irodalom 6. tankönyv*, 20–22.

Relkovic, "Adalékok a Somlóvidék folklorejához," 106.

Réső, *Magyarországi népszokások*.

Szendrey Á., "A napforduló és a mágikus állatvédés összekapcsolásának kérdése," 318, 331.

Szendrey Zs., "A varázslatok eszközei," 388–91.

Tankó, "A 'guzsalyaskodás' Gyimesben," 72.

Tolnai, "Nagyfalusi babonák," 396.

Wlislockiné, "Kakas, tyúk, és tojás a magyar néphitben," 205–6.

Chapter 9: Sacred Food and Drink

MKL Articles: Benedekhagyma

MNL Articles: Alma; Bor; Első tej; Lakodalmi kalács; Mágikus eljárás; Szent Antal tüze; Szépségvarázslás; Tej; Vadrózsa

Bellosics, "Magyarországi adatok a nyári napforduló ünnepéhez (Harmadik közlemény)," 118–19.

Bellosits, "Délvidéki magyar babonák," 309, 311.

Bosnyák, "A moldvai magyarok hitvilága," 45.

Bosnyák, "Napkorona, aranyalma, pásztorbot, suba," 7.

Dömötör, *A magyar nép hiedelemvilága*, 164.

Makkai and Nagy, *Adatok téli néphagyományainkhoz*, 140.

Paládi-Kovács, *Magyar néprajz nyolc kötetben*, vol. 7, 175, 257.

Szendrey, "A növény, állat, és ásványvilág a varázslatokban," 162.

Szendrey, "A varázslatok eszközei," 387–88, 403.

Szendrey, "Őszi jelesnapjaink," 45.

Vajkai, *Népi orvoslás a Borsavölgyében*, 51.

Versényi, *Bányák, bányászok, hagyományok*, 84.

Chapter 10: The Witch

MNL Articles: Boszorkány; Boszorkányperek; Fokhagyma

Benkóczy, "Egervidéki babonák," 99.

Dömötör S., *Szent Gellért hegye és a boszorkányok*, 94.

Dömötör T., *A magyar nép hiedelemvilága*, 56–57.

Erdész, "Állattá változások a nyírségi nép hiedelmekben," 216, 218.

Gáll, "Magyarországon megérte boszorkánynak lenni, illetve…."

Klaniczay, "Boszorkányhit boszorkányvád, boszorkányüldözés a XVI–XVIII. században," 285.

Kolumbán, "Babonás hiedelmek a dévai csángóknál," 37–38.

Komáromy, *Magyarországi boszorkányperek oklevéltára*, xxii, xvii.

McCarthy, "The Death Toll of Europe's Witch Trials."

Miklós, "A 16–17. századi baszkföldi és erdélyi boszorkányperek összehasonlítása," 31.

Pócs, "A boszorkányszombat és ördögszövetség népi alapjai Közép-Délkelet-Európában," 48.

Pócs, *Hiedelemszövegek*, 359.

Rajšp, "Boszorkányperek Szlovéniában," 523, 530.

Rédéyné Hoffman, "Egy bujdosó naplójából," 27.

Solymossy, "A 'Vasorrú bába' és mitikus rokonai."

Szendrey, "A varázslatok eszközei," 388.

Szendrey, "Évnegyedi szokásaink és babonáink," 14.

Szendrey, "Szalontai jeles napok," 77, 81–89.

Szendrey, "Tiltások és tiltott cselekvések," 247.

Tóth, *Boszorkánypánik és babonatéboly*, 272.

Tóth, *Szegedi Boszorkányperek*, 15.

Chapter 11: Other Magical Persons

MNL Articles: Beng; Csordásfarkas; Halottlátó; Tolvajlás a tudóstól

Agócs, "A szlovákiai magyarok hagyományos hangszeres zenei kultúrája," 18.

Benkóczy, "Egervidéki babonák," 102.

Diószegi, *A pogány magyarok hitvilága*.

Diószegi, *A sámánhit emlékei a magyar népi műveltségben*, 227–69.

Diószegi, *Az ősi magyar hitvilág*, 55.

Diószegi, *Sámánizmus*, ch. 4.

Dömötör, *A magyar nép hiedelemvilága*, 75–77, 118–20.

Dömötör, *A népszokások költészete*, 63.

Fogarasi, *Sámánok és táltosok*, 8.

Herkely, "A gyermeknevelés szokásai és babonái a matyóknál," 224.

Hesz, "Álom halottakkal, mint élők és holtak közt kommunikáció," 353.

Kiss, "A szüléssel, kereszteléssel és felneveléssel járó szokások, babonás hiedelmek Hódmezővásárhelyről," 86.

K. Kovács, *A kolozsvári hóstátiak temetkezése*, 130.

Ortutay, *Kis magyar néprajz*, 106–7.

Paládi-Kovács, *Magyar néprajz nyolc kötetben*, vol. 7, 604.

Pócs, "A boszorkányszombat és ördögszövetség népi alapjai Közép-Délkelet-Európában," 70.

Pócs, "A magyar táltos és a honfoglaláskori samanizmus. Kérdések és feltevések," 6–10, 27.

Pócs, "Az asztal és a tűzhely, avagy hol van a szentsarok?" 379.

Pócs, *Népi vallás és mágia Közép-Kelet-Európában - Válogatott tanulmányok II*, 12.

Róheim, *A magyar sámánizmus*, 10.

Róheim, *Magyar néphit és népszokások*, 9–10, 15, 95.

Sitkei, "A honfoglaló magyarok hitvilága és a magyar nyelv," 218–19.

Chapter 12: Magical Techniques

MNL **Articles:** Átok; Átokdal; Bekerítés; Böjtölés; Füstölés; Köpés; Kötés; Lakodalmi tűz; Nyomfelszedés; Ráolvasás; Szótlanság

Dienes, *A honfoglaló magyarok*, 47.

Diószegi, *Az ősi magyar hitvilág*, 22–23.

Dömötör, *A magyar nép hiedelemvilága*, 61, 152, 155–59.

Jankó, "Kalotaszegi babonák," 281.

Kovács, *Szeged és népe*, 345–46.

Kurocskin, "A boszorkány alakja az ukrán folklórban," 519.

Lajos, *Este a fonóban*, 135.

Olosz, "Fehér László."

Ortutay, *Kis magyar néprajz*, 105, 109–13.

Pócs, "A kimondott szó varázsereje."

Pócs, *Magyar ráolvasások I*, 70–71, 101.

Róheim, *Magyar néphit és népszokások*, 9–10, 15, 95.

Szendrey Á, "A napforduló és a mágikus állatvédés összekapcsolásának kérdése," 326.

Szendrey Á., "Az újtűz," 153.

Szendrey Zs., "Műveltségtörténet és babonafejlődés," 60.

Szendrey Zs., "Nyomfelszedés."

Szendrey Zs., "Szalontai jeles napok," 76.

Szendrey Zs., "Tiltások és tiltott cselekvések," 248.

Vajkai, *Népi orvoslás a Borsavölgyében*, 23–24.

Chapter 13: Talismans and Beyond

MKL **Articles:** Rózsafűzér

MNL **Articles:** Akasztott ember; Amulett; Bodza; Boszorkányper; Első tej; Halál; Hetedik gyerek; Koponya; Olvasó; Ostya; Számok; Szenteltvíz; Tolvajlás; Vadrózsa; Vasfű

Bálint, *Boldogasszony vendégségében*, 3.

"Ballagási tarisznya tartalma mi mit jelképez?"

Bellosits, "Délvidéki magyar babonák," 309.

Berze Nagy, *Égigérő fa*, 46, 130.

Csiszár, "Gyógyítás emberkoponyával Bergen."

Dömötör, *A magyar nép hiedelemvilága*, 167.

Fehér, "Bíbájosok, boszorkányok Recskén és környékén," 222.

Gönczi, "A gyermek születése és szoptatása körül való szokások Göcsejben és Hetésben," 49–50.

Kiss, "A szüléssel, kereszteléssel és felneveléssel járó szokások, babonás hiedelmek Hódmezővásárhelyről," 91.

Kiss, *Hódmezővásárhelyi temetkezési szokások*, 14–16.

Lakatos, *Vadászhit*, 17–18.

Pávay, "Oláhlapádi babonák és népies gyógymódok s földrajzi elterjedésük," 297.

Rapaics, *A magyarság virágai*, iii, chap. 3.

Singer, "Gömörmegyei babonák," 376.

Szendrey Á., "A napforduló és a mágikus állatvédés összekapcsolásának kérdése," 319–20, 330.

Szendrey Á. and Szendrey Zs., "Részletek a készülő babonaszótárból," 200.

Szendrey Zs., "A növény, állat, és ásványvilág a varázslatokban," 157, 159.

Szendrey Zs., "Népszokásaink lélektani alapjai," 7.

Szendrey Zs., "Szalontai jeles napok," 77.

Szendrey Zs., "Vadász babonák," 29.

Szojka, *A természet a néphitben*, 15.

Takács, "Nagy Szent Mária egy nagy asztalt terített...A hegyen végzett lóáldozat és a betegségdémonok megvendégelése egy különös ráolvasócsoportban," 72.

Vajkai, *Népi orvoslás a Borsavölgyében*, 42, 98, 129, 132, 147.

Viski, "A tulipán szó történetéhez."

Wlislockiné, "Jósló állatok a kalotaszegi néphitben," 52, 54.

Chapter 14: Divination

MKL **Articles:** Méh

MNL **Articles:** Álom; Előjel; Halál előjelei; Istenítélet; Szerelmi jóslás; Szerencsejóslás

Bálint, *Karácsony, húsvét, pünkösd*, 18.

Bálint, *Népünk ünnepei*, 40.

Bellosits, "Délvidéki magyar babonák," 310–11.

Dömötör, *Magyar népszokások*, 44.

"Ha felmegyünk Boszorkánykőre soha nem felejtjük el, amit onnan látunk."

Jankó, "Kalotaszegi babonák," 285.

Kiss, *Hódmezővásárhelyi temetkezési szokások*, 3–4.

K. Kovács, *A kolozsvári hóstátiak temetkezése*, 10–11.

Lajos, *Este a fonóban*, 134–35.

Nagy, "Hegyhátvidéki hangutánzók, mondák és babonák," 71.

Paládi-Kovács, *Magyar néprajz nyolc kötetben*, vol. 7, 119, 210, 216, 226, 248, 261–64.

Sebestyén, "Az időrendbe szedett váradi tüzesvaspróba-lajstrom," 400.

Szendrey, "Népszokásaink lélektani alapjai," 7.

Tóth, *Boszorkánypánik és babonatéboly*, 89.

Virt, *Elszakasztottad a testemtől én lelkemet: a moldvai és a Baranya megyei csángók halottas szokásai és hiedelmei*, 4.

Wlislockiné, "Jósló állatok a kalotaszegi néphitben," 48–55.

Wlislocky, "Szerelmi jóslás és varázslás az erdélyi sátoros czigányoknál," 275.

Chapter 15: Healing Magic

MNL **Articles:** Árpa; Bekerítés; Fürösztés; Ijedtség; Népi gyógyászat; Sárgaság; Szent Antal tüze; Szemverés; Színek

Balassa and Ortutay, *Magyar néprajz*, 67.

Bellosits, "Délvidéki magyar babonák," 20.

Bosnyák, "Napkorona, aranyalma, pásztorbot, suba," 9.

Diószegi, *Az ősi magyar hitvilág*, 196.

Dömötör, *A magyar nép hiedelemvilága*, 147, 149.

Dömötör, "Népi embergyógyítás."

Fogarasi, *Sámánok és táltosok*, 85.

Gönczi, "Az emberi betegségek gyógyítása a göcseji népnél, harmadik közlemény," 129, 215.

Gulyás, "Adventi és karácsonyi népszokások a Jászságban," 108.

Haynal and H. Orosz, *1998. esztendei kalendárium és szakácskönyv magyar háziasszonyok számára*, 21.

Kis-Halas, "Átformált hagyomány," 5.

Kiss, "A szüléssel, kereszteléssel és felneveléssel járó szokások, babonás hiedelmek Hódmezővásárhelyről," 89.

Kunkovács, *Táltoserő*, 69.

Pávay, "Oláhlapádi babonák és népies gyógymódok s földrajzi elterjedésük," 294, 296, 299.

Pócs, "Evil Eye in Hungary," 205, 212–13.

Pócs, *Magyar ráolvasások I*, 38, 49, 54, 66, 71.

Pócs, "Szócikkek egy mágiaenciklopédiához," 3.

R. Várkonyi, "Közgyógyítás és boszorkányhit," 403–4, 408.

Szendrey, "A növény, állat, és ásványvilág a varázslatokban," 158.

Szendrey, "Szalontai jeles napok," 76, 78–79, 84.

Szendrey, "Tiltások és tiltott cselekvések, 246–49.

Takács, "Nagy Szent Mária egy nagy asztalt terített…A hegyen végzett lóáldozat és a betegségdémonok megvendégelése egy különös ráolvasócsoportban," 49.

Vajkai, *Népi orvoslás a Borsavölgyében*, 23, 128.

Chapter 16: Sacred Time

MNL **Articles:** Hét napjai; Kalács; Kedd asszonya; Nevezetes időpontok; Mosás; Szent Antal tüze; Takarítás; Tilalom

Balassa, "Hagyományos időjóslás, időmágia Magyarországon a 18-20. században," 573–81.

Berde, *A magyar nép dermatológiája*, 40.

Gönczi, "A gyermek születése és szoptatása körül való szokások Göcsejben és Hetésben," 46.

Jankó, "Kalotaszegi babonák," 281.

Kálmány, *Boldogasszony*, 8–10, 25.

Kiss, "A szüléssel, kereszteléssel és felneveléssel járó szokások, babonás hiedelmek Hódmezővásárhelyről," 89–90.

Kolumbán, "A hosdáthiak népszokásai," 120.

Máté-Tóth and Rosta, "Vallási riport, 1991–2022."

Róheim, "Kedd asszonya," 90–95.

Singer, "Dunántúli babonák," 234.

Szabó, "Az oláhok 'Kedd asszonya,'" 52–53.

Szendrey, "Meztelenség a magyar néphitben," 130.

Chapter 17: Winter

MKL **Articles:** Téltemetés

MNL **Articles:** Busójárás; Farsang; Időjóslás; Téltemetés, télkiverés, télkihordás; Újév, újesztendő, kiskarácsony; Zajkeltés

Andrić, "Busójárás, Busók," 481–82.

Balassa, "Hagyományos időjóslás, időmágia Magyarországon a 18-20. században," 580, 586.

"Bálint napi népszokások, február 14."

Bálint, *Népünk ünnepei*, 69.

"Busó festivities at Mohács."

Dömötör, *A magyar nép hiedelemvilága*, 43, 72.

Halász, "Mohácsi Busójárás."

Licskay, "2021 Busójárás Is Cancelled."

Makkai and Nagy, *Adatok téli néphagyományainkhoz*, 13, 20.

Manga, "Szlovák kapcsolatok a palóc karácsonyi szokásokban," 100.

Paládi-Kovács, *Magyar néprajz nyolc kötetben*, vol. 7, 109–11, 127–38, 263–64.

Szendrey, "A 'kongózás,'" 21–23.

Szendrey, "Évnegyedi szokásaink és babonáink," 15, 18.

Szendrey, "Szalontai jeles napok," 74.

Szendrey, "Tiltott és előírt ételek a magyar népszokásban," 15.

Chapter 18: Eastertide

MKL Articles: Hamvazószerda, Házszentelés

MNL Articles: Aratás; Húsvét; Húsvéti korbácsolás; Húsvéti locsolás; Húsvéti ünnepkör; Karikázó; Korbácsolás; Nagyböjt; Nagyhét; Nagypéntek; Nagyszombat; Sajbózás; Új tűz; Virágvasárnap

Bálint, *Karácsony, húsvét, pünkösd*, 187, 198–99.

Bálint, *Népünk ünnepei*, 75.

Berki, "Babonák a tűzről – Mivel csillapítsuk a tűz éhét?"

Halász, "A moldvai magyarok tavaszi ünnepköréről."

Nemes, "Pásztor-babonák," 170.

Paládi-Kovács, *Magyar néprajz nyolc kötetben*, vol. 7, 127, 148–50, 154–57, 159–60, 166.

Pesovár, "Körtánchagyományunk," 85.

Réső, *Magyarországi népszokások*.

Simon, "Cibereleves, ahogy nagyanyáink készítették - Így készül a hagyományos böjti étel."

Szendrey, "Szalontai jeles napok," 74.

Varga, "Húsvéti dülőkerülés, didergés és hajnalozás," 269–70.

Versényi, *Bányák, bányászok, hagyományok*, 43.

Wlislockiné, "Kakas, tyúk, és tojás a magyar néphitben," 209–10.

Chapter 19: Spring

MNL **Articles:** Boszorkány; Bújj, bújj zöld ág; Flórián-nap; Harmatszedés; Határjárás; Pünkösdi királyság; Tolvajlás; Villőzés

Bálint, *Karácsony, húsvét, pünkösd*, 10, 336–37.

Bálint, *Népünk ünnepei*, 79.

Berki, "Babonák a tűzről – Mivel csillapítsuk a tűz éhét?"

Dömötör, *Magyar népszokások*, 11.

Fogl, "Sárkányölő Szent György ünnepe."

Gubrán-Nagy, "Pünkösd jelképei."

Lakatos, *Vadászhit*, 18.

Makkai and Nagy, *Adatok téli néphagyományainkhoz*, 140.

Paládi-Kovács, *Magyar néprajz nyolc kötetben*, vol. 7, 145–46, 172, 176–77, 180.

Pócs, *Magyar ráolvasások I*, 102.

Réső, *Magyarországi népszokások*.

Róheim, *Magyar néphit és népszokások*, 49.

Sebestyén, "A pünkösdi király és királyné," 35–36.

Szendrey, "Az újtűz," 153–54.

Chapter 20: Summer

MNL **Articles:** Aratás; Aratókoszorú

Bálint, *Karácsony, húsvét, pünkösd*, 357.

Bálint, *Népünk ünnepei*, 107–9.

Bellosics, "Magyarországi adatok a nyári napforduló ünnepéhez (Harmadik közlemény)," 118–19, 124, 126–27.

Bellosits, "Délvidéki magyar babonák," 308.

Berki, "Babonák a tűzről – Mivel csillapítsuk a tűz éhét?"

Dömötör, *Magyar népszokások*, 41.

Gunda, "Szent Iván napi tűzcsóválás Törökkoppányban."

Madarassy, "Magyar aratószokások," 85–86.

Paládi-Kovács, *Magyar néprajz nyolc kötetben*, vol. 7, 186–87, 193–98.

Richter, "Évi szokások, babonák és szólás-mondások Német-Prónán és vidékén," 221.

Szendrey, "Szalontai jeles napok," 77.

Chapter 21: Autumn

MKL Articles: Halottak napja; Halottak miséje; Vendel

MNL Articles: Halott etetése; Karácsonyi asztal; Szent Mihály lova; Szent Mihály napja; Vetés

Balassa, "Hagyományos időjóslás, időmágia Magyarországon a 18-20. században," 572–73.

Benedek and Kürtössy, "Szeptember 8. Kisasszony napja," 3.

Bosnyák, "A moldvai magyarok hitvilága," 125, 220.

Farkas, "Néprajzi vonatkozások a múlt századi nagykőrösi sajtóban," 158.

Kálmány, *Boldogasszony*, 5.

Lajos, *Este a fonóban*, 11.

Lükő, "A jávorcsillag-mítosz ábrázolása az Urál vidéki sziklarajzokon," 441.

Paládi-Kovács, *Magyar néprajz nyolc kötetben*, vol. 7, 128, 200–201, 207, 209.

Szendrey, "A növény, állat, és ásványvilág a varázslatokban," 255.

Szendrey, "A varázslatok eszközei," 387–99.

Szendrey, "Őszi jelesnapjaink," 45.

Szendrey, "Tiltások és tiltott cselekvések," 249.

Szendrey, "Tiltott és előírt ételek a magyar népszokásban," 15.

Tánczos, "Angyalkultusz a moldvai csángó folklórban," 16.

Chapter 22: Advent

MNL Articles: Disznóölés; Előjel; Kivirágoztatott ág; Lucabúza; Luca napja

Balassa, "Hagyományos időjóslás, időmágia Magyarországon a 18-20. században," 585.

Bálint, *Karácsony, húsvét, pünkösd*, 72.

Bálint, *Népünk ünnepei*, 40.

Barna, "A lucadiszno hiedelme Jánoshidán."

Dömötör, *A magyar nép hiedelemvilága*, 99–100.

Dömötör, *Magyar népszokások*, 47.

Gulyás, "Adventi és karácsonyi népszokások a Jászságban," 96.

"Körömből itták a pálinkát."

Paládi-Kovács, *Magyar néprajz nyolc kötetben*, vol. 7, 210, 218–21, 225–28.

Sebestyén, *Dunántúli gyűjtés*, 426.

Szendrey, "A 'kongózás,'" 23.

Szendrey, "Tiltott és előírt ételek a magyar népszokásban," 16.

Chapter 23: Christmas

MNL **Articles:** Karácsonyfa; Karácsonyi abrosz; Karácsonyi asztal; Karácsonyi morzsa; Ostya

Agócs, "A szlovákiai magyarok hagyományos hangszeres zenei kultúrája," 11.

Balassa, "Hagyományos időjóslás, időmágia Magyarországon a 18-20. században," 586.

Bálint, *Karácsony, húsvét, pünkösd*, 18, 31, 33.

Bálint, *Népünk ünnepei*, 49.

Dömötör, *Magyar népszokások*, 18, 25, 45–46.

Makkai and Nagy, *Adatok téli néphagyományainkhoz*, 54.

Manga, "Szlovák kapcsolatok a palóc karácsonyi szokásokban," 98.

Paládi-Kovács, *Magyar néprajz nyolc kötetben*, vol. 7, 244–48, 258–60.

Pócs, "A karácsonyi vacsora és a karácsonyi asztal hiedelemköre," 21–22, 61–63, 69–71, 76, 85.

Richter, "Évi szokások, babonák és szólás-mondások Német-Prónán és vidékén," 231.

Sarosácz, "Baranyai délszláv népszokások. I. Karácsonyi és lakodalmi szokások a sokacoknál és bosnyákoknál," 104.

Szendrey, "A füstölés a magyar néphitben," 43.

Chapter 24: Coming of Age

MNL **Articles:** Hajviselet; Komatálküldés; Konfirmáció; Leányavatás; Legényavatás; Párta

Balassa and Ortutay, *Magyar néprajz*, 61.

Kis-Halas, "Átformált hagyomány," 15.

Morvai, "Azt tartották, hogy akinek lánya van, hamarabb öregszik."

Réső, *Magyarországi népszokások*.

Ruitz, "A parasztifjúság társasélete a Bódva vidékén (1880-1950)," 577.

Szendrey, "A társadalmi érintkezés formái," 377–78.

Temesváry, *Előítéletek, népszokások és babonák a szülészet körében Magyarországon*, 9.

Vörös, "Kutyaáldozatok és kutyatemetkezések a középkori Magyarországon I," 179.

Chapter 25: Love and Marriage

MNL **Articles:** Álmenyasszony; Búsanya, búsapa; Eljegyzés; Esküvő; Eső; Fonó; Gyertyás tánc; Házasságkötés szokásköre; Házasságon kívül elismert nemi kapcsolat; Hívatlanok; Hozományvitel; Kontyolás; Lakodalmi étkezések; Lakodalmi tűz; Megetetés; Menyasszony befogadása; Menyasszony búcsúztatása; Menyasszonytánc; Menyasszonyvitel; Párnás tánc; Próbaházasság; Szépségideál; Szépségvarázslás; Szerelmi varázslás; Szerelmi ajándék; Vadházasság; Vőfély; Vőfélybot; Vőfélypálca; Vőfélyvers

Berde, *A magyar nép dermatologiája*, 38.

Csáky, "Szerelemmel és születéssel kapcsolatos szokások és hiedelmek az Ipoly mentén," 31–32.

Kiss, "A szüléssel, kereszteléssel és felneveléssel járó szokások, babonás hiedelmek Hódmezővásárhelyről," 84.

"Menyasszonyfektetés és felkontyolás."

Ortutay, *Az ősi magyar hitvilág*, 25.

Paládi-Kovács, *Magyar néprajz nyolc kötetben*, vol. 7, 14, 46, 60–66, 192.

Réső, *Magyarországi népszokások*.

Róheim, *Magyar néphit és népszokások*, 61–66.

Szendrey and Szendrey, "Részletek a babonaszótárból," 198.

Wlislocky, "Szerelmi jóslás és varázslás az erdélyi sátoros czigányoknál," 276–77.

Chapter 26: Pregnancy and Childbirth

MNL **Articles:** Anyajegy; Csecsemőkor; Elvetélt gyerek; Fürösztés; Gyermekágy; Kereszteletlen gyerek; Kígyó; Lélek; Magzatelhajtás; Meddőség; Szépségideál; Szülés; Terhesség; Újszülött; Üszöggyerek; Vámpír

Balásy, "Székely kincsásó babonák," 296–97.

Berde, *A magyar nép dermatológiája*, 38.

Csáky, "Szerelemmel és születéssel kapcsolatos szokások és hiedelmek az Ipoly mentén," 32.

Dömötör, *A magyar nép hiedelemvilága*, 101.

Gönczi, "A gyermek születése és szoptatása körül való szokások Göcsejben és Hetésben," 44–47, 52.

Gönczi, "Az anyajegy a somogyi néphitben," 163–64.

Herkely, "A gyermeknevelés szokásai és babonái a matyóknál," 224.

Herkely, "Az elásott kincs a Bán völgyi néphitben."

Kálmány, *Boldogasszony*, 12–19, 23.

Kiss, "A szüléssel, kereszteléssel és felneveléssel járó szokások, babonás hiedelmek Hódmezővásárhelyről," 85, 87.

Kolumbán, "A hosdáthiak népszokásai," 119.

Paládi-Kovács, *Magyar néprajz nyolc kötetben*, vol. 7, 14, 18, 19.

Pócs, *Hiedelemszövegek*, 145.

Pócs, *Népi vallás és mágia Közép-Kelet-Európában - Válogatott tanulmányok II*, 19.

Pócs, *Magyar néphit Közép-és Kelet-Európa határán*, 96.

Pócs, *Magyar ráolvasások I*, 77.

Sántha Attila, "Ő, akit Babbának neveznek (a vasorrú bábától Babba Máriáig)," 59–60.

Szendrey, "Tiltások és tiltott cselekvések."

Vajkai, *Népi orvoslás a Borsavölgyében*, 94, 98.

Chapter 27: Postpartum and Infancy

MNL **Articles:** Keresztelő; Köldökzsinór; Szoptatás; Váltott gyerek

Balassa, *Karcsai mondák*, 29.

Bellosits, "Délvidéki magyar babonák," 304.

Bora Das, "As Cultures Worldwide Seek to Peek into a Child's Future."

Diószegi, *Az ősi magyar hitvilág*, 201–2.

Dömötör, *A magyar nép hiedelemvilága*, 105, 139.

Dömötör, *Magyar népszokások.*

Endrei, "Somogy vármegye népe," 206.

"Fehérlófia."

Gönczi, "A gyermek születése és szoptatása körül való szokások Göcsejben és Hetésben," 44.

Haynal and H. Orosz, *1998. esztendei kalendárium kalendárium és szakácskönyv magyar háziasszonyok számára*, 21.

Jankó, "Kalotaszegi babonák," 285.

Kálmány, *Boldogasszony*, 14.

Kiss, "A szüléssel, kereszteléssel és felneveléssel járó szokások, babonás hiedelmek Hódmezővásárhelyről," 87, 89–90.

László, "Az 'agos' (szőrösen született) gyermek megfőzése," 186–87.

Moór, "A gyermekneveléssel járó szokások és babonák," 179–80.

Nagy, "Hegyhátvidéki hangutánzók, mondák és babonák," 69.

Paládi-Kovács, *Magyar néprajz nyolc kötetben*, vol. 7, 27–29.

Pócs, *Magyar néphit Közép-és Kelet-Európa határán*, 96.

Pócs, *Népi vallás és mágia Közép-Kelet-Európában - Válogatott tanulmányok II*, 39, 42.

Szendrey, "A varázslatok eszközei," 390.

"Virág Péter."

Zsilák, "Betegségek okozói," 128.

Chapter 28: Death: The Final Passage

MNL **Articles:** Akasztott ember; Gyász; Halál; Halál előjelei; Halott búcsúztatása; Halott etetése; Halott kivitele; Halott lakodalma; Halotti készületek; Halotti papucs; Halotti ruha; Halotti tor; Koporsó; Ravatalozás; Siratóének; Szemfedél; Temetés; Temető; Túlvilág; Virrasztás

"A sírjeltől a nemzeti szimbólumig."

Balassa, "A magyar gyász-színek kérdéséhez."

Balassa, "A magyar temetők néprajzi kutatása," 229.

Bosnyák, "Visszasírás."

Diószegi, *Az ősi magyar hitvilág*, 196.

Dömötör, *A magyar nép hiedelemvilága*, 217–19, 222–26.

Erdmann, "Szokás, hagyomány, hiedelmek."

Fél, "Adatok a gyászszínekhez és párhuzamok," 12.

Hesz, "Álom halottakkal, mint élők és holtak közt kommunikáció," 354.

Kiss, *Hódmezővásárhelyi temetkezési szokások*, 3–5, 7–9, 12–13, 15.

K. Kovács, *A kolozsvári hóstátiak temetkezése*, 27–30, 34, 47, 49–53, 60, 84, 104, 110, 118, 161, 217–18, 261, 263.

Kunt, "Temetkezési szokások Pányokon II," 499, 512, 515.

Lim, "Belly Dancing for the Dead."

Paládi-Kovács, *Magyar néprajz nyolc kötetben*, vol. 7, 71–75, 79, 83–85, 99.

P. Lator: *"Kimegy a lelke..."* 210–13, 295.

Ökrösné Bartha, "Köznépi temetők, pásztorsírjelek Anatóliában," 172.

Ortutay, *Kis magyar néprajz*, 126–27.

Pócs, "Az asztal és a tűzhely, avagy hol van a szentsarok?" 379.

Róheim, *Magyar néphit és népszokások*, 166–67, 173, 176–77, 182, 266.

Szendrey Á., "Az ősmagyar temetkezés," 17, 21.

Szendrey Zs., "Őszi jelesnapjaink," 47.

Vincze and Pilling, "A cigányság jelenkori halotti és gyászszokásai," 5, 14.

Virt, *Elszakasztottad a testemtől én lelkemet*, 6, 9.

BIBLIOGRAPHY

Hungarian naming conventions lead with the surname and are followed by the given name—the reverse of what English speakers expect a "first" and "last" name to be. In this bibliography, all the names are given surname first; names listed without a comma are Hungarian authors.

Abkarovits Endre. "A székelykapu." *Most Magyarul! Hongarije Magazine* (2020): 16–19. Accessed November 16, 2023. https://hagyomanyok haza.hu/sites/default/files/2020-02/a_székelykapu.pdf.

Agócs Gergely. "A szlovákiai magyarok hagyományos hangszeres zenei kultúrája." PhD diss. Budapest: Irodalomtudományi Doktori Iskola, 2010.

"A kezdetek…(Legendák és a feltételezett valóság)." *Galgahévíz község ingyenes közéleti havilapja* 25, no. 1 (January 2014): 13.

"A Korondi Likaskő." *Térj haza, vándor!* Accessed October 6, 2023. https://www.terjhazavandor.ro/a-korondi-likasko.

Andrić, Jasna. "Busójárás, Busók." *Ethnographia* 105 (1994): 477–89.

"A sírjeltől a nemzeti szimbólumig." *Új Szó Online.* Accessed November 17, 2023. https://ujszo.com/kozelet/a-sirjeltol-a-nemzeti-szimbolumig.

Balassa Iván. "A magyar gyász-színek kérdéséhez." *Ethnographia* 56 (1945): 69–70.

———. "A magyar temetők néprajzi kutatása." *Ethnographia* 84 (1973): 225–40.

———. "Hagyományos időjóslás, időmágia Magyarországon a 18-20. században." Accessed December 17, 2022. https://epa.oszk.hu /02000/02030/00029/pdf/HOM_Evkonyv_35-36_567-594.pdf.

———. *Karcsai mondák*. Budapest: Akadémiai Kiadó, 1963.

Balassa Iván and Ortutay Gyula. *Magyar néprajz*. Budapest: Corvina, 1979.

Balásy Dénes. "Székely kincsásó babonák." *Ethnographia* 8 (1897): 296–98.

"Bálint napi népszokások, február 14." Nepszokasok.hu, January 3, 2023. https://nepszokasok.hu/balint-napi-nepszokasok.

Bálint Sándor. *Boldogasszony vendégségében*. Budapest: Veritas, Hungária, 1944.

———. *Karácsony, húsvét, pünkösd: A nagyünnepek hazai és közép-európai hagyományvilágából*. Budapest: Neumann Kht., 2004.

———. *Népünk ünnepei: az egyházi év néprajza*. Budapest: Szent István-Társulat, 1937.

"Ballagási tarisznya tartalma mi mit jelképez?" Accessed November 14, 2023. https://mrsale.hu/ballagasi-tarisznya-tartalma.

Barna Gábor. "A lucadiszó hiedelme Jánoshidán." *Ethnographia* 85 (1974): 89–90.

Bathó Edit H. "Gyermekijesztők a Jászságban." In *Gyermekvilág a régi magyar falun*, edited by T. Bereczki Ibolya, vol. 50 of *A Jász-Nagykun-Szolnok Megyei Múzeumok közleményei*, 621–27. Szolnok, Hungary: Damjanich János Museum, 1995.

Bellosics [Bellosits] Bálint. "Magyarországi adatok a nyári napforduló ünnepéhez (Harmadik közlemény)." *Ethnographia* 13 (1902): 117–27.

Bellosits [Bellosics] Bálint. "Délvidéki magyar babonák." *Ethnographia* 10 (1899): 304–13.

Benedek Csaba and Kürtössy Péter. "Szeptember 8. Kisasszony napja." Accessed September 5, 2022. http://karpatmedence.net/jeles-napok /127-szi-unnepkor/519-szeptember-8-kisasszony-napja?format=pdf.

Béni Alexandra. "Genetic Study Proves that Hungarians Are the Descendants of the Huns." *Daily News Hungary*, October 2, 2017. https://dailynewshungary.com/genetic-study-proves-hungarians -descendants-huns.

Benkóczy Emil. "Egervidéki babonák." *Ethnographia* 18 (1907): 99–102.

Berde Károly. *A magyar nép dermatológiája*. Budapest: Magyar Orvosi Könyvkiadó Társulat, 1940.

Berki Imre. "Babonák a tűzről – Mivel csillapítsuk a tűz éhét?" Accessed November 17, 2023. https://www.vedelem.hu/letoltes/anyagok/665 -babonak-a-tuzrol-mivel-csillapitsuk-a-tuz-ehet.pdf.

Berze Nagy János. *Égigérő fa: Magyar mitológiai tanulmányok*. Pécs, Hungary: Tudományos Ismeretterjesztő Társulat Baranya Megyei Szervezete, 1961.

Bora Das, Rashmi. "As Cultures Worldwide Seek to Peek into a Child's Future." *Rashmi Writes* (blog), August 29, 2021. https://rashmiwrites .com/2021/08/29/as-cultures-worldwide-seek-to-peek-into-a-childs -future.

Bosnyák Sándor. "A moldvai magyarok hitvilága." *Folklore Archívum* 12 (1980).

———. "Napkorona, aranyalma, pásztorbot, suba." *Országépítő* 1, no. 3 (1990): 5–11.

———. "Visszasírás." *Kharón - Thanatológiai Szemle* 2, no. 1 (Spring 1998). https://kharon.hu/docu/1998-tavasz_bosnyak-visszasiras.pdf.

"Busó Festivities at Mohács: Masked End-of-Winter Carnival Custom." UNESCO. Accessed November 14, 2023. https://ich.unesco.org/en /RL/buso-festivities-at-mohacs-masked-end-of-winter-carnival -custom-00252.

Csáky Károly. "Szerelemmel és születéssel kapcsolatos szokások és hiedelmek az Ipoly mentén." *Honismeret: a hazafias népfront folyóirata* 12 (1984): 30–33.

Csiszár Árpád. "Gyógyítás emberkoponyával Bergen." *Ethnographia* 76 (1965): 602–3.

Csonka-Takács Eszter. "A születési rítusok és hiedelmek szerepe a közösség kapcsolatrendszerében Gyimesközéplokon." PhD diss. Budapest: Eötvös Loránd Tudományegyetem Bölcsészettudományi Kar, 2006.

Daczó Árpád. "A Gyimesi Babba Mária." In *Népismereti Dolgozatok*, 79–86. Bucharest: Kriterion Könyvkiadó, 1980.

Dám László. "A kővé vált kenyér." *Ethnographia* 79 (1968): 429–30.

Dénes Gabriella. "Boldogasszony Papucsa." *Romkat.ro*, August 15, 2021. https://romkat.ro/2021/08/15/boldogasszony-papucsa.

Dienes István. *A honfoglaló magyarok*. Budapest: Hereditas Press, Corvina Kiadó, 1972.

Diószegi Vilmos. *Az ősi magyar hitvilág: Válogatás a magyar mitológiával foglalkozó XVIII–XIX. századi művekből*. Budapest: Gondolat Kiadó, 1971.

———. *A pogány magyarok hitvilága*. Budapest: Akadémiai Kiadó, 1967.

———. *A sámánhit emlékei a magyar népi műveltségben*. Budapest: Akadémiai Kiadó, 1958.

———. *Samanizmus*. Budapest: Gondolat Könyvkiadó, 1962.

Domokos Pál Péter. "Hajnal, hajnalnóta, hajnalozás." *Ethnographia* 72 (1961): 237–65.

Dömötör Sándor. "Szent Gellért hegye és a boszorkányok." *Tanulmányok Budapest múltjából* 7 (1939): 92–111.

Dömötör Tekla. *A magyar nép hiedelemvilága*. Budapest: Corvina Kiadó, 1982.

———. *A népszokások költészete*. Budapest: Akadémiai Kiadó, 1974.

———. *Magyar népszokások*. Budapest: Corvina Kiadó, 1972.

———. "Népi embergyógyítás." *Magyar Néprajz Nyolc Kötetben*. Budapest: Akadémiai Kiadó, 1990.

Elek Zoltán. "Gömörmegyei népmondák." Magyarországi Néprajzi Társaság, *Ethnographia* 7 (1896): 380–83.

Endrei Ákos. "Somogy vármegye népe." In *Magyarország vármegyei és városai: A Magyar koronai országai történetek, földrajzi, és közgazdasági állapotának encziklopédiája*. Budapest: Országos Monográfia Társaság, 1914. https://www.arcanum.com/hu/online

-kiadvanyok/Borovszky-borovszky-samu-magyarorszag-varmegyei
-es-varosai-1/somogy-varmegye-153D7/somogy-varmegye-nepe
-irta-endrei-akos-tanar-15837/szuletes-kereszteles-15883.

Erdész Sándor. "Állattá változások a nyírségi nép hiedelmekben." *A Nyíregyházi Jósa András Múzeum évkönyve* 1 (1958): 215–26.

Erdmann Gyula, ed. "Szokás, hagyomány, hiedelmek." *Doboz (Száz magyar falu)*. Budapest: Száz Magyar Falu Könyvesháza, 2002. https://www
.arcanum.com/en/online-kiadvanyok/SzazMagyarFalu-szaz-magyar
-falu-1/doboz-2622/szokas-hagyomany-hiedelmek-28BB.

Farkas Péter. "Néprajzi vonatkozások a múlt századi nagykőrösi sajtóban." *Studia Comitatensia* 24 (1994): 137–65.

Fáy Zoltán. "Harry Potter magyar sárkánya." *MANDA Magyar Nemzeti Digitális Archívum és Filmintézet*, February 23, 2012. http://mandar
chiv.hu/cikk/209/Harry_Potter_magyar_sarkanya.

Fehér Gyula. "Bíbájosok, boszorkányok Recskén és környékén." *Ethnographia* 48 (1937): 220–24.

Fehér Jenő. *Középkori magyar inkvizíció*. Buenos Aires: Transylvania könyvkiadó vállalat, 1956.

"Fehérlófia." Accessed November 16, 2023. https://www.arcanum.com
/hu/online-kiadvanyok/Szoveggyujtemeny-szoveggyujtemeny-1/a
-magyar-oskolteszet-emlekei-2/magyar-mese-es-mondavilag-29
/feherlofia-467.

Fél Edit. "Adatok a gyászszínekhez és párhuzamok." *Ethnographia* 46 (1935): 6–17.

Felföldi László. "Rituális táncok a magyar néphagyományban." *Ethnographia* 98 (1987): 207–26.

Fogarasi István. *Sámánok és táltosok*. Szentendre: Interpopulart Könyvkiadó, 1993.

Fogl Krisztián Sándor. "Sárkányölő Szent György ünnepe." Laczkó Dezső Múzeum, April 24, 2021. https://www.ldm.hu/hu/blog/sarkanyolo
-szent-gyorgy-unnepe.

Foreign Service Institute. "Foreign Language Training." US Department of State. Accessed November 17, 2023. https://www.state.gov/foreign -language-training.

Gáll Anna. "Magyarországon megérte boszorkánynak lenni, illetve…." *Index*, November 1, 2021. https://index.hu/kultur/2021/11/01/magyar orszagon-megerte-boszorkanynak-lenni.

Gönczi, Ferenc. "A gyermek születése és szoptatása körül való szokások Göcsejben és Hetésben." *Ethnographia* 17 (1906): 44–52.

———. "Az anyajegy a somogyi néphitben." *Ethnographia* 44 (1933): 163–64.

———. "Az emberi betegségek gyógyítása a göcseji népnél, harmadik közlemény." *Ethnographia* 13 (1902): 214–24.

———. "Az emberi betegségek gyógyítása a göcseji népnél, második közlemény." *Ethnographia* 13 (1902): 128–32.

Gubrán-Nagy Anna. "Pünkösd jelképei." Pünkösd Info, May 24, 2019. https://punkosd.info/punkosd-jelkepei.

Gulyás Éva. "Adventi és karácsonyi népszokások a Jászságban." In *Jászsági Évkönyv*. Jászberény, Hungary: Jászsági Évkönyv Alapítvány, 2013.

Gunda Béla. "Szent Iván napi tűzcsóválás Törökkoppányban." *Ethnographia* 49 (1938): 213.

Gyallay Domokos. "A fehér ló szerepe a székely hagyományban." *Ethnographia* 73 (1962): 389–99.

"Ha felmegyünk Boszorkánykőre, soha nem felejtjük el, amit onnan látunk." *Sokszínű Vidék*, June 27, 2022. https://sokszinuvidek.24.hu /viragzo-videkunk/2022/06/27/boszornyko-panorama.

Halász Gabi. "Mohácsi Busójárás: érdekességek a mohácsi télkergetésről." *Csodálatos Magyarország*, February 10, 2021. https://csodalatos magyarorszag.hu/hirek/mohacs/mohacsi-busojaras-erdekessegek -a-mohacsi-telkergetesrol.

Halász Péter. "A moldvai magyarok tavaszi ünnepköréről." Kolozsvár (Cluj-Napoca): *Kriza János Néprajzi Társaság Évkönyve* 8 (2000): 233–75.

———. "Hagyományos méhészet a moldvai magyaroknál." *Erdélyi Múzeum* 78, no. 2 (2016): 60–88.

Haynal Kornél and H. Orosz Mária. *1998. esztendei kalendárium és szakácskönyv magyar háziasszonyok számára.* Budapest: Greger-Delacroix, 1998.

Herkely Károly. "A gyermeknevelés szokásai és babonái a matyóknál." *Ethnographia* 49 (1938): 223–25.

———. "Az elásott kincs a Bán völgyi néphitben." *Ethnographia* 48 (1937): 475.

Hesz Ágnes. "Álom halottakkal, mint élők és holtak közt kommunikáció." *Ethnographia* 116 (2005): 349–63.

Holló Domokos. "A garabonciás diák alakja a magyar néphagyományban." *Ethnographia* 45 (1934): 19–34.

"Illés próféta ünnepe." *Magyar Kurír, Katolikus Hírportál,* July 20, 2021. https://www.magyarkurir.hu/kultura/illes-profeta-unnepe.

Ilyefalvi Emese. "'Ebszar, kutyaszar, semminek tartom, meggyógyítom...' Egy gyógyító ráolvasástípus a magyarországi boszorkányperekben." In *Boszorkányok, Varázslók és Démonok Közép-Kelet-Európában,* edited by Klaniczay Gábor and Pócs Éva, 411–55. Budapest: Balassi Kiadó, 2014.

Ipolyi Arnold. *Mythológia.* Pest, Hungary: Heckenast Gusztáv Kiadása, 1854.

Istvánffy Gyula. "A borsodi matyó nép élete." *Ethnographia* 7 (1896): 364–73.

Jankó János. "Kalotaszegi babonák." *Ethnographia* 2 (1891): 273–85.

Jones, W. Henry, and Lewis L. Kropf, eds. "The Folk-Tales of the Magyars." London: Elliot Stock, 1889. https://www.gutenberg.org/files /42981/42981-h/42981-h.htm.

Kálmány János. *Boldogasszony: Ősvallásunk istenasszonya.* Budapest: A magyar tudományos akadémia, 1885.

———. "Gyermek-ijesztők és rablók nyelvhagyományainkban." *Ethnographia* 4 (1893): 225–47.

Kandra Kabos Jakab. *Magyar mythologia*. Eger, Hungary: Beznák Gyula Könyvkereskedő Bizománya, 1897.

"Kihirdették, melyik lett Magyarország tortája 2019-ben." *Sokszínű Vidék*, July 31, 2019. https://sokszinuvidek.24.hu/otthon-keszult/2019/07/31/magyarorszag-tortaja-2019.

Kis-Halas Judit. "Átformált hagyomány: a töröcskei öntőasszonyok." *Tabula: A Néprajzi Múzeum online folyóirata* 7, no. 2 (2004): 191–208.

Kiss Géza. *Ormányság*. Budapest: Sylvester R. T., 1937.

Kiss Lajos. "A szüléssel, kereszteléssel és felneveléssel járó szokások, babonás hiedelmek Hódmezővásárhelyről." *Ethnographia* 30 (1919): 84–91.

———. *Hódmezővásárhelyi temetkezési szokások*. Budapest: Hornyászky Viktor Magyar Királyi Udvari Könyvnyomdája, 1921.

K. Kovács László. *A kolozsvári hóstátiak temetkezése*. Budapest: Gondolat Könyvkiadó Kft., 2004.

Klaniczay Gábor. "Boszorkányhit, boszorkányvád, boszorkányüldözés a XVI–XVIII. században." *Ethnographia* 97 (1986): 257–95.

Kolumbán Samu. "A hosdáthiak népszokásai." *Ethnographia* 6 (1895): 119–23.

———. "Babonás hiedelmek a dévai csángóknál." *Ethnographia* 15 (1904): 35–42.

Komáromy Andor. *Magyarországi boszorkányperek oklevéltára*. Budapest: Magyar Tudományos Akadémia, 1910.

"Körömből itták a pálinkát." *Kolorline*, February 25, 2018. https://kolorline.hu/hirek/kazincbarcika/2018-02-25/korombol-ittak-a-palinkat.

Kovács János. *Szeged és népe*. Szeged, Hungary: Dugonics Társaság, 1901.

Kovács S. János. "Az Méhekrül való hasznos beszéd." *Ethnographia* 2 (1891): 18–21.

Központi Statisztikai Hivatal. "Tudom, hol nyaraltál tavaly nyáron." *Központi Statisztikai Hivatal Infografika*. Accessed November 17, 2023. https://www.ksh.hu/infografika/2021/belfoldi_turizmus.pdf.

Kunkovács László. *Táltoserő*. Budapest: Masszi, 2006.

Kunt Ernő. "Temetkezési szokások Pányokon II.: Szokásvizsgálat." *A Herman Ottó Múzeum Évkönyve* 28–29 (1991): 497–522.

Kurocskin, A. V. "A boszorkány alakja az ukrán folklórban." *Ethnographia* 101 (1990): 514–19.

Lajos Árpád. *Este a fonóban.* Budapest: Népművelési Propaganda Iroda, 1974.

Lakatos Károly. *Vadászhit. (A magyar vadászbabonák és hiedelmek kultusza.)* Második bővített kiadás [2nd ed]. Szeged, Hungary: Engel Lajos kiadása, 1910.

Lang'at, Vic, Jr. "What Is Tengrism?" *World Atlas*, May 10, 2018. https://www.worldatlas.com/articles/what-is-tengrism.html.

László Gyula. "Az 'agos' (szőrösen született) gyermek megfőzése." *Ethnographia* 45 (1934): 186–87.

Licskay Péter. "2021 Busójárás Is Cancelled—But What Is Behind This Tradition?" *Daily News Hungary*, February 10, 2021. https://daily newshungary.com/2021-busojaras-is-cancelled-but-what-is-behind -this-wild-tradition.

Lim, Louisa. "Belly Dancing for the Dead: A Day with China's Top Mourner." National Public Radio, June 26, 2013. https://www.npr .org/2013/06/26/195565696/belly-dancing-for-the-dead-a-day-with -chinas-top-mourner.

Lükő Gábor. "A jávorcsillag-mítosz ábrázolása az Urál vidéki sziklarajzokon." *Ethnographia* 73 (1962): 437–47.

Madarassy László. "A palóc mennykő." *Ethnographia* 44 (1933): 75.

———. "Magyar aratószokások." *Ethnographia* 39 (1928): 83–93.

Magyar Katolikus Lexikon. Based on the Szent István Társulat version, 1980–2013. https://lexikon.katolikus.hu.

Magyar Néprajzi Lexikon of 1977–1982. MTA Néprajzi Kutató Csoport. Budapest: Akadémiai Kiadó, 1982.

Makkai Endre and Nagy Ödön. "Adatok téli néphagyományaink ismeretéhez." *Erdélyi Tudományos Füzetek* 103, edited by Dr. György Lajos. Kolozsvár (Cluj-Napoca): Erdélyi Múzeum-Egyesület, 1939.

Manga János. "Szlovák kapcsolatok a palóc karácsonyi szokásokban." *Ethnographia* 59 (1948): 94–102.

Máté-Tóth András and Rosta Gergely. "Vallási riport, 1991–2022. Magyarországi trendek nemzetközi összehasonlításban." In *Társadalmi Riport 2022*, 457–72. Budapest: Tárki Társadalomkutatási Intézet, 2022.

McCarthy, Niall. "The Death Toll Of Europe's Witch Trials." Statista, October 29, 2019. https://www.statista.com/chart/19801/people -tried-and-executed-in-witch-trials-in-europe.

"Medve." *Magyar etimológiai szótár*. Arcanum Adatbázis Kiadó. Accessed December 16, 2023. https://www.arcanum.com/hu/online-kiadvanyok /Lexikonok-magyar-etimologiai-szotar-F14D3/m-F2FC3/medve-F30E9.

"Menyasszonyfektetés és felkontyolás: Régi magyar esküvői szokások, amelyek feledésbe merültek." *Secret Stories*, January 3, 2018. https:// secretstories.hu/interjuk/regi-magyar-eskuvoi-szokasok-2.

Miklós Eszter. "A 16–17. századi baszkföldi és erdélyi boszorkányperek összehasonlítása." *Orpheus Noster* 9, no. 3 (2017): 29–44.

Moór Elemér. "A gyermekneveléssel járó szokások és babonák." *Ethnographia* 45 (1934): 178–80.

Morvai Linda. "Azt tartották, hogy akinek lánya van, hamarabb öregszik." *Sokszínű Vidék*, April 24, 2022. https://sokszinuvidek.24.hu/eletmod /2022/04/24/nepviselet-napja-viselet-hagyomany.

Muraközi Ágota. "A lidérc a nyírségi néphitben." *A Nyíregyházi Jósa András Múzeum évkönyve* 10 (1967): 183–202.

Nagy József. "Hegyhátvidéki hangutánzók, mondák és babonák." *Ethnographia* 3 (1892): 64–73.

Nemes Elek. "Pásztor-babonák." *Ethnographia* 18 (1907): 169–70.

Nickel Réka Zsuzsanna. "Reám vicsoritotta az fogait." *Ethnographia* 119 (2008): 299–322.

Nyáry Albert. "A halottlátó." *Ethnographia* 19 (1908): 91–96.

Ökrösné Bartha Júlia. "Köznépi temetők, pásztorsírjelek Anatóliában." *Ethnographia* 108 (1997): 165–73.

Olosz Katalin. "Fehér László." *Balladatár*. Kolozsvár (Cluj-Napoca): Kriza János Néprajzi Társaság, 2017. Accessed November 17, 2023. http:// www.kjnt.ro/balladatar/ballada/feher-laszlo-1-1-1-1-1-1-1.

Oravecz Hargita and Zalai-Gaál István. "Burial Rites of the Neolithic." In *Hungarian Archaeology at the Turn of the Millennium*, edited by Visy Zsolt, 107–12. Budapest: Ministry of National Cultural Heritage, 2003.

Ortutay Gyula. *Kis magyar néprajz*. Budapest: Gondolat, 1966.

Ortutay Gyula and Diószegi Vilmos, eds. *Az ősi magyar hitvilág*. Budapest: Gondolat Könyvkiadó, 1978.

Paládi-Kovács Attila, ed. *Magyar néprajz nyolc kötetben*, vol. 7. Budapest: Akadémiai Kiadó, 1990.

Patay Pál. *Zempléni harangok*. Miskolc, Hungary: Nemzeti Kulturális Alapítvány, 2009.

Pávay Ferencz. "Oláhlapádi babonák és népies gyógymódok s földrajzi elterjedésük." *Ethnographia* 18 (1907): 294–99.

Peisner Ignácz. "Die Volkskunde." *Ethnographia* 15 (1904): 76–78.

Pesovár Ernő. "Körtánchagyományunk: Epilógus a Körtánc-monográfiához." *Iskolakultúra: pedagógusok szakmai-tudományos folyóirata* 2, no. 21 (1992): 83–86.

P. Lator Ilona. *"Kimegy a lelke, marad a test."* Uzhhorod, Ukraine: Intermix Kiadó, 2005.

Pócs Éva. "A boszorkányszombat és ördögszövetség népi alapjai Közép-Délkelet-Európában." *Ethnographia* 103 (1992): 28–88.

———. "A karácsonyi vacsora és a karácsonyi asztal hiedelemköre." *Néprajzi Közlemények* 10, no. 3–4 (1965).

———. "A kimondott szó varázsereje." *FolkMAGazin* 27, no. 6 (2020): 16–17. Excerpted from *Kis magyar néprajz a rádióban*, edited by Jávor Katalin, Küllős Imola, and Tátrai Zsuzsanna, 318–22. https://issuu .com/folkmagazin/docs/mag20_6/s/11508128.

———. "A magyar ősvallás." In *Lélekenciklopédia III*, edited by Simon-Székely Attila, 433–79. Budapest: Gondolat Kiadó, 2019.

———. "A magyar táltos és a honfoglaláskori samanizmus. Kérdések és feltevések." *Ethnographia* 128, no. 1 (2017): 1–46.

———. "Az asztal és a tűzhely, avagy hol van a szentsarok?" In *Számadó: Tanulmányok Paládi-Kovács Attila tiszteletére*, edited by Hála József,

Szarvas Zsuzsa, and Szilágyi Miklós, 375–87. Budapest: MTA Néprajzi Kutatóintézet, 2001.

———. "Élők, holtak és a víz mitológiája." Paper presented at "Magyar Tudomány Ünnep: A víz kultúrája konferencia." Accessed November 17, 2023. https://mta.hu/data/dokumentumok/i_osztaly/1_Eloadasok _tara/A viz kulturaja_2008/A_viz_PocsE.pdf.

———. "Evil Eye in Hungary: Belief, Ritual, Incantation." In *Charms and Charming in Europe*, edited by Jonathan Roper, 205–27. Houndmills, England: Palgrave Macmillan, 2004.

———. *Fairies and Witches at the Boundary of South-Eastern and Central Europe*. Helsinki: Academia Scientiarum Fennica, 1988.

———. *Hiedelemszövegek*. Budapest: Balassi Kiadó, 2012.

———. *Magyar néphit Közép-és Kelet-Európa határán*. Budapest: L'Harmattan Kiadó, 2002.

———. *Magyar ráolvasások I*. Budapest: Magyar Tudományos Akadémia Néprajzi Kutatócsoport, 1985.

———. *Népi vallás és mágia Közép-Kelet-Európában - Válogatott tanulmányok II*. Studia Ethnologica Hungarica. Budapest: L'Harmattan Kiadó, 2018.

———. *Néprajzi Közlemények. A karácsonyi vacsora és a karácsonyi asztal hiedelemköre*. Budapest: Néprajzi Múzeum, 1965.

———. "Szócikkek egy mágiaenciklopédiához." *Ethnographia* 115 (2004): 1–46.

———. "Zagyvarékas néphite." *Néprajzi Közlemények* 9, no. 3–4 (1964).

Post, Helen, Endre Németh, László Klima, Rodrigo Flores, Tibor Fehér, Attila Türk, Gábor Székely, Hovhannes Sahakyan, Mayukh Mondal, Francesco Montinaro, Monika Karmin, Lauri Saag, Bayazit Yunusbayev, Elza K. Khusnutdinova, Ene Metspalu, Richard Villems, Kristiina Tambets, and Siiri Rootsi. "Y-Chromosomal Connection Between Hungarians and Geographically Distant Populations of the Ural Mountain Region and West Siberia." *Scientific Reports* 9 (2019). https://doi.org/10.1038/s41598-019-44272-6.

Radóczné Bálint Ildikó. *Irodalom 6. tankönyv.* Budapest: Oktatási Hivatal, 2020.

Rajšp, Vinko. "Boszorkányperek Szlovéniában." *Ethnographia* 101 (1990): 521–31.

Rapaics Raymund. *A magyarság virágai: A XX. (1932–1934 évi) ciklus első kötete.* Budapest: Természettudományi Könyvkiadóvállalat, 1932.

Rédéyné Hoffman Mária. "Egy bujdosó naplójából." *Ethnographia* 37 (1926): 20–28.

Relkovic Davorka. "Adalékok a Somlóvidék folklorejához." *Ethnographia* 39 (1928): 94–107.

Réső Ensel Sándor. *Magyarországi népszokások.* Pest, Hungary: Kugler Adolf Kiadó, 1866. Accessed November 11, 2023. https://mtda.hu /books/Magyarorszagi_nepszokasok.pdf.

Richter Magyar István. "Évi szokások, babonák és szólás-mondások Német-Prónán és vidékén." *Ethnographia* 9 (1898): 221–32.

Róheim Géza. "A halálmadár." *Ethnographia* 24 (1913): 23–36.

———. *A magyar sámánizmus: a táltos.* Budapest: Nemzeti Örökség, 1925.

———. "Kedd asszonya." *Ethnographia* 24 (1913): 90–95.

———. *Magyar néphit és népszokások.* Budapest: Nemzeti Örökség, 1925.

Ruitz Izabella. "A parasztifjúság társasélete a Bódva vidékén (1880-1950)." *Ethnographia* 76 (1965): 572–601.

R. Várkonyi Ágnes. "Közgyógyítás és boszorkányhit." *Ethnographia* 101 (1990): 384–436.

Sántha Attila. "Ő, akit Babbának neveznek (a vasorrú bábától Babba Máriáig)." *Székelyföld* 16, no. 7 (2012): 54–70.

Sarosácz György. "Baranyai délszláv népszokások. I. Karácsonyi és lakodalmi szokások a sokacoknál és bosnyákoknál." *Janus Pannonius Múzeum Évkönyve* (1967): 103–22.

Schwarz Elemér. "A nagyfalvai bolygó vadászról szóló monda." *Ethnographia* 31 (1920): 91–94.

Scott-Macnab, David. "The Many Faces of the Noonday Demon." *Journal of Early Christian History* 8, no. 1 (2018): 22–42.

Sebestyén Gyula. "A magyar néphagyomány emlékeinek országos gyűjtéséről." *Ethnographia* 23 (1912): 193–99.

———. "A pünkösdi király és királyné." *Ethnographia* 17 (1906): 32–43.

———. "Az időrendbe szedett váradi tüzesvaspróba-lajstrom." *Ethnographia* 14 (1903): 396–401.

———. *Dunántúli gyűjtés*. Magyar népköltési gyüjtemény VIII. Budapest: Athenaeum, 1906.

Seres András. "Erdők, vizek csodás lényei Háromszéken és a környező vidékeken." In *Népismereti Dolgozatok*, edited by Kós Károly and Faragó József, 185–96. Bucharest: Kriterion Könyvkiadó, 1981.

Simon Dorina. "Cibereleves, ahogy nagyanyáink készítették - Így készül a hagyományos böjti étel." *Femina*, February 4, 2021. https://femina.hu /recept/cibereleves-recept.

Singer [Székely] Leó. "Dunántúli babonák." *Ethnographia* 9 (1898): 233–36.

Sitkei Dóra. "A honfoglaló magyarok hitvilága és a magyar nyelv." *Ingenia Hungarica* 3 (2017): 213–28.

Solymossy Sándor. "A 'Vasorrú bába' és mitikus rokonai." *Ethnographia* 38 (1927): 217–35.

Stöckert Gábor. "Miért hétszünyű a kapanyánimonyók?" Index.hu, August 29, 2016. http://index.hu/tudomany/til/2016/08/29/miert _hetszunyu_a_kapanyanimonyok.

Szabó Imre. "Az oláhok 'Kedd asszonya.'" *Ethnographia* 17 (1906): 52–55.

Szakács Gábor. "Boldogasszony, Anyánk!" Accessed November 11, 2023. http://magtudin.org/Szakacs_Gabor_Lukacs_Atya_2010-es%20cikk.pdf.

Székely [Singer] Leó. "Gömörmegyei babonák." *Ethnographia* 7 (1896): 374–79.

Szendrey Ákos. "A füstölés a magyar néphitben." *Ethnographia* 46 (1935): 42–48.

———. "A magyar lélekhit." *Ethnographia* 57 (1946): 34–46.

———. "A napforduló és a mágikus állatvédés összekapcsolásának kérdése." *Ethnographia* 70 (1959): 313–43.

———. "A társadalmi érintkezés formái." *Ethnographia* 48 (1937): 372–85.

———. "Az ősmagyar temetkezés." *Ethnographia* 39 (1928): 12–26.

———. "Az újtűz." *Ethnographia* 42 (1931) 153–54.

———. "Meztelenség a magyar néphitben." *Népünk és nyelvünk* 2 (1930): 129–33.

Szendrey Ákos and Szendrey Zsigmond. "Részletek a készülő magyar babonaszótárból." *Ethnographia* 51 (1940): 195–210.

Szendrey Zsigmond. "A 'kongózás.'" *Ethnographia* 42 (1931): 21–27.

———. "A nép élő hitvilága." *Ethnographia* 49 (1938): 257–73.

———. "A néphit mennykője." *Ethnographia* 44 (1933): 163.

———. "A növény, állat, és ásványvilág a varázslatokban." *Ethnographia* 48 (1937): 154–66.

———. "A varázslatok eszközei." *Ethnographia* 48 (1937): 386–404.

———. "Évnegyedi szokásaink és babonáink." *Ethnographia* 52 (1941): 10–23.

———. "Műveltségtörténet és babonafejlődés." *Ethnographia* 54 (1943): 56–63.

———. "Népszokásaink lélektani alapjai." *Ethnographia* 45 (1934): 3–19.

———. "Nyomfelszedés." *Ethnographia* 47 (1936): 220.

———. "Őszi jelesnapjaink." *Népünk és nyelvünk* 8 (1936): 43–49.

———. "Szalontai jeles napok." *Ethnographia* 27 (1916): 73–80.

———. "Szatmár megye néphagyományai." *Ethnographia* 39 (1928): 27–38.

———. "Tiltások és tiltott cselekvések." *Népünk és nyelvünk* 9 (1937): 246–50.

———. "Tiltott és előírt ételek a magyar népszokásban." *Ethnographia* 43 (1932): 15–19.

———. "Vadász babonák." *Népünk és nyelvünk* 4 (1932): 28–29.

Szojka Gyula. *A természet a néphitben.* Debrecen, Hungary: Debreczeni Könyvnyomda, 1884.

Takács György. "Nagy Szent Mária egy nagy asztalt terített…A hegyen végzett lóáldozat és a betegségdémonok megvendégelése egy különös ráolvasócsoportban." *Erdélyi Múzeum* 74, no. 4 (2012): 46–84. Accessed November 11, 2023. https://eda.eme.ro/handle/10598/26337.

———. *Babba Mária: Adalékok a Magyarság őshitének istenanya-alakjához*. Debrecen, Hungary: Főnix Könyvműhely, 2002.

Tánczos Vilmos. "Angyalkultusz a moldvai csángó folklórban." Accessed November 17, 2023. https://tanczosvilmos.files.wordpress.com /2011/09/angyalkultusz.pdf.

Tankó Gyula. "A 'guzsalyaskodás' Gyimesben." *Honismeret Magazin* 49, no. 1 (2021):71–74.

Temesváry Rezső. *Előítéletek, népszokások és babonák a szülészet körében Magyarországon*. Budapest: Dobrowsky és Franke, 1899.

Tolnai Vilmos. "Nagyfalusi babonák." *Ethnographia* 10 (1899): 395–97.

Tomán Erzsébet. "A kegytárgyak élete." *Ethnographia* 106 (1995): 673–91.

Tóth G. Péter, ed. *Szegedi Boszorkányperek*. Budapest: Balassi Kiadó, 2016.

———. *Boszorkánypánik és babonatéboly*. Budapest: Balassi Kiadó, 2020.

Váczy, András. "Csodakövek a Bükkben." Accessed November 17, 2023. http://gil.hu/kulonleges-helyek-es-jelkepek/boldogasszony-ko.

Vajkai Aurél. *Népi orvoslás a Borsavölgyében*. Kolozsvár (Cluj-Napoca), Romania: Nagy Jenő és Nagy Sándor Könyvnyomdája, 1943.

Varga Lajos. "Húsvéti dülőkerülés, didergés és hajnalozás." *Ethnographia* 9 (1900): 268–70.

Versényi György. *Bányák, bányászok, hagyományok: Válogatott tanulmányok és költemények*. Rudabánya, Hungary: Érc-és Ásványbányászati Múzeum Alapítvány, 2011.

Vikár Béla. "A szentiváni ének." *Magyar Nyelvőr* 30, no. 9 (1901): 401–14.

Vinci Balázsné Bálint Juliánna. "Klára, Dála, Ramocsa." Oral history recorded by Lőrincz József, Székelydálya, 1977. Accessed November 14, 2023.

Vincze Zoltán and Pilling János. "A cigányság jelenkori halotti és gyászszokásai: Egy mélyinterjús kutatás tapasztalatai." *Kharón - Thanatológiai Szemle* 19, no. 1–2 (2015): 1–24.

"Virág Péter." Népmese.hu. Accessed November 14, 2023. https://www .nepmese.hu/mesetar/mesek/virag-peter.

Virt István. *Elszakasztottad a testemtől én lelkemet: a moldvai és a Baranya megyei csángók halottas szokásai és hiedelmei.* Kolozsvár (Cluj-Napoca), Romania: Kriza János Néprajzi Társaság, 2001.

Viski Károly. "A tulipán szó történetéhez." *Népünk és nyelvünk* 4 (1932): 28.

Vörös István. "Kutyaáldozatok és kutyatemetkezések a középkori Magyarországon I." *Folia Archaeologica* 41 (1990): 117–45.

Wass Albert. *Selected Hungarian Legends.* Translated by Elizabeth M. Wass de Czege. Astor Park, FL: Danubian Press, 1971.

Wlislockiné Dörfler A. Fanni. "Jósló állatok a kalotaszegi néphitben." *Ethnographia* 3 (1892): 47–55.

———. "Kakas, tyúk, és tojás a magyar néphitben." *Ethnographia* 6 (1895): 205–13.

Wlislocky Henrik. "Szerelmi jóslás és varázslás az erdélyi sátoros czigányoknál." *Ethnographia* 1 (1890): 273–76.

Zágorhidi Czigány Balázs. *Oszkó.* Budapest: Száz Magyar Falu Könyvesháza, 2002.

Zentai János. "Alsómocsoládi hiedelemmondák." *Janus Pannonius Múzeum Évkönyve* (1967): 81–87.

Zimonyi István. *A magyarság korai történetének sarokpontjai: Elméletek az újabb irodalom tükrében.* Magyar Őstörténeti Könyvtár 28. Budapest: Balassi Kiadó, 2014.

Zsigmond Győző. "Népi kozmogónia és égitestmagyarázás a mezőségi Magyarszováton." *Ethnographia* 105 (1994): 541–82.

Zsilák Mária. "Betegségek okozói: mitikus lények, betegség démonok: adatok a magyarországi szlovákok hiedelmeihez és népi orvoslásához." In *Test, lélek, természet: tanulmányok a népi orvoslás emlékeiből,* edited by Barna Gábor and Kótyuk Erzsébet, 127–32. Szeged, Hungary: Néprajzi és Kulturális Antropológiai Tanszék, 2002.

INDEX

Florian's Day, 200

flour, 2, 38, 90, 104, 144, 167, 247

flowers, 2, 11, 14, 16, 21, 29, 56, 64, 96, 103, 105, 108, 109, 140,
146, 147, 171, 185, 198–201, 203–205, 207, 215, 227, 230, 237,
243, 247, 270, 277–279

flutes, 232

flying lard , 114

főkötő, 242, 253, 299

fonó, 81, 82, 127, 151, 172, 223, 238, 239, 299, 324

Friday, 135, 172, 187, 206, 223, 295

fright, 56, 59, 160, 259, 299

frogs, 14, 40, 65, 73, 74, 84, 114, 132, 144, 145, 161, 187

funeral feast, 67, 73, 181, 223, 278–280, 303

G

garabonciás, 38, 76, 112, 299, 307

garden, 2, 29, 30, 37, 74, 80, 81, 91, 97, 107, 135, 147, 162, 163,
173, 185, 189, 196, 203, 204, 207, 253, 264, 278

garlic, 51, 56, 94, 102, 106, 115, 117, 143, 157, 159, 187, 197, 213,
221, 230, 250, 256, 261, 262, 265, 271, 281

gate, 31, 73, 87, 93, 102, 114, 144, 220, 250, 251, 278

gazda, 70, 80, 93, 96, 97, 106, 125, 135, 147, 167, 177, 200, 207,
213, 214, 216, 220, 221, 228, 229, 231, 233, 299

gazdasszony, 41, 80, 90, 93, 95, 98, 101, 107, 114, 143, 177, 185,
187, 195, 197, 221, 228–230, 233, 299

Gellért, 115, 313

gentian, 161

ghost, 33, 57–60, 126, 158, 170, 215, 231, 256, 257, 277, 281, 300,
302

giants, 44–47, 126, 179, 301

gnome, 16, 35, 45, 301, 303

goat, 127

moon, 10, 12–14, 30, 31, 35–37, 39, 72, 96, 102, 130, 131, 170, 171, 206, 213, 223, 246, 260, 289, 295

moon craters, 36

Moon King, 36

moon phases, 30, 36, 170, 213

morzsa, 140, 230, 301, 323

Mother Wind, 38

mourning, 31, 39, 56, 58, 188, 215, 240, 250, 275–281

mouse, 32, 65

mumus, 55

N

Nagyböjt, 183–185, 301, 320

Nagyhét, 185, 187, 301, 320

Nagypéntek, 90, 187–189, 286, 295, 320

Nagyszombat, 189, 295, 320

nails, 33, 49, 132, 145, 171, 221, 224, 227, 255, 269, 274, 279

name days, 168, 169, 301

naming, 151, 161, 168

nature spirits, 19, 20, 28, 31, 43, 65, 308

new fire, 133, 189, 303

New Year's, 6, 112, 116, 132, 175–178, 222, 293, 294

nora, 258

nyavalya, 54, 309

O

oldás, 134

olvasó, 146, 301, 302, 316

omens, 40, 71, 73, 129, 130, 149, 153, 169, 177, 259

Óperencia Sea, 179

ördög, 53, 54, 60, 267, 301

óriás, 45, 301

T

Z

To Write to the Author

If you wish to contact the author or would like more information about this book, please write to the author in care of Llewellyn Worldwide Ltd. and we will forward your request. Both the author and publisher appreciate hearing from you and learning of your enjoyment of this book and how it has helped you. Llewellyn Worldwide Ltd. cannot guarantee that every letter written to the author can be answered, but all will be forwarded. Please write to:

Margit Tóth
℅ Llewellyn Worldwide
2143 Wooddale Drive
Woodbury, MN 55125-2989
Please enclose a self-addressed stamped envelope for reply,
or $1.00 to cover costs. If outside the U.S.A., enclose
an international postal reply coupon.

Many of Llewellyn's authors have websites with additional
information and resources. For more information,
please visit our website at http://www.llewellyn.com.